The Parent Test

How To Measure and Develop Your Talent for Parenthood

Ellen Peck and Dr. William Granzig

G. P. PUTNAM'S SONS
NEW YORK

To the family, with faith in its survival

Excerpts from the following works are reprinted by permission:

How to Help Your Child Get the Most out of School, Dr. Stella Chess. Doubleday & Co., Inc.
How to Survive Parenthood, Eda J. Le Shan. Random House, Inc.
Mother's Day Is Over, Shirley Radl. Charterhouse Books
My Heart's in the Highlands, William Saroyan. George Braziller, Inc.
A Nation of Sheep, William J. Lederer. W.W. Norton & Company, Inc.

Contents

"I'm Somebody Besides Mommy"
No Illusions, Please!
The Quest for Experience
The Need for Laughter

With grateful acknowledgment for aid in conceptualizing and developing THE PARENT TEST,

Dr. Ruth Hunt, Planned Parenthood/World Population
Dr. Louise B. Tyrer, Vice-President, Planned Parenthood/World Population
Dr. Jessie Bernard
Dr. Richard Stander, Director of Education, American College of Obstetricians and Gynecologists
Dr. James Lieberman, American Public Health Association
Dr. Teresa Marciano, Fairleigh Dickinson University
Mr. Alvin Toffler
Mrs. Nancy Cox
Dr. Sylvia Wassertheil-Smoller, Albert Einstein College of Medicine
Dr. Rebecca Liswood
Dr. Stella Chess, New York University School of Medicine
Reverend William H. Genne, National Council on Family Relations
Dr. Patricia Schiller, Executive Director, American Association of Sex Educators, Counselors and Therapists
Dr. Thelma Dixon Murphy, American Association of Marriage and Family Counselors
Dr. Adele Hofmann, American Academy of Pediatrics
Dr. Bertrand New, American Academy of Child Psychiatry
Dr. Charles Arnold, American Public Health Association
Dr. John M. Wozniak, Dean of Graduate School of Education, Loyola University
Dr. Michael Carrera, President, American Association of Sex Educators, Counselors and Therapists
Mrs. Corky Hale Stoller
Dr. Herbert Robbins

Foreword

parent/ˈpar-ənt [L. *parens* (orig. ppr. of *parere*, to beget]
1: one that begets or brings forth offspring **2a:** an animal or plant that is regarded in relation to its offspring **2b:** the material or source from which something is derived
[Webster's New Collegiate Dictionary]

One glance at a dictionary tells you why this book is needed. In our society we define parenthood as a biological act instead of a behavioral process. We equate family planning with contraception instead of contemplation. We become parents without knowing what parents do. We have children without knowing what children are like. And we make mistakes without knowing why.

Back and forth we careen between the examples set by our well-meaning, but inexperienced, parents and the model set by the always perfect, but unreal, media mothers and fathers. Impatiently we wait for our children to become the bright, beautiful, well-mannered youngsters who grace the glàmour pages and smile at us from the TV screens. But what we see is *not* what we get. Real children have runny noses and temper tantrums and they spill things all over our best clothes.

Must we be so ill-prepared for the real children we get? Not any more, because Bill Granzig and Ellen Peck have captured the essence of real parenthood and put it between the covers of this book. They did it by doing research with real parents. Using their book, you can try the parenting role on for size, and you don't have to make mistakes on real children to see if it fits.

What's more, you can trust the information you get, because this book is not based on speculation or theory. The authors have accumulated data to support the material they present, and their data come from the people who really know the answers—parents.

This book won't tell you whether or not to be a parent. It's not supposed to do that. But it will help you learn what is needed to become a *successful* parent. That's why I believe this book is so important. Just being a parent isn't enough.

Not all candidates for parenthood will profit from a book like this. Those who can learn only by trial and error will have to practice on a child (or two) of their own. Those who were fortunate enough to have perfect parents themselves need only copy their parents' example to the letter (or let their parents bring up the children). Forgive my tongue-in-cheek approach—what I'm really trying to say is that being a successful parent is so difficult that we can all use any help we can get. If you're thinking about taking on the role of parent, this may be one of the most important books you ever read. And by the way, it's never too late to learn how to be more successful as a parent. I believe this book is just as valuable for people who are already parents.

It's also never too early to learn about being a parent. Next time my kids tell me how they are going to raise *their* kids, guess what I'm going to do?

I'm going to give them a copy of this book to read.

—ARTHUR ULENE, M.D.
Today Show Family Physician

The Parent Test

Introduction

Should I Be a Parent? What Aptitude Is All About

Let's say it's five P.M.

Not too far from where you live, a mother named Nancy Carr is teaching her daughter Janny to separate egg whites and yolks for a cheese soufflé (which Janny until recently has called a puffy). Janny's starting to try out the right name for it, though, her mother has noticed: She seems fascinated that the word comes from another language, fascinated, in fact, to start to understand that other languages exist.

Making the soufflé is taking somewhat longer than it would if Nancy did it herself—if you're five, it's a little scary to try to control the contents of a breaking egg. Also, some flour has spilled onto the counter and at least one spoon of shredded cheese has found its way to the floor. But Janny's having fun, and Nancy doesn't mind the time it takes. She has a rigid teaching schedule all day, but it really doesn't matter if dinner isn't ready just at six P.M.

Suddenly Janny stops talking about dinner and says, "Mommy, I admire the way you're going to let me quit piano lessons."

Surprised—recognizing a motivational technique she herself has used for years ("Janny, I admire the way you put your toys away," "I admire the way you're going to take your own bath tonight")—Nancy laughs and demands, "Young lady, are you using psychology on me?"

"What's psychology?" Janny asks.

Nancy starts to explain . . .

13

* * *

Several blocks away, also not too far from where you live, Frieda Jennings and her daughter Susan are in their kitchen. Susan would like to help make dinner. But her mother, having learned that "help" means "mess," carefully assigns only very safe tasks to Susan: carrying nonbreakable items like napkins and silverware to the table and putting bread on plates.

Trying to ignore Susan's chatter on her little trips between the kitchen and dining room about how she will plan dinner when she's bigger (Susan has started to use the word *plan* in interesting ways, but her mother hasn't noticed), Frieda concentrates on getting the family meal together with as little fuss as possible.

Suddenly, the bowl in which she is tossing the salad slips precariously across the counter due to a small puddle of apple juice she hadn't noticed. "Susan," she calls, her voice on edge, "haven't I told you often *not* to get your own juice because you always spill it? Don't you feel bad at always causing people more work? When will you learn responsibility for following instructions? And speaking of responsibility, you can just get to your room and make your bed like you were supposed to this morning . . . !''

Both Nancy Carr and Frieda Jennings have been mothers for about five years, but their reactions are quite different. Nancy is generally delighted. Frieda, if she were free to, might well consider walking out tomorrow.

Which mother's experience is more typical? Unfortunately, with few exceptions, major studies of recent years indicate that there are more Friedas than Nancys—more unhappy than happy parents. Eda LeShan recently commented, "Raising a child seems to have become as pleasurable as building a house without blueprints," and this remark may clearly point to what the major problem of family life is today: There are no blueprints for parenthood.

There are handy hints on structural specifics (comparable perhaps to how to patch a roof or fix a faucet), but no overall design to let people know what the task of parenthood is like *before they take it on.* Thus, where Nancy and Frieda are concerned, we might say that one mother lucked out, the other didn't—for neither of them, before they had a child, had much of an idea of what parenthood was really like. Neither of them really thought to ponder such a question very much—which is a little astonishing if you stop to think about it.

Probably no one would take an office job without asking:

How many hours a day will I work?
What office machines must I know how to use?
How many vacation days will I get?
Will there be co-workers I can call on to help me?
What new skills will I have to develop?

It would also make sense to want to know:

How many diapers a day will I change?
How many hours of sleep will I lose?
How do you help a preschooler make friends and learn skills?
What changes in my present life-style are likely?
If I get into trouble, will someone help me?

before taking on the "job" of parenthood.

Parenthood? *A job?*

Since it requires time and the application of personal skills, it could be called a job; but it might be more accurate to call parenthood a profession (the often-explained difference being that a profession is a job you love so much that, if nobody paid you to do it, you would pay somebody to let you). Parenthood fits that definition, since its successful practice calls for more than time and skills—it requires interest, commitment, and love.

Parenthood could be called the world's newest profession, since it hasn't been considered a profession for very long.

And though the profession is an exciting one, the pay isn't good. In fact, a small initial investment on your part will be required (about $2600 the first year, with an additional eighteen to twenty years to pay the remaining $98,000 or so—in convenient installments, of course).

On the brighter side, nobody can fire you.

And to some extent you can make your own hours: There is no rigid nine-to-five time clock. As a parent, you're technically free to take a nap or see a movie at three in the afternoon if you can manage it. (And maybe you should try to take one hour off now, if you can, since you may be on duty for the next twenty-three!)

If the picture sounds like a mixed one, with every possible delight cunningly counterbalanced with a probable disadvantage, that's all the more reason for thinking very carefully before putting yourself in that picture: because parenthood has one unique feature among other professions. It's permanent.

You may be a salesclerk this season; but next year you may be a buyer. You might be an attorney at this moment; but there may be a moment when you leave law practice and decide to teach. However, once you have had a child, you will never again not be a parent! As Jean Kerr once remarked, "The thing about children—and I can't be the first to have noticed this—is that, after you have them, thereafter you HAVE THEM!"

As might be expected, this sort of job security carries a built-in system of guaranteed promotions. Once you have served just a few years as parent of an infant, you are assured placement as parent of a toddler; then as parent of a school-age child. After accumulating eight to twelve years of further job seniority, you will again automatically advance, this time to the highest, most risk-laden but potentially rewarding levels of parenthood service. You will first be the parent of a teenager who will be voted Most Likely to Succeed (or who will not), then the parent of a young adult who indeed *seems* likely to succeed (or who does not). And just to keep things from getting dull for parents, the job description of things they must do will change regularly (or irregularly); sometimes from year to year, sometimes, it will seem, on the hour.

From the evidence, very few people know beforehand what they're getting into. In an often-quoted statement of bewilderment, one young mother told sociologist E. E. LeMasters, "We knew where babies came from, *but we didn't know what they were like.*"

What children are like is one central informational factor that is shrouded in mystery for those who are not yet parents. Art through the ages has taught us much about the nature of human life but has failed utterly to capture the activity level of children. The "art" form that twentieth-century technology has unleashed among us, television, is even more untrustworthy, portraying as it does only children who are physically beautiful and appealingly active (and who seldom sulk). Even firsthand data from those who are already parents is unreliable: It is frequently severely edited. Bobby's father will tell you about Bobby's perfect spelling score and stunning batting average, but will remain mum about Bobby's behavioral demerits. Denise's parents will show you an editorial Denise wrote that transcends Lippman and a poem she wrote that rivals Frost, but neglect to mention that Denise screams and breaks things if politely requested to write a thank-you note.

Children are, of course, angels. They are beings whose natural habitat is the stratosphere of human personality, unpolluted by common responsibilities and compromises. With astral innocence, they bestow roughly scissored Mother's Day cards upon the favored individual nearest them in mid-May, create a new breed of paper elf or reindeer in December, and at any season may bring tears to the eyes of us bystanders with their pure delight at things we've stopped even noticing.

But children also tend to make the elevator stop at every floor when we're in a hurry, love to carry small radios that turn a simple adult stroll into an exercise in decibel tolerance, and like to peer around corners to watch the fun after they've left their tricycles where they're sure to be tripped over.

Children require lots of physical care when young, and lots

of psychological nurturing when young *and* older. Children are like foreign visitors to a country where we, the adults, are experienced natives, and we must act as their interpreters, explaining the language and customs of this less-than-logical land that we have brought them into. Having a child thus means not only changing diapers and teaching to walk, but explaining love and social justice, war and crime and energy policy, diets and starvation, racism and sexism, algebra and why Ehrlichman went to jail but Nixon didn't have to, and why you can't stay out till eleven P.M. even if everybody else can.

From another perspective, children are a biological investment that will reach maturity (perhaps bringing hoped-for dividends) when parents are no longer young: not dividends in the sense of a 7 percent per annum return in perpetuity on a $98,000 investment; nor necessarily in the sense of grandchildren who call for far less expenditure of personal capital and time and worry than the children themselves did (for even if one has children these days, the odds that they will in their turn give us grandchildren are far from secure); nor even dividends in the form of blocks of time that we have given them returned to us graciously, say at holidays or on our birthdays. The dividends the best of parents get might seem meager to an outsider. They largely have to do with the pleasure that can be taken in seeing a child catch on to something we've known for decades. Often these are simple things: the meaning of a new word, the mastery of a small skill like separating eggs. And they can have to do with the satisfaction of seeing a child do something honorable or courageous or kind, and feeling that you may have had something to do with that action. Such satisfactions may sound like minor ones to you, or they may seem very important and desirable indeed.

There's one inescapably shocking thing about having a child. From the first moment of parenthood, you are suddenly part of another generation—specifically, the older generation. Though there's a widespread notion that children keep you young, most parents know better. The constant comparisons you cannot avoid making between yourself and your child (children do not have lines around the eyes) are fairly insistent reminders of parents' own advancing age. Children almost inevitably force parents to acknowledge their own mortality.

Given all this, the thought of having a child logically inspires a bit of caution. Creating a new life is nothing to be taken lightly. In fact, for many couples today the question of whether or not to have children has become *the* question of the early phases of marriage. More and more, it's also a question raised during premarital conversations, as part of that process by which men and women evaluate one another's ideas and values (and in fact evaluate one another as potential long-term partners). "What would it be like?" is a central concern.

From the standpoint of parenthood as profession, the answer to that question might be approached by comparing parenthood to a few other, better-known and better-defined occupations and activities.

Being a parent might be seen as a little like being an astronaut, in that no matter how much you are told, how much training and instruction you receive, your own experience can't really be predicted: It will be new, uncharted, uniquely yours. Being a parent is also akin to being a nurse or doctor, because of the patience and selflessness required (and the long hours)! Being a parent is somewhat like being a teacher, too, since you continually need to impart knowledge, evaluate learning, and hold eventual "graduation" in sight.

Parenthood is a little like all these occupations.

And it's a little like swimming.

Some people plunge in without thinking and do a beautiful breast stroke; others just barely manage a "survival float"; and still others can't manage even *that* and have to call for help. Some wait until the hottest day of summer and even then test the water carefully to the ankle prior to a more deliberate immersion; others will swim in any season (and some simply won't go near the water).

In a way, what this book is advising is swimming lessons.

Not that the final chapter contains Red Cross badges for those who complete the course or Olympic medals for those who excel. (It's not necessary that all swimmers be merit-badge winners or Olympic medalists, anyway.) But one premise of this book is that *preparation for anything important is well worth the time it takes.* Thus the fact that you are reading this book probably says something important about you. You evidently value parenthood enough to think carefully about it and consider what people who have devoted much of their lives to it (in theory, or practice, or both) believe.

One recent but very important belief that has emerged about parenthood is that parenthood is not something that "comes naturally." It does for other, luckier species who can rely on instinct, with no need at all for parenthood-effectiveness training! The notion that parenthood comes naturally for humans too doubtless results from the fact that natural, biological processes precede it.

But parenthood itself is not a simple, biological phenomenon. There are important differences between procreation and parenthood. The processes of procreation are biological: Conception is biological. Gestation is biological. Birth is biological. But parenthood is psychological in its application—and if natural instincts ever guided humans through any part of it, those instincts lie dormant now. We have taken such large steps away from a natural environment that probably no instincts survive. Not even childbirth is instinctive anymore: "Natural childbirth" these days is something that has to be taught. "If parenthood came naturally," one psychiatrist explained simply, "the world wouldn't be in the mess it's in."

Still, there are many who assume that a strong connection exists between the ability to give birth and the ability to parent; many who assume that since nearly everybody is naturally able to procreate, nearly everybody should naturally be a parent. Such assumptions are dangerous and can court risk and carelessness, because if these assumptions are accepted, any thoughtful planning for parenthood, including birth control, can be seen as irrelevant.

Obviously, this book firmly rests on a different foundation of thought: not only the thought that every child should be planned but, in fact, should be planned in a more careful way than anyone has ever previously suggested.

For, to some parents, not only does parenthood fail to come naturally, it does not even come with effort.

The truth is that parenthood is a very tough job, one that even the experts haven't figured out. One of the most undisputed of experts, Eda LeShan, addresses that point meaningfully:

> Sex education by itself didn't guarantee happier marriages; kindly discipline didn't eliminate the bully; demand feeding didn't create anxiety-free, stable young people. I know good, decent, intelligent parents who cared deeply, tried hard to learn the best new, modern ways to raise children, and who are horrified and ashamed because their children are not at all what they expected them to be. They are sometimes mean, unhappy, bratty kids; they are sometimes dishonest, irresponsible, and unkind. They hate and distrust adults a lot of the time. And these are children around whom there has been love and understanding.
>
> We have all known and thought about these facts, but we are all being quietly bothered and bewildered. *It is time we stopped the pretense.* Child-raising is more complicated than we dreamed and we have not found the magic key. (emphasis ours)

Just how tough a job parenthood is can be partly surmised from the sheer number of recent efforts mounted to find that "magic key." One single New York bookstore has on its shelves 164 different book titles relating to child-raising. At last count more than half a million parents had been through a course based on one of them, Parenthood Effectiveness Training; and one West Coast book distributor remarked that he believed the only reason total sales of the Bible were still ahead of Dr. Spock's *Baby and Child Care* was because of mass sales of the former to motels. Columnists and booksellers alike have described the sudden influx of parent-advice books as an endless deluge or tidal wave.

There are advice books which aim to provide an in-depth understanding of one particular age of childhood (as *The Child from Birth to Three*) and others which address the situation of the child with a particular congenital or psychological problem (as *Understanding Your Autistic Child*).

There are ambitious volumes which appeal to a parent's understandable desire to maximize his or her child's achievement potential, such as Dr. Glenn Doman's *How to Teach Your Baby to Read*. Books of this genre typically spark controversy: "Like automobiles and toothpaste, one supposes that the next batch of children will be 'new and improved,'" commented columnist George F. Will with unconcealed disapproval.

And there are books for parents which hold out, not hints for getting through the job enviably or extraordinarily, but simply hope for getting through the job, period! *How to Survive Parenthood* outsells *How to Raise a Brighter Child*. Coping, not competing, seems to be the basic skill that parents are in pursuit of, for this category of books is the most popular of all.

Are parents who read these books finding what they are looking for? Is anybody really unearthing discoveries or secrets that will unlock the complexities of parenthood?

It should be clear that, if any one of the books available (or, for that matter, any group of them in combination) worked, the word would spread like electricity. There would be such clear and dramatic differences between parents who had read, say, *Child Rearing in Ten Easy Lessons* and those who had not, that soon all parents would. Were such a happy scenario to occur, we would then sense all around us a general letting out of held breath—a general easing of the tensions which presently surround the process of raising children.

But there must be some reason why these books, sincere and sensible though most of them are, don't work—or at least don't work for everyone. Why does "active listening" prove effective for Parent A but not for Parent B? Why do both Parent A and Parent B flunk "childrenese"? Why do Parents C and D find almost all their attempts to follow advice unsuccessful, often, in fact, leaving them more frustrated than ever?

The reason, we suggest, is that the books attempt to offer "job help" to a broad and diverse audience of "job holders," many of whom are inappropriately placed in their jobs! Thus it is small wonder that they are unable to put potentially useful and relevant advice into action.

Under the best of circumstances it is a little hopeless to try to help someone succeed at a job he or she is not suited for.

Sociologist and author Jessie Bernard has commented:

> If we forced every girl to become, say, a librarian or nurse or secretary or what-have-you, we would not be surprised if some performed well or others poorly. Or that some enjoyed their work while others did not. We would recognize that they are all different and that a common career would not be equally congenial to all. We show no such logic in the case of mothers.

Pursuing this line of thinking, one member of the American College of Obstetricians and Gynecologists wrote:

> If everyone were urged to become a doctor, and if then in fact virtually everyone did set up a medical practice, we would see predominantly UNHAPPY men and women struggling to meet the demands of a complex profession—with widespread lack of success. Doubtless in such a situation we would then see a proliferation of books on Physician Effectiveness Training— which wouldn't have any more general curative result than the parent advice books do now.

Just as there are people who are not cut out to be physicians, it is reasonable to assume that there are people who are not cut out to be parents. And, just as the concept of aptitude is used to help predict which medical-college applicants have the basic qualities needed to be good doctors, it could be that the concept of aptitude can help those interested in becoming parents predict their probable success and happiness in that role.

This brings us to a second, also recent and very important, emerging belief about parenthood: *Some individuals have a greater aptitude for parenthood than others.*

Aptitude is a word with a relatively recent history. In its applied sense, it refers to a branch of psychology designed to assess whether a given individual is suited for a certain occupation. Oddly enough, the principle of aptitude has been applied to just about every field of productive adult endeavor except the most important one: the one most directly involving the rearing of children.

There exist mechanical aptitude tests, teacher aptitude tests, clerical aptitude tests, musical aptitude tests—but no parent aptitude tests.

There are aptitude tests which predict your ability to be a baker, optician, physician, credit manager, millwright or locksmith, piano tuner or police officer, architect or social worker or dramatist—but none to forecast your ability to be a good mother or father. And in fact there have been very few hints from the professions most closely involved with aptitude—psychology and counseling—that there is any sense of urgency about coming up with one.

A few isolated suggestions have come from authorities in other fields. George Bernard Shaw, in one of his essays, remarked, "Parenthood is an important profession; yet what test of fitness is imposed in the interests of children?" In *Future Shock* Alvin Toffler strongly suggested that parenthood should be accorded the status of a specialized occupation. Charlotte Perkins Gilman, arriving at this insight long before either of them, insisted in an 1898 issue of the *Woman's Journal* that "Motherhood is a profession."

But the concept of parenthood aptitude seems most often touched on in casual, usual, everyday conversations in which nonfamous men and women talk about parenthood. How often has each of us heard or said something like:

I should be a parent because I can offer a child a lot.
He shouldn't be a parent because he travels all the time.
Jim and Sue should have children because they have sunny dispositions.
Cheryl would be a marvelous mom if she could control her temper.
Sam should have a kid because he needs to settle down.
Linda shouldn't because she'll never settle down.
He's in too poor health . . .
She's not stable enough . . .
They don't have any money . . .
We should because we want to . . .
They shouldn't because they don't want to . . .

Such statements contain the central assumption of the concept of aptitude, the assumption that *there are differences between those individuals who should be parents and those who shouldn't!*

Could an aptitude test for parenthood help people determine what those differences are, and consequently who should and should not consider having a child?

Ongoing discussion surrounded that question during 1975 and 1976. Though the subject of parent aptitude was part of no formal conference program, it began to be on an unofficial agenda during private, after-hours talks at annual meetings of such organizations as the American Psychological Association, the National Council on Family Relations, the American College of Obstetricians and Gynecologists, Planned Parenthood, and similar groups.

For about a year these talks were just straws in the wind, not woven into any structure. But more and more private communications among professionals began to form a pattern. From family planner to sociologist, pediatrician to child psychiatrist, population leader to family counselor, more and more letters about other matters entirely began to carry a similar postscript: "By the way, as regards the concept of parent aptitude which we were recently discussing . . ." One family counselor, Dr. Charles Figley, phoned three other family counselors on receipt of his new anthology in human relationships to point out, "There's a half-page that reads like a definition of parent aptitude; take a look at it." Dr. Louise B. Tyrer and Ellen Peck spent five evenings over a period of as many months drafting questions which should be raised if the concept of parenthood aptitude ever found a professional or public forum.

Eventually, in June of 1976, an interdisciplinary research and study group called the Consortium on Parenthood Aptitude was formed. The statement of belief of the consortium founders is also the underlying philosophy of this book, and therefore worth repeating:

> We share a faith in parenthood. Though, like other institutions, it is being questioned, rethought, and redefined, this to us seems a positive process, not a discouraging one. It seems to us if we can regard parenthood as option, not obligation, the result will be happier parents, children, and families.
>
> To have a child can be an act of affirmation, courage, and wisdom. Yet the decision *not* to have a child can also be made responsibly, joyfully—and wisely. How, then, does one decide?
>
> While rejecting simplistic notions which hold that one criterion (say, intelligence or income) is an all-important predictor for success in the role of parent, we do look forward to developing a valid concept of *parenthood aptitude.*

The consortium founders intended to investigate the concept of parent aptitude and to create an instrument to measure it, stating as their premise and working goal:

> It is both possible and desirable to construct a measurement in-

strument predictive of an individual's probable success and happiness in the role of parent.

That goal is an ongoing one, but this book represents one significant outgrowth of consortium work. It is not, however, an aptitude *test* as usually defined. It is rather a parenthood aptitude questionnaire or guide that is based on beliefs of consortium members and consultants across the disciplines as to what factors determine successful parenting and what qualities good parents tend to have.

Aptitude, of course, is not a one-dimensional concept. It is not a simple matter of "you've got it or you don't." Though it is generally considered to be at least in part innate, aptitude should be seen as an innate or inborn potential which can be exercised or developed in a number of ways.

Let's suppose, for instance, that ten different people we know have unusually high musical aptitudes. There would probably be great differences among those ten people. Sally, who enjoys research and scholarship, may write a book on music; Mike, who likes to attend live musical events, particularly opera, may be a critic; Jerry, who is gregarious and enjoys late hours, may exercise his aptitude for music by playing in a dance band; Kent may prefer a quiet studio where he gives lessons to private students; Larry may never enter a musical profession at all but he does sing at weddings once in a while.

So, too, aptitude for parenthood can vary greatly.

You may have an aptitude for dealing sensitively and patiently with one child but not with more. You may be able to handle parenthood in an urban setting with convenient day care but not in a small town as a twenty-four-hour-a-day parent. You may be impatient with infants but superb at stimulating the thinking of a preschooler (or wonderful with infants but impatient with a preschooler's chatter). Or you may have an overall aptitude for parenthood *but not yet* because of too many unfulfilled dreams and commitments of your own. It's even possible that you may choose to exercise parenthood aptitude in some way other than by becoming a parent—by choosing a career, perhaps, as a teacher or counselor.

Since aptitude is multidimensional, it can be broken down into certain *components of capability.* If Jim, for instance, wonders if he has an aptitude for a given profession, we might examine these aptitudinal components one by one.

1) Expectations.   What expectations does Jim have about this profession? How realistic are they?

2) Resources.   What resources are needed for success in this profession? How do Jim's resources measure up to generally accepted requirements?

3) Skills.   What skills does the profession demand? Does Jim presently have the needed skills? If not, can they be developed?

4) Motivations.   How strongly and for what reasons does Jim want to enter this profession?

5) Traits.   What personal characteristics do successful members of this profession possess? Do Jim's personal traits seem similar?

6) Interests.   How sincere are Jim's interests in most or all elements of this profession?

Though an ideal aptitude test would embrace all of the above components of aptitude, in fact no existing aptitude test does. Often, practically speaking, some components may be of little relevance. If Jim wants to be a painter, the nature of his motivation may not be crucial. It may not matter why he wants to paint if all indications are that he has the ability to.

Still, sometimes the limitations of existing tests are obvious.

The National Teacher Examination, for instance, evaluates teachers' mastery of subject matter, reasoning, and judgment. These are obviously only intellectual aspects of the ability to teach. They do not include interest in children, emotional stability, expectations, or other factors which would seem to matter greatly!

Sometimes, recognizing such limitations, vocational counselors try to supplement formal tests with practical questions and suggestions. For example, Walter D. Myers in *The World of Work* asks aspiring teachers to look at their expectations:

> Is your vision of teaching a real or fanciful one? Some people envision themselves teaching in a classroom of extremely cooperative and receptive children, only to be appalled when they have to face a disruptive, disorderly class. There are thus many people who have entered teaching only to find that they do not care for it at all. . . .

Obviously, Myers's statement could very easily apply to parenthood as well as to teaching.

The aptitude measurement guide in this book, however, includes direct consideration of expectations. In fact, it includes all the components of aptitude listed above. We might discuss each of these very briefly.

Expectations about parenthood should be realistic. Parenthood seems to get a lot of people in trouble because they go into it blindfolded—or at least with poor vision due to thick, rose-colored glasses. Many expect too much of parenthood. They expect it to provide instant identity, fulfillment, or other lavish emotional benefits. Many also have too ideal a concept of children, expecting them to be always or at least mostly docile and adorable.

With just a little critical thinking, one would realize that parenthood is not psychic magic, that children aren't always angels. Still, the airy expectations persist because we're not encouraged to approach parenthood critically; in a sense, society fits us with those rose-colored glasses.

Sociologist E.E. LeMasters has pointed out that when a social role is difficult (as parenthood certainly is in our society), a romantic mythology grows up around it. The myth is not needed when the role is simple. Parenthood, for instance, was never romanticized in a simpler era. In early, isolated, uncomfortable settlements, nobody had children because it was glamorous or fulfilling or romantic or fun, or because children were innocent and appealing or cute and adorable. People simply had children, with very little fuss (and no great expectations). With the increasing complexities of a modern age, however, child-raising has come to mean more than simple care and nurture and teaching of rural-settlement skills.

Values are in flux. Peer groups can corrupt, TV can mesmerize; new math bemuses, new morality frightens. In this century, probably for the first time in all of history, it has become necessary to ask, Do you know where your children are tonight? The times they are a-changin', all right, and in the clear direction of hazardous uncertainties. According to LeMasters's widely accepted view, the growth of the "parenthood as fulfillment" idea and other too-high expectations for the parent role have been in direct proportion to the increasing difficulty of raising children!

Therefore, if in this book we do not seem to treat the processes of parenthood and child-raising with the gently glowing words which often surround these subjects, that is NOT due to any antichild or antiparenthood bias on our part. We do want to avoid reinforcing the process LeMasters describes, however. Anyone growing up in this society has, prior to reading this book, received predominantly warm, romantic impressions of parenthood and children. The unromantic approach in this book's vocabulary will not take away those romantic impressions; indeed, may not even seriously challenge them—but it will perhaps fail to *reinforce* them.

Similarly, if the overall tone of some questionnaire items and surrounding discussion seems less than firmly proparenthood, it is again not the result of bias, but with the same view toward counterbalancing, even if only slightly, the fairly one-sided cultural cues that all of us have received for so long.

Our own bias is that we feel parenthood should be respected. But respect is not the same as adulation. In fact, adulation cannot coexist with true respect. At the same time that our culture generally regards motherhood as sacred, for instance, we deny it the respect a profession of its importance deserves ("What do you do?" "I'm a mother." "Oh. But what do you *do?*"). Placing parenthood on a pedestal involves false respect and real risk. The pedestals are shaky, the parents on them fall down, families break. Oddly enough, if we stop worshipping parenthood, we may find that we can then respect it. That is, in fact, our hope.

Besides expectations, interests are important. Wanting to have a child should logically be intimately connected to interest in children. Just how crucial a matter this is can be seen by overviewing the quality of parenting that behavioral psychologists Sylvia Brody and Sidney Axelrod reveal in their discussion of "maternal types," based on the observation of many mothers.

> Mothers of *Type I* take pleasure in observing and reporting about their infants and give information agreeably. . . . They are genuinely interested in their infants' moods and activities and physical needs for care. . . .
>
> *Type II* mothers observe their infants casually. . . . They

can seem serious caretakers but show little interest in matters of child raising. Their handling of their infants is dispassionate, impersonal. . . .

Type III mothers are unwilling observers and poor reporters. They barely show interest in their infants' development and have almost no curiosity about child-rearing methods. Tenderness is manifested only briefly or sporadically.

Type IV mothers are either tense or angry, or they are flippant and nonchalant about their maternal role. All assert disinterest in learning about infant care, and all refer to their infants critically, sarcastically, or with open hostility. . . .

If, right now, we were to circle the words *interest* and *disinterest* wherever they appear in those descriptions of maternal types, the importance of maternal interest might almost seem to rise up from the page (and maybe simultaneously the idea of maternal *instinct* would be laid to rest)! The "nonmaternal" mothers described above might possess the ability to be good mothers, but it seems they are just not interested!

And even if aptitude exists, it must be activated by interest!

Norman Munn's classic psychology reference, in fact, states, "A person who pursues a certain type of work because he is interested in it comes closer to reaching his potential than someone with less interest; and, also, through engaging in the activity, raises his potential."

Are *you* interested in children?

Can you imagine yourself immersed in the world of a child—the feeding, bathing, and snuggling of the infant giving way to the teaching of the alphabet and numbers to the preschooler; and that in turn being replaced by playing outdoor games with an eight-year-old and interestedly talking about who tripped whom at school?

Or do you feel of like mind with the young women who, explaining to sociologist Jean Veevers why they did not want children, said:

Look, let's face it, nobody ever says it, but children are stupid.

When a six-year-old has an IQ of 120, that means he's very smart *for a six-year-old!* But compared to even a slow grown-up person he is stupid. I guess I like kids as well as I like other stupid people. I mean—I know it's not their fault, but all the same I don't want to spend much time talking with them. And even bright people may be ignorant. Teenagers are as smart as adults, but they haven't lived long enough to know much. They are smart, but they are not informed. I like people who are both, and I guess that means adults.

With children, you are always going over the same things. I don't like to deal with people who know less than I do. I like to deal with people who know more than I do.

Interest in children has an early and prominent position in this book's parent aptitude questionnaire. If you find yourself *disinterested* in that section of the questionnaire, perhaps you'll have told yourself something important.

A desire to enter any occupation is important, too—so important that it can sometimes outweigh all other factors! Both history books and our own personal experiences contain many examples of men and women who achieved success in a given field (often against great odds and negative predictions) because their desire to succeed in that field overcame any obstacles. There is at least one Pulitzer novelist who flunked high-school English and one Nobel physicist who was considered dull in the sciences by his teachers. For that matter, next door to some of us probably lives a successful accountant who was once assured he had no aptitude for math, or a happy and admired fashion designer whose clothes were once generally laughed at. They wanted to succeed—and did.

But while desire to have a child can likewise be more important than any other factor in predicting your success as a parent, *don't count on that being true unless you really know* why *you want to be a parent.*

Want is a complex term. Count how many times you use the word during one day and see how varied its meanings seem. "I want more attention around here" is different from "I want to leave for lunch now" or "I want to watch the news on Channel X not Channel Y" (and all are much, much less significant than "I want to have a child").

Carrying just one of the above *wants* a step further: why might you want more attention around here—say, around the office? On a whim? Due to some discontent that may be momentarily eased if others look at you? So you will be promoted? So you will feel admired or important? Or so you can gain attention not just for yourself but for an employee-reform policy you feel is needed? (And why might you want a child? On a whim? Due to some discontent . . . So you will feel admired or important . . . Or so you can raise a child not just for yourself but with qualities you feel that others, too, have need of?)

The questionnaire that follows will try to focus very intently on your possible motivations for wanting a child.

Common sense would also quickly tell us that aptitude for parenthood involves a few specific skills (like the ability to mediate when two children are claiming possession of one toy) and personal traits (like patience, which comes in handy when a child's method of washing the dinner dishes extends till the "Late Show") and many others that you could list. In fact, you could probably make your own list of prerequisites to parent aptitude as easily as we did.

What we have tried to do, as well, is add the weight of professional experience to common sense within a framework that involves some testing principles.

The result may or may not tell you whether you would be a successful parent, but it should at least tell you some things you didn't know before.

One thing this book's aptitude questionnaire will tell you is how you compare (in terms of resources, traits, skills, interests, and expectations) with parents who have felt happy and successful in their role.

Most aptitude tests involve this kind of comparison. In fact, most aptitude tests are partially constructed after determining the characteristics of successful practitioners of a given occupation. The test is then constructed with a view toward seeing how those who aspire to that given occupation compare.

We have followed such an approach. Our successful practitioners of the profession of parenthood had certain characteristics which were felt to provide good evidence of their success:

1) *They were self-assessed as good parents.*
    They professed an overall feeling of satisfaction with the entire parenthood experience.
    They had no doubt that they would repeat the experience of having a child or children if they had the choice again.
    They had maintained a happy marriage through the process of raising children.

2) *They were assessed by others as good parents.*
    Their children rated them as good parents.
    At least two professionals such as a physician, priest or rabbi, or counselor evaluated them as good parents.
    A variety of normal acquaintances reinforced the "good parent" assessment, these acquaintances typically including: two neighbors; two co-workers; one relative from each side of the family; one teacher for each child.

3) They had entered what are generally considered to be parenthood's most difficult years: all had at least one child who had reached mid-adolescence.

Virtually all had nonhandicapped children, but there were slight physical handicaps (speech impediments) and learning disabilities within the children of this sample population.

The average number of children precisely echoed the current national average of approximately 2.1 (however, this indicated somewhat smaller than average family size during the time these couples were forming their families). Also, there were more only children among the sample than in the national average (12 percent, as opposed to 5 percent within the United States population as a whole).

This group of successful parents responded to the same questionnaire items that you are about to see.* So did a group of admittedly unhappy parents, many of whom stated unequivocally that, given the choice, they would not have children again! Responses of the two groups of parents were compared, and the final construction of this questionnaire (including both the discussion which will follow each section of questions and the final scoring) was significantly based on *differences in responses* of the two groups.

In addition, parent populations were encouraged to respond to each questionnaire item with marginal notes. We have reproduced some comments which are particularly illuminating, and at times we have relied significantly on judgments and ideas contained in them.

In cases where the two groups did not respond very differently, or in cases where responses varied within either group (for example, if responses to certain discipline questions varied within the group of successful parents or were not significantly distinguishable from the responses of the unsatisfied

---

*There was, of course, one obvious difference: a constantly called-for change in verb tense. For example, a questionnaire item that you will read as, "I believe children should be seen and not heard," was revised for our parent groups to mean, *Before I had children I believed that* . . . , since the obvious benefit lies in comparing these successful parents' past, preparental attitudes and characteristics with your present ones. Accuracy of remembered preparental situations was insured insofar as possible by pretesting interviews and instructions and spouse collaboration when this proved useful. Also, some questionnaire items which you will read as hypothetical ("I would put my living room off-limits to a toddler") were matters of actual experience for the sample parent groups, who responded by indicating what they *had* done. Parents taking this questionnaire now should make these same adjustments whenever necessary.

parents), the item has either been left unscored or, in a few cases, scoring has been determined based on a consensus of opinion within the Consortium on Parenthood Aptitude.

In our discussions of questionnaire items, when we say that "Successful parents felt . . ." or "Successful parents indicated . . ." what we are essentially doing is using shorthand for something like, "A statistically significant number of members of the successful-parent group compared to an equivalent number of members of the unsatisfied-parent group felt that . . ." or "indicated that . . ." and so on.

In many cases there was a remarkable consistency of response among members of both parent groups. As an example, even though the successful parents now have at least one teenager (and thus began their parenthood careers twelve to seventeen years ago, when birth control was less reliable and less easily obtainable), virtually all of our successful parents had planned their children.

You should relax a little before responding to the questions and statements that follow. Deciding to have a child may be a profound and portentous matter; deciding to fill out a questionnaire isn't. No one will be looking over your shoulder to say "tsk, tsk" or hand you a pass/fail grade.

In fact, the very idea of grade or score seems to imply a test: but as we have indicated, what follows is more properly to be seen as a guide to self-knowledge. And it is for you alone—or for you and your spouse—to help you foresee what kind of parent you might be.

If you are already a parent, don't fear finding out that you are wrong for the job. In fact, the knowledge you gain here can easily help you be a better, happier parent by helping you understand why you became one. You may gain reassuring knowledge about basic qualities that are necessary or helpful for successful parenting, qualities you possess but may not be fully utilizing. Or you may learn about some areas of aptitude where "retroactive readiness" can be exercised.

It's likely, in fact, that you will learn something about yourself as a person (your values, your priorities, your attitudes toward self and others) in addition to things you will learn about yourself as a parent or a possible parent.

Here are a few hints about responding to the questionnaire:

Spouses should respond to all items individually, not in collaboration. You will notice that almost all items are phrased "*I* feel . . ." "*I* would. . . ." Even though we hope and assume that all prospective parents are involved in the sort of ongoing man-woman relationship that makes parenthood easier, part of the purpose of the questionnaire is to identify individual strengths and weaknesses, for example, "I would be better with infants and teenagers than he would, whereas he seems to have better responses to preteens"; and part of the purpose of many of the items is to offer a chance to compare personal expectations and viewpoints.

Answer *all* questions (with the exception of one brief section with separate items for men and women) even if it seems to you that "That question isn't for me—it's for my spouse." Men may be particularly inclined to want to skip some items which may seem as if they are for women only. But they are for *parents*, and though to some extent, functionally, we have made the words *parenthood* and *motherhood* interchangeable and left most parenting to mothers, potential fathers should know what parenthood involves in order to assess whether it is something they feel interested in or suited for.

Remember that no one area of the questionnaire is crucial. False expectations don't mean a lack of aptitude for parenthood (expectations can be changed). Lack of skills is not necessarily serious, either (skills can be developed). Neither will failure to have certain resources that raising children requires disqualify anyone (resources have a way of accumulating over time). Even traits of character can change with time.

Try to respond to the statements as naturally and spontaneously as possible. In general, your first response will be your truest.

Don't try to second-guess the right response to any question or statement. This can not only waste your time but possibly distort your self-knowledge profile. Besides, very often *there is no right or wrong response.*

To demonstrate this point, let's suppose you encounter a questionnaire item that says:

My spouse and I find pleasure in time spent alone together

and shrewdly guess that a True response will win points, since surely being a contented marital partner forecasts being a happy parent.

But a True response would earn no points there (since children are shown in various studies to lessen the time spouses spend alone and therefore threaten closeness), just as you would earn no points for a response of False (since, though the presence of a child can interfere with closeness, a motive of using a child in an attempt to overcome isolation must be guarded against). The above is one of a good number of questionnaire items which will be unscored. Its point is to simply prompt your own thinking as to why you answered as you did. We guarantee that there will be many, many unscored questionnaire items, so you might as well be honest—it really will be easier.

Finally, don't spend too much time analyzing every word. One young woman who responded to the questionnaire prior to publication contemplated the statement "I could live on half my present income without distress" for about five minutes, wondering what *distress* meant and how it should be specifically defined! Whether you define *distress* as mild annoyance or screaming indignation, respond according to what it means to you, not what you imagine it might mean to us.

Here we go . . .

Chapter 1

Do I Have the Basics? Health, Maturity, Home, Money

Questionnaire 1

T or F responses should be given to all items except those which are multiple choice.

1. I don't believe in stocks or savings but in living for today.

2. I have a pretty clear idea of where I'm going in life; I have certain goals in mind.

3. I love to sleep late.

4. I rarely have an illness so severe that I am kept from functioning at home or work for more than a day.

5. I am prone to small maladies such as nervous stomach, tension headache.

6. What I'm doing in life matters, is making a difference.

7. I usually have enough energy to get through the day and enjoy some leisure activity in the evening.

8. I sometimes feel I am about to go to pieces.

9. I look for extra projects, things to do, to use my time and energy.

10. When I have a cold I:
    a) can keep going pretty easily
    b) can keep going but it's an awful struggle

c) use this as a reason to take a break from work
d) love to pamper myself, have others pamper me

11. My age is:
    a) under 21
    b) 21–25
    c) 25–29
    d) 30–or over

12. My marriage or current relationship has lasted:
    a) more than two years
    b) more than four years
    c) more than six years

13. I have been living on my own, away from my parents, for at least two years.

14. I sometimes rely on loans from my parents to solve temporary budget problems.

15. I sometimes feel so full of pep that sleep does not seem necessary for several days.

16. I am a high-strung person.

17. I enjoy at least one outdoor sport on a regular basis.

18. I (my spouse and I) have enough income to live comfortably.

19. I (we) could live on half our present income without distress.

20. I am known for a stylish way of dressing.

21. I yearn for certain luxuries which I cannot now afford.

22. When shopping for small items (groceries, cosmetics, or men's toiletries), I do not bother to comparison shop.

23. My economic future looks pretty secure.

24. I enjoy being able to spend $10 on impulse for an

accessory, an item for the home, or a new best-selling book.

25. I (my spouse and I) have more than $2000 in savings.

26. It is important to me (us) that a set percentage of income be set aside each pay period.

27. My spending habits are sensible, not impulsive.

28. I do not enjoy baseball, ballet, and the like unless I have good seats.

29. I would love to travel extensively.

30. Possessions and material goods are relatively unimportant to me.

31. I prefer eating out to having dinner at home.

32. I know, or could figure out, almost exactly how much money my spouse and I spent last year and what we spent it on.

33. I don't like to go to a party unless I'm wearing something new.

34. If we had a child, our present living quarters would feel cramped.

35. Our house or apartment is decorated to our taste and satisfaction.

36. I find I've been unconsciously arranging our present home with the eventual presence of a child in mind.

37. I find my house or apartment somewhat stifling, *therefore* I am not happy when some circumstance (as waiting for a delivery) keeps me home.

38. I find my house or apartment pleasant, *still* I am not happy when some circumstance keeps me home.

39. My favorite belongings and personal possessions are:
    a) more of real than of sentimental value
    b) more of sentimental than of real value
    c) both of real and of sentimental value

40. A child is more valuable than any possession he or she could possibly destroy.

41. Our present neighborhood is not a "children's" neighborhood: Schools far away, playmates few.

42. If I had a child the living room or perhaps another area of our house or apartment would be placed off limits during toddler years.

43. If I were magically handed $2000 in cash today, I would *most* like to:
    a) take a trip
    b) buy something expensive (car, stereo) with no time-payment worries
    c) invest in bonds at 10 percent interest
    d) buy country property
    e) buy gifts for friends
    f) use it for home furnishings
    g) contribute to a worthy cause
    h) use for maternity costs of having a baby
    i) use for continuing education of self or spouse

44. I've never really thought about what my primary life goals are.

45. I can more than hold my own in a discussion of what life is going to be like in the next twenty-five years.

Do I Have the Basics?
Health, Maturity, Home, Money

Emily Post seems to be selling less briskly these days. The women's liberation movement tossed a lot of rules about who opens doors for whom up into the air, and until those rules drift down again into some new pattern, we're all relaxing a little.

But while etiquette may be out, a less formal, less artificial concept of courtesy is still something most people try to operate by.

It would be considered a breach of courtesy to invite someone to your home for dinner and have no food in the house; to ask an out-of-town guest to stay overnight and put no towels on the rack; to offer a ride to a friend in a hurry when you know there's a good chance you'll run out of gas. In short, you don't offer hospitality that you know you don't have the resources to provide.

Yet a lot of people who would never dream of committing any of those small violations of courtesy will, in effect, invite into their homes a long-term "houseguest" who will be completely dependent upon them without any assurance but blind faith that they can provide for him or her during the long visit.

Only in a large, complex, optimistic, affluent, and credit-happy society could people behave so unrealistically. In smaller communities caution would be required.

For example, at Twin Oaks, considered the paradigm of rural communes during the sixties, the presence of small, dependent "houseguests" proved a formidable problem. Over a period of five years, the occasional presence of as many as nine children at one time meant that about fourteen hours a day of adult supervision of the children was necessary. With urgent needs to construct houses, build furniture, install electricity, and get a sustainable food-production system going, child care seemed an extravagant way to spend so many hours of adult time. As Jessie Bernard explains it in *The Future of Motherhood*:

> In 1969 the community clamped down. No more children until the children's house was ready and there was some assurance of permanence. The failures to date had not been due to people so much as to the difficulty of supporting small children when the community could hardly support itself.
>
> It was 1972 before Twin Oaks felt it could "afford" children.

Within the small-community unit of the family, too, it is realistic to evaluate the needs of children in terms of available resources to make sure their needs can be met. Here, too, it makes sense to wait until children can be afforded.

Not having money or a place to raise children doesn't by any means disqualify you for parenthood—any more than having no food in the house disqualifies you from having people over for dinner. It simply means you might be wise not to invite them over tonight.

It is becoming increasingly usual for couples to not simply have a child but to consider seriously whether they can afford to have a child. In supporting the wisdom of doing this, we don't mean to view a child as a commodity or to frame reproductive issues in purely economic terms. But when a couple cares enough to look ahead to the needs a child will have, it is certainly an indication of thoughtfulness and responsibility.

On the other hand, just as having a lavish supply of food on hand will not automatically make you a good host, having large amounts of cash in the bank doesn't necessarily mean you are ready for parenthood. It simply means you'll be able to pay the hospital bills.

If you have $1000 to $2000 saved, you are fairly well prepared to pay for the first week of your child's life (at least according to the Health Insurance Institute, which estimates that cost to average $1600). The HII includes a few prenatal costs in that figure, such at $500 for a basic layette (wardrobe, bathing items, nursery equipment) and a modest $200 for a maternity wardrobe.

Hospital costs in a major city easily run to $150 per day, obstetrical services from $300 to $600, and such things as delivery room, anesthesia, medication, and hospital telephone are extra. These costs do not anticipate any unusual complications such as a cesarean operation, blood transfusions, or special treatment for premature infants. Although about 90 percent of births are normal, if a delivery is complicated—if the baby is born with special problems requiring surgery, transfusions, or a special environment due to prematurity or some other factor—bills can rise from 50 percent to 200 percent!

According to other sources, some of those figures just given seem to be overoptimistic underestimates. In some major cities $1600 cannot be expected to cover natal costs (in New York City hospital and obstetrical costs alone can run $2250).* And—a maternity wardrobe for $200?

What a woman spends on maternity clothes may depend on what she has to spend or decides to spend; but the following items listed by William and Joanna Woolfolk in *The Great American Birth Rite*, seem standard and not extravagantly priced:

3 everyday dresses @ $25	$75
1 dress for evening @ $50	50
2 jacket-pants outfits @ $30	60
3 "separates" outfits, 3 ea pants, tops @ $15	90
1 pair flat-heeled shoes @ $30	30
1 bathrobe @ $20	20

*For the record, the cost of adopting a baby through a private agency seems fairly reliably set at around $1500.

2 nursing nightgowns @ $15	30
3 maternity bras @ $7	21
6 maternity panties @ $2.50	15
2 slips @ $6	12
3 pr support hose @ $6, 4 pr maternity hose @ $2.50	28
2 girdles @ $12	24

and add up to about $455, not $200.

There's a psychological element, too, that might cause more than $200 to be spent on maternity clothes. The period of pregnancy is a time when couples are either happily looking forward to the coming birth or have accepted the fact of pregnancy but are not happy about it. In either case, spending mechanisms may surface.

The happy mother-to-be feels special and may want to treat herself to items not budgeted for (most budgets don't foresee impulse spending for chic little items like a French T-shirt saying BABY in rhinestones). And a woman unhappy about her pregnancy may spend money on the accoutrements of her condition in order to try to reconcile herself to its reality.

We don't mean to be placing inordinate emphasis on such a relatively unimportant item as a maternity wardrobe. But the wardrobe does give an easy-to-check example of how official estimates of what a baby costs (which many couples accept on faith and use as a basis for their budgeting) can so very easily be exceeded.

The Health Insurance Institute figures, which are the one Sylvia Porter chooses to trust in *Sylvia Porter's Money Book*, seem very low. We'll use the layette as just another quick example. According to the HII, this should cost $500. Again, the Woolfolks raise the estimate to about $825; and, again, the breakdown for the more expensive estimate looks reasonable:

6 doz. diapers @ $8.50 per doz.	$51.00
4 sacque sets @ $4.50	18.00
4 waterproof panties @ 1.75	7.00

1 sweater set @ $8	8.00
3 stretch terry coveralls @ $6	18.00
5 blankets @ $2	10.00
2 thermal sleepers @ $5	10.00
6 pr booties @ $1.25	7.50
3 crib blankets @ $10	30.00
6 knitted crib sheets @ $4	24.00
3 flannelette waterproof sheets @ $4	12.00
6 waterproof lap pads (3 for $1.50)	3.00
1 comforter @ $12	12.00
2 heavyweight outdoor or travel wraps @ $15	30.00
Stroller	50.00
Crib	100.00
Crib mattress	30.00
Crib bumpers	10.00
Infant seat	12.00
Chest of drawers	80.00
Nursery lamp	20.00
Playpen	50.00
Highchair or feeding table	50.00
Bassinet	50.00
Diaper pail	5.00
Baby swing	25.00
Car seat	35.00

A carriage would add another $100 or so, for a total of almost $900.

Some items listed can be kept for future use, thus lowering the relative cost of future pregnancies. Some can be sold to friends and neighbors when no longer needed.

Conversely, such items can be borrowed, bought second-hand, or obtained as outright gifts from others—including items of maternity and infant clothing. But the fact seems to be that most couples are no more willing to seek secondhand baby or maternity items than they are to seek used or donated furniture or clothing not related to pregnancy and birth. In fact, our interviews indicate a somewhat greater reluctance to think that birth-related, used goods are good enough. It seems typical for prospective parents to feel that, for their own baby, "only the best" is adequate.

Ask yourself very carefully what your own feelings about the economics of childbirth are. Would your personal budget and income dictate practicality and ingenious dollar-stretching? Or allow all-new items? Are you willing to be as practical as necessary? Or are you apt to want to be extravagant?

Somewhere along the way, if you have acquaintances or friends close to the population movement (or, increasingly, even if you don't) somebody is apt to mention to you that the U.S. Commission on Population Growth and the American Future estimated in 1971 that the cost of raising just one child through one year of college could reach $103,023 for a middle-class family, including lost-income costs for one nonworking spouse but not adjusting for inflation. Somebody's bound to look at your baby and say something like, "Well, gee, this little fella looks like he's worth every penny he's going to cost over the years!"

Someone may also mention the biggest item—college. In a typical story told to us, a friend of new parents who happened to work with the Oakland Financial Group delivered some advice along with the baby gift he brought: Given the estimated four-year cost of state university attendance by the time their baby reached age eighteen, he advised the new parents to begin at once to save $3,250 per year! What such informants may have in mind is reinforcing their own hesitation about having children (if they do not) or hastening your full-fledged membership into their situation of budget problems—or they may simply think they are being helpful.

However, from our interviews with new parents, it would seem that these stunning far-range figures will have less immediate impact than the weekly diaper service or Pampers bill or some other small detail you hadn't thought of in advance—perhaps the fact that your wallet will be thinner by $12 to $22 (depending on your baby-sitting arrangement) when you go out for an evening from now on. Or two mobiles at $16.95 to hang above the baby's crib may prove an irresistible expenditure when you learn that infants respond to and receive sensory stimulation from moving objects and that they can distinguish shape and color.

From a Michigan mother comes another typical example. "We hadn't planned that a baby would mean $10 extra per week on our food bills. Not that our tiny baby consumes $10 worth of food a week! But I'm not free to go to the discount supermarkets anymore whenever I please. They are simply too crowded, take too much time, and fatigue both the baby and me too much. I'm sure you're going to ask why my husband can't shop there for us, but since the hours he could shop after work (5 to 7 P.M.) are the most crowded, and since once he is home his presence is important to the baby and me, it just doesn't seem to work. We're trying to learn to do once-a-month shopping on Saturdays. Meanwhile I am having groceries delivered by a smaller, and of course more expensive, food shop." (We quote that experience as a typical example, not an insoluble problem, of course. Though Joan Bowker's studies on "Crisis and Coping in the First Three Months" indicate such levels of fatigue to be far from unusual, they doubtless do not always prevent occasional supermarket forays.)

Even if that mother's extra $10 per week now spent for food results from some variation of postpartum depression or fatigue, it still could interfere with former, less-than-careful spending habits such as impulse spending, failure to comparison shop, and so on.

Later on, so will other little things a child will need at different ages. Even children under six require books and playthings, paints and crayons, and gifts for parties. Later, magazines, hobbies, club dues, sports equipment, carfare and school lunches, movies and other amusements prove significant additions. For preteens and teenagers, clothing and grooming aids, savings for special purposes such as travel or future education can bring about a sharp reduction in parents' own standard of living.

Money isn't everything of course. But it can easily become something significant when it's not plentiful. And thinking about dollars-and-cents child-related expenses is important for reasons that go beyond planning.

Not only were there significant differences between our groups of satisfied parents and dissatisfied parents in terms of how well each group had planned for the costs of children (yes, the more satisfied parents had budgeted more carefully and had saved money over a longer period of time prior to childbirth), but analysis of "crisis" scores within the "Childbirth as Crisis" studies according to four income categories indicated that twice as many couples with incomes under $10,000 faced crisis as did those with incomes of over $13,000.*

A similar crisis can recur long after childbirth if either spouse's field of employment proves vulnerable to periodic layoffs or industry-wide shutdowns due to energy shortages or similar increasingly likely economic factors. A 1977 Mervin Field Poll conducted in California showed that, of persons interviewed who lost their jobs during 1976, only 37 percent succeeded in finding other jobs.

It is impossible to predict any of our individual economic futures with certainty, but for obvious reasons prospective parents should ask if their economic future looks reasonably stable and secure.

You would also be wise to ask yourself whether you have other basic resources your child will need. Do you have the resources of personal space and a suitable environment: a room where he can sleep; an area where she can play; a neighborhood which he can share with other children; a plan for her day care if both you and your spouse intend to keep outside jobs after her birth. After surveying the day-care situation in

*Figures adjusted to 1976 dollar value.

the United States, noted child educator Dr. Stella Chess flatly declared, "I would plan for day care before I planned a child." And overall, can you provide a home where a child will be welcome.

The welcome must be wholeheartedly extended even in the face of some inevitable disruptions. Unless you have an extremely roomy house or apartment, some disorder will naturally occur even in the earliest days and weeks of your child's life. Be prepared to find small towels and diapers encroaching onto formerly clear counter space in bathrooms, baby clothing atop dressers; formula and baby food in evidence in the kitchen or dining room; extra amounts of laundry erupting from hampers; boxes of Pampers spilling from closets; and later, of course, toys everywhere.

You will not encounter every one of these inconveniences, but you will face enough of them to test your tolerance. At the same time that you will almost inevitably be staying home more, your home will be less tidy. Within your home, your own personal space will be diminished.

You may find your delight in your child and his or her development mingled with a tense effort to defend personal belongings you are fond of against assaults of youthful exuberance. Are you sure that your delight in your child will predominate? The excited look in an infant's face when she or he first tastes something that will later become a favorite food—say, strained raspberries—should mean more to a parent by far than the fact that raspberry stains have just gotten onto his or her shirt or that milk is spilled at the same meal at which raspberries are discovered!

Among many new parents, a tolerance for furniture slipcovers is hastily developed. One mother commented, "Before I had Christian, I disdained plastic slipcovers for furniture. I think I even remarked once I'd rather die than cover a pleasant sofa texture with something so disagreeable to sit on. Well, if I once preferred death to plastics, I now prefer plastics to spills," she concluded.

From the standpoint of child development, slipcovers are preferable to off-limits areas within the home. Dr. Burton White, director of Harvard University's Preschool Project, has found that restrictive practices in the home can delay a child's fundamental sensory, motor, and even intellectual development. Dr. White reported in a newsletter of the American Psychological Association that children who are given free access to all living areas of their homes seem to develop more quickly and easily than those whose movements and exploratory play are restricted.

Not surprisingly, parents who were satisfied with their experiences in raising children indicated a need to become less materialistic during years of early childhood: "You can't be 'thing-oriented,'" wrote one. Many others wrote of at least one treasured belonging that had been innocently destroyed by a child. One parent wrote, "Everyone talks about the need to child-proof a home. Nobody is very specific as to how to do it. We locked up all harmful or poisonous substances, put sharp and breakable objects out of reach, but somehow left a photograph album in its usual place on our coffee table. As a result, most of our wedding pictures were destroyed."

Almost all satisfied parents apologized for any expressed concern over material goods. Several stressed that they were of course not blaming the child, yet practically speaking, everyone has possessions they value. The wisdom seems to lie in accepting this rather than claiming that "a child is more valuable than any possession he could possibly destroy"—which of course is true. Yet at some moment this is probably going to be severely tested. A particularly poignant incident related by Shirley Radl in *Mother's Day Is Over* is worth sharing in this regard:

> Sometimes the resentment over the loss of an object is all the more galling when love for the children figured so strongly in owning it. One Christmas season before we had children, my husband and I found an exquisite crèche in a little antique store. The manger was made of wood and straw, and the

figures were ceramic and beautifully painted. The crèche came from a small village in Italy, and we were told that the village had since been flooded and that the craftsmen who made the figures had died or disappeared. No more of these would ever be available.

The proprietor of the shop treasured the crèche. He seemed about to refuse to let it go after he told us the story, but he relented when he realized that we appreciated its beauty as much as he did. With a deep sigh, he carefully wrapped each figure, boxed up all the pieces, and wished us a merry Christmas.

When we got home, we unwrapped everything carefully, set up the figures and manger, and talked about the day when we would have children. As we readied the place for the season and sipped our hot buttered rums, we talked about the fun and the fullness that would be ours when we were truly a family. We talked about how much our children would enjoy the tradition of putting this together each year.

And after the children were born, putting up the crèche at night and enjoying their reaction in the morning became a part of our happy Christmases. A few nights before last Christmas, we waited until the children were in bed, and then contentedly set about our sentimental task, anticipating the smiles of delight when Adam and Lisa would wake up and discover this annual surprise. We spent wonderful family moments as they asked the questions about each figure the next morning.

Two days later, the children were peacefully sitting and coloring in the room where the crèche was. I was clearing up the breakfast dishes when suddenly a wrestling match broke out. Before I could get there, the Three Wise Men and two sheep had made it crashingly to the floor.

Five ceramic figures do not constitute a tragedy, but as I was picking up the pieces, I remembered our conversation the day we bought this last-of-a-kind Christmas decoration—the conversation about how wonderful it would be to share the crèche with our children . . .

We might sum up the topic of material possessions with the simple suggestion that, if your home is your castle and you are contemplating having a child, you must prepare for a gentle invasion. Children have needs to be active, to explore, to reach, to grasp, to push, to experiment. These are learning activities, not mischief. A child who wonders, What will happen if I throw this little vase on the floor—will it break or bend or melt or disappear? and who then proceeds to throw the vase to the floor, is learning something about physics and the behavior of matter (though the lesson may not be to our liking). One of the smaller tasks of parenthood is to look beyond occasional destructiveness to the needs for activity that underlie it.

A child has one need, however, that is more important than anything else mentioned so far. A child's most basic need is for parents. While that might seem too obvious to mention, it is worth reflecting, in the most general terms at least, on what a parent is or should be.

A parent should be someone with good health and energy.

Dr. Carl Faber of Los Angeles is among the counselors who place great importance on the energy dimension of child-raising:

> A potential parent must have an area of free energy left over from his or her own concerns and conflicts—energy to freely give and invest in tasks and concerns, large and small, that parenthood will bring. Without this 'free energy' to give to the needs of a child, I question whether it's fair at all to have a child. The person who now needs every bit of available energy just to keep himself going just isn't likely to make it.

Several physicians, too, have suggested that a parent's innate energy level bears a direct relationship to being able to adjust well to parenthood. Anecdotal evidence from counselors reinforces this. An almost universal complaint of new parents who have severe adjustment problems is fatigue. Certainly all of us can and have weathered an occasional night without sleep, but a continuous pattern of interrupted rest can both tax patience and distort judgment, and can even lower tolerance to other physical ailments such as the minor but inevitable illnesses that children are vulnerable to. ("When my kids were younger, I never felt really well," one mother recalled. "I was almost always slightly ill.")

Dr. Thomas Holmes, in his investigation of life stress factors (circumstances which create ongoing stress in men and women), places "disruption of sleep patterns" on his list of significant stress-producing occurrences, right along with such things as "loss of a job," "illness of spouse," and "sudden financial emergencies."

Energy, of course, is not only affected by basic good health, but perhaps is so closely dependent upon it as to be almost synonymous with it. In fact, in several languages the semantic relationship between the two is interesting; the Japanese word for good health, for example—*genki*—also means "not tired." But there are important psychological factors, as well. As one successful mother observed, no doubt correctly, "The energy level itself is affected by depression. Unhappiness is more debilitating than doing a lot of things you want to do. I lost as much sleep as any of my neighbors—I just wasn't as *unhappy* as they were about what I faced when I woke up in the morning!"

You should ask yourself how easily you become tired; yet weigh this against your desire to add to your present schedule the energy demands that parenthood would bring.

A successful parent should have another important quality as well, one hinted at by Eda LeShan's matter-of-fact remark, "If you are a parent, it helps if you are grown up." A good parent should possess maturity.

Fine, but how do you assess whether or not you have maturity?

We've gathered suggestions from two groups of people who should know best: professionals who counsel parents in trouble, and the successful parents on whose experiences this book is in large part based. Combining the ideas of these two groups, a fairly widespread agreement on a few simple guidelines was found.

To be mature, most felt, you should have achieved *indepen-*

dence from your own family, so that you no longer rely on mother, father, or relatives for basic financial and emotional support. Living with your parents indicates lack of independence. So does relying on family members for job situations or "sure thing" job recommendations. There was divided opinion as to whether accepting financial help for major start-of-adult-life purchases such as furniture, a car, or financial help with a baby violated a necessary principle of independence: Most felt it did, and even minority voices felt that such loans should be made by a family member only on the same basis as they would be made by a lending institution, that is, to be repaid in full with interest. Occasional borrowing "when things get tight," a common practice of young people in their early to mid-twenties, was seen as thwarting independence. Emotionally, your family should not be relied on to provide comfort when things go wrong. "That is not standing on your own two feet," someone observed, "and it can lead to real trouble in marriage." A rule of thumb suggested was "being able to regard your parents as friends, not protectors."

To be mature, you should also have *come to grips with something else in life since achieving autonomy from your family*. This might be a job, schooling in a field you've selected, exploration of a talent you thought worth developing, or prolonged travel. You should have *known success and coped with failure* within this endeavor, whatever it is. Surviving a major setback was mentioned by many people as a maturing experience.

You should have *learned to live intimately with a roommate*, that is, a spouse, or a romantic partner, not a roommate in the college-dormitory sense of the word. Doing so develops the ability to share; to adapt one's schedule, needs, and priorities to those of another; to develop tolerance for differences of habit and preference; and to develop the knack for structuring your own behavior based on the ability to anticipate the behavior of your partner. Living with a roommate in this intimate sense should also allow you to develop habits of sensitive observation: "This will please her . . . " "This will not

DO I HAVE THE BASICS?

please him . . . " "When he/she is preoccupied, the unexpected is bound to be upsetting . . . " and so on. The art of learning to live with one other adult was, most successful parents felt, a prerequisite for being able to live with two or more other people, of whom at least one is a child.

A mature person is able to *like and respect herself or himself* and, as a consequence, to *have confidence in her or his own choices, opinions, and judgments.* "You can have achieved 'independence' according to many external criteria," observed New York psychologist Dr. Herbert Robbins. "But if something inside you rejects the value system you are following then you lack one very important basis of internal independence—that is, self-respect."

Maturity also involves having a pretty clear idea of the direction you are going in life, and having set short- and long-range goals in that direction. This gives roots to the personality, gives something to weigh and measure options against, including such options as marriage and parenthood. Are these things in line with, or do they conflict with, personal goals that are important to you?

A mature person, most felt, has established a *strong marital bond* or its noncontractual equivalent. While most felt it was not necessarily true that "If you're a successful spouse, you'll be a successful parent," nearly everyone thought it would help! One counselor had an interesting suggestion in line with this requirement of maturity. "The idea of 'building a marital bond' sounds like a very dull thing to have to do," he wrote. "The question is *what goes into the bond?* I would suggest that the most vital thing is for the husband and wife to have a several-years-long *fling* together. The best thing for a couple to do to strengthen their relationship is to do whatever they want to do—explore their dreams, follow their impulses."

A final indicator of maturity suggested by several leading sociologists was: having *an understanding of one's society and its probable future direction.*

This may seem to give an edge to recent college grads who

majored in history and political science, but the kind of social understanding referred to can in fact probably be better gained from keen attention to the six o'clock news than from a hasty course in "Problems of Modern Civilization"! There are lots of people full of accreditation in social theory who fail utterly to understand society—who fail to have a mature comprehension of the present and future problems we will all share.

Of course, a mature view of the future is difficult to bring into focus. We all vaguely know that water tables are falling, populations rising, the job market toughening, nonrenewable natural resources dwindling, and multinational corporations acquiring unprecedented powers, yet most of us at this moment have our minds on our bank balance, our hair color, a shopping list, or what the guy in the next office thinks of us.

Like the motorist who assumes that if his gas tank is full, the road ahead is safe, most of us find the short-range assumption (based on a little bit of functioning machinery, a few handy facts) a lot more manageable than trying to peer around the corners of the globe.

An interesting representation of how we human beings look at our world was shown a few years ago by the authors of a world study called *The Limits to Growth*.

Without the aid of the computer banks that top researchers and national leaders have at their disposal, of course, a totally global perspective is not only an unrealistic goal for most of us, but in fact it's an impossible one. The human brain, remarkable as it is, can only keep track of a few of the thousands of intricate and intertwining dynamic forces that, at any given moment, are acting to shape our future.

Still, there are differences between those who at least attempt the struggle to understand the world and those who instead snuggle within yesterday's worn but comfortable assumptions. There are differences between an individual who assumes that, if he is making $100 a week this year in a steady job, he will make $125 a week next year and $150 a week the

Figure 1 HUMAN PERSPECTIVES

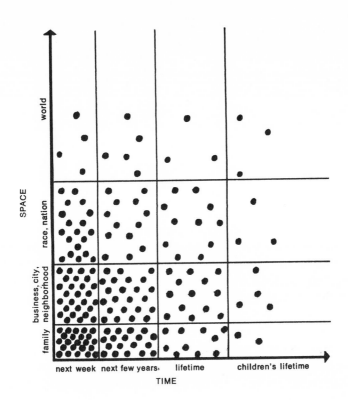

The graph has two dimensions: time and space.

Although people's perspectives vary in space and in time, every human concern falls somewhere on the space-time graph. The majority of the world's people are concerned with matters that affect only family or friends over a short period of time. Others look further ahead in time or over a larger area—perhaps a city or nation. Only a very few people have a global perspective that extends far into the future.

Reprinted by permission, from Dennis and Donella Meadows. *The Limits to Growth.* Potomac Associates, 1972, p. 19.

year after that, and the individual who knows that that is no longer the way things work and who in some measure will thus be better able to cope with future probabilities.

The latter individual has some advantages as a potential parent. He in some way comprehends that he is not just bringing a child into his household, but into a world ever so slightly out of control; and, knowing this, he can maximize his personal control in ways available to him.

He knows life will change dramatically within both his lifetime and his child's: jobs, politics, education, housing, crime, day care, the role of women—all are just a few issues which will affect both him and his child directly.

What protective gestures will he be able to make toward his family's future? If he sees that our affluence rests on a crumbling foundation and suspects that his own job field may be in for massive layoffs at some futurè time, he may begin to lay the groundwork for supplementing income in other ways and investigate other occupational areas such as exploring the possibilities of subsistence farming or farm-lot sharing.

If he perceives that, given escalating energy problems, his present home could become far too expensive to heat and maintain, he may become involved in local politics to the extent of urging utility-rate control, join with others to advocate the national energy policies he sees as most hopeful, or try to build a solar reflector.

If he strongly intuits that two income-producing adults will be necessary to support a family of three or four members, he may become fervent in his efforts to change the thinking of his congressman, who last week voted against a national day-care program of federally sponsored centers for preschool children.

These are just a few ways in which a mature, wide-ranging, and farsighted outlook on the part of a prospective parent can increase the chances a child will have for happiness and well-being.

An extremely logical question that might be raised at this

point would be, Is there any simple rule as to just how old someone would have to be to have achieved all these experiential components of maturity? The expected reply—maturity is not a matter of chronological age . . . maturity can't be measured in years alone—we feel to be inadequate. Based both on common sense and expert opinion, and perhaps more importantly, based on the age of our successful-parent population when they had their first children, we'd like to suggest a specific answer to the above question: *You have to be at least twenty-five years old.*

We find that parents who have a first child before they are twenty-five years old often regret it later, and they have directly expressed this regret to us. One father in our group of admittedly unhappy parents said, "If I were having Timmy now, I'd appreciate him. If I could see him as a baby again, I'd pay some attention; I wouldn't be so impatient." The father speaking was twenty-eight years old.

This only confirms what counselors with years of experience report as standard. Eda LeShan reports that younger parents commonly, almost universally, feel, "Why was I in such a hurry? Why didn't I wait another year? Why didn't we take a trip instead? Now I'm a prisoner forever—this baby owns me body and soul—I'm finished, all washed up!"

Director of Purdue University's Marital Counseling Service Dr. Charles Figley recommends that "Waiting until age twenty-five gets you out of several 'time traps.' After twenty-five, you're more likely to be responding to your *own* feelings than just reacting to some cultural alarm clock that says, 'After high school you're old enough,' which would be at age eighteen or nineteen, or 'After college you're old enough,' generally age twenty-one or twenty-two. Age twenty-five increases the odds that the decision you're making is your own."

Dr. Jessie Bernard, a highly respected sociologist who has explored reproductive issues at great range and great depth in such landmark works as "The Future of Marriage" and "The

Future of Motherhood,'' can be very short-spoken at times. Asked whether parenthood after age twenty-five compares well in terms of parents' adjustment to parenthood before that age, she simply replied, ''That's not even a question. Raise the age by five years, or ten—then maybe there'll be be something to talk about.''

Our group of satisfied parents also stood firm in advocating first pregnancy after age twenty-five. The demographics of this group are atypical, but may well relate to their success as parents. Since this group has at least one child who has reached adolescence, they generally had a first pregnancy in the years immediately surrounding 1960. At that time, fewer than 20 percent of women waited until after age twenty-five to have their first children. However, for our successful parents, the statistic almost reversed itself. More than 80 percent of our satisfied parents *did* wait until after age twenty-five.

Comments of this group included:

''We managed better than those we knew who had their first child when they were younger. The younger ones had a tendency to expect the baby to take care of them rather than the other way around.''

''To use a modern-day phrase,'' said another, ''you have to do your own thing first. Be an adult before you have a child. That way, you'll never need to be the kind of bitter parent who, denying himself some pleasure, looks at his child and says, 'If it weren't for you I could be doing what I want to.' Because, you see, you'll have *already* done what you want to.''

''Within reasonable limits, it is better the longer you wait.''

Many echoed that feeling. ''My wife and I had our first and only child when we were both thirty-six years old. We are happier about parenthood than anybody else we know. We think it's because we waited. In general, we think the longer you wait, the better. The longer you wait, the more of life you have experienced. The longer you wait, the more ready you are.''

Since there has popularly been considered to be a biological barrier making childbearing unwise after about age thirty, some wonder if later childbearing has physical disadvantages for the mother. But the majority of obstetricians and health professionals seem to see positive factors associated with pregnancy postponement.

National health statistics show that pregnancy complications are most common among women in their adolescence and early twenties: toxemia, prolonged labor, and nutritional problems are more common then, in part due to environmental factors and in part due to relative physical immaturity of the younger mothers. The risk of pregnancy-related death is also greater for younger mothers.

The infant's chances, too, for a sound start in life increase with the mother's age increment. Infant mortality for babies born to mothers under fifteen is more than twice as high as for mothers in their early twenties; infants born to mothers under nineteen have less of a chance for survival than do babies born to mothers in their twenties and thirties.

As age forty is approached, certain physical risks such as birth defects do rise sharply. The most certain example is the increased risk of Down's syndrome, or mongolism. According to the latest (1970) edition of Novak's *Textbook of Gynecology*, mothers twenty years old have only a 1 in 2000 chance of bearing a mongoloid child. At thirty-five, the risk is still only about 1 in 1000. But between the years thirty-five and forty, the chances increase to 1 in 100, and rise to 1 in 50 for the forty-five-year-old first-time mother.

Still, New York gynecologists and obstetricians Drs. David James and Frederick Silverman say that 15 percent of their practice consists of women over forty having their first babies. In their practice there have been no birth defects and no abortions due to the possibility of defective birth. (A preventive check on the unborn infant, *amniocentesis,* is becoming more and more routinely used: It allows accurate prediction of any birth defects which may exist by examination of a small amount of amniotic fluid.)

Physicians point to the following advantages for delayed

first pregnancies: an older mother gets much more concerned and attentive prenatal care; she is more self-solicitous as well; her personal circumstances are apt to be more affluent and comfortable; she undergoes more frequent testing. Says Dr. James of the over-forty first-time mother, "If there's even a slight complaint, we'd be much quicker in seeing her." It all adds up to very good chances for having a healthy child and ending up as a healthy mother.

Might an older woman have to worry more about energy, about keeping up with a child? Commented one of our successful parents on this point, "You don't generally chase your child through forests, do you? Ten years or so shouldn't make that much difference in your ability to get around an average house or apartment."

In general, there seems no question that the biological boundary for childbearing, once considered to coincide rigidly with a woman's thirtieth birthday, can be and is being pushed back. Gail Sheehy's conclusion after extensive study, as stated in her book *Passages,* is that *"thirty-five* brings the biological boundary into sight" (emphasis ours).

Certainly women in their thirties can well have the same advantageous situations physicians describe as typical of the over-forty mother.

And within reasonable limits, the woman who postpones having a child will enjoy physical advantages. Most experts interviewed would place psychological factors above physical ones, in any case. Commented Dr. Louise B. Tyrer, an obstetrician-gynecologist with almost a full generation of medical experience, "Sensitivity tends to accompany a woman's maturity, as do wisdom and self-knowledge. The mature woman is ready to be sensitive to the needs of a child—because she is *ready to have* a child. The kind of readiness she enjoys ripens slowly, over the years. It just cannot be rushed."

Chapter 2

Am I Interested in Children?

Questionnaire 2

1. Kids today get away with murder.

2. I have enjoyed working with children in some way in the past few years.

3. There is one child who is my special friend.

4. At adult social gatherings, children should be:
   a) seen and not heard
   b) treated politely
   c) interacted with, paid attention to
   d) absent

5. When visiting friends who have children, I tend to ignore the children.

6. I enjoyed baby-sitting as a teenager.

7. I wouldn't mind driving a school bus.

8. I have cared for a child *in my home* for a day or more during the past year.

9. It's not necessary to like children in general to be able to love your *own*.

10. It's been my experience that people fall in love with photographs of children more than they like them in the flesh.

11. My spouse and I are at our favorite, quiet restaurant. Nearby sit a mother, father, and two children. The

children are cutting up and being loud. They distract my attention first by shouting "Soup!" when the soup arrives, then by shouting "Souper!" (variation of "supper"? approval of the soup?) and make more noise in appreciation of their own wit. Among their other activities (though the parents did quiet them during the main course) were sword fights with the silverware and hiding behind the napkins. My reaction to this is:

    a) fancy restaurants can use a dash of children's spontaneity.

    b) parents shouldn't bring young children to places where the clientele expects a subdued atmosphere.

    c) parents should exercise control over their children in public places.

    d) I wish my spouse and I had asked to be moved to a quieter table at the beginning of our meal!

12. Most of my friends who have children have children I wouldn't want.

13. Of all people, children are the most imaginative.

14. You can do anything with children if you only play with them.

15. It is important to keep grandparents, other relatives, and friends from spoiling your children with too much attention.

16. I always pause to admire infants.

17. I love to hold infants and small children.

18. There are magic moments for a parent—such as a child's first step, a child's first word—which both represent parenthood's real meaning and which compensate for any number of sleepless nights and other hardships.

19. I'd draw a line between the interesting, meaningful parts of infant care (which appeal to me) and the maintenance tasks (which don't).

20.   Here is the way I feel about diapers:

    a) Even changing diapers can be a beautiful expression of love for your child.

    b) Let's face it: changing diapers isn't pleasant but it is something you must do because it is a necessary part of infant care.

    c) I would expect my spouse to be primarily responsible for this task.

    d) Willingness to change diapers has absolutely nothing to do with whether or not one can be a good parent.

21.   *My First Book* was recommended by the children's librarian as excellent for my little girl who is two. Sturdy, brightly colored, each page pictures three objects to point to so that she can learn the names of objects as I pronounce them. My daughter does not respond to the book at all. My reaction is most likely to be:

    a) My daughter may have a vision problem—I'll call the pediatrician.

    b) My daughter may be a slow learner—I'll find a specialist.

    c) The librarian must have been wrong about the age level for which this book is appropriate.

    d) Children's rates of development and interest vary enormously; there is no cause for concern.

    e) I think I'll see if she responds to other books or real objects.

22.   My three-year-old daughter is standing facing the toilet, naked, pelvis thrust forward, trying to hold her clitoris like a penis so she can "pee like a boy does . . . " My reaction is:

    a) amusement

    b) concern

    c) alarm

    d) nonchalance

    e) horror
    f) disgust

23.   I would not mind being almost exclusively responsible
      for infant care if my spouse were not interested in
      helping or sharing at this stage.

24.   I would be able to take it if an infant of mine cried often,
      woke often during the night.

25.   When I think about a baby, it's a mixed picture: Babies
      are messy sometimes, have colic and fever and drippy
      noses sometimes, spit up sometimes, not always clean
      and sweet.

26.   While riding along, Curious George kept thinking of boats. It
      would be such fun to have a boat. But how could he get one?
      He thought and thought—and then he had an idea! He got off
      his bicycle, took a newspaper out of his bag, and began to fold
      it. First he folded down the corners, like *this*, then he folded
      both edges *up*, brought the ends together, and flattened it
      sidewise. Then he turned one corner up, then the other one,
      again brought the ends together and flattened it sidewise. Then,
      gently, he pulled the ends *open*—and there was his *BOAT!*
      [*Curious George Rides A Bike* by H.A. Rey]

The response to the above story that is closest to my
own response is:
    a) I think it would be fun to read this story to a young
child of mine and make a paper boat.
    b) If my child wanted this story read and a paper boat
made every night for a week, it would still be fun.
    c) If *Curious George* remained my child's favorite
bedtime story for an entire summer, paper boats and all,
I still would not be bored.
    d) If I had carefully selected for my child a stimulating
variety of books to read, I would subtly discourage an
exclusive preference for *Curious George.*

e) If I had obtained for my child a stimulating variety of books to read, I would *firmly* discourage an exclusive preference for *Curious George*.

f) After I had made about five paper boats, I would expect my child to make the boat himself.

g) I have frankly no interest in this situation at all.

27. The idea of teaching addition and subtraction by creating games, perhaps like, "Freddie the Frog jumps two steps forward. Now *if* Freddie the Frog jumps *one* jump back . . . " would be a challenge I'd enjoy.

28. My four-year-old will not nap today. First it's "I'm thirsty," and "I'm thirsty again, my throat's dry," then "The blanket's too heavy," then "I need Petey Puppet," then "I'm hungry, then "I need . . . " My reaction is likely to be:

a) I spank: enough is enough

b) I order child to stay in room and sleep.

c) I explain "quiet time" and that no more requests will be answered for now.

d) I accede to all requests.

29. Small children should be firmly discouraged from masturbatory play.

30. Dr. Stella Chess of New York City tells this story:

A young mother was walking slowly down the street pushing a stroller full of groceries. She got to the steps of her apartment building, pulled the stroller up, opened the door and pushed it in. Then she stood on the steps watching. I followed her glance. Down the sidewalk came her two-year-old, strutting as if he owned the city.

He gets to the steps. Each one is as high as his legs are long. He has a cracker box in his hand. He tries to lift his leg to mount the step. He can't make it. The grown-up watches and waits. He looks at her for help. She smiles and waits. He tries again. No luck. He looks at the box.

He looks at the railing. He looks at the grown-up again. She smiles. He takes hold of the railing and tries. No good. Still holding the railing, he stops to think. He looks at the box. He puts it down on the step. Now he leans on the steps with his free hands and balances himself so he can make the step. He's up. He looks at his mother, smiling now himself. She smiles again. He picks up the box, recognizes he's got the same problem again. But this time he doesn't give up the box. He gets up the next step leaning on the box in his hand. Next step he tries without using the box hand at all. Can't make it. Legs are too short. He leans on the box again. He's up. He's made all the steps. His mother hugs him to her, impulsively, and carries him through the door.

The reaction to the above story that is closest to my own reaction is:

a) Why on earth was that mother walking a block ahead of her *two-year-old*? City streets and sidewalks are dangerous.

b) The process described must have taken twenty minutes! I would feel too busy for all that trial-and-error to go on and would have picked up the child and carried him up the steps.

c) The mother was risking giving her child a sense of failure if he could not in fact manage to climb the steps.

d) The mother is not a good mother; she didn't offer to help her little boy.

e) What a nice example of the magic an encouraging smile can work!

f) That mother has an enviable sense of what her child can do on his own.

g) For the life of me, I cannot see myself in such a picture.

31. Following is a capsule example of how children learn.

PARENT (to Johnny, four months old, in carriage): Look, Johnny, there's a dog. See him? Woof, woof!

JOHNNY: Smiles, giggles.

PARENT (to Johnny in high chair, six months old): Hear that, Johnny? Bow, wow! What's that? That's the dog barking outside.

JOHNNY: More smiles and giggles.

PARENT (to Johnny in stroller, twelve months): Here comes the dog, Johnny. Want to pat him? (You take his hand and rub it over the dog's soft fur.) Nice soft doggy.

JOHNNY: Mmmm (laughing and looking at parent).

JOHNNY (riding in car, sixteen months old, jumping up and down in his seat): Dog, dog! Woof! Woof!

PARENT: That's right, Johnny. That's a nice soft dog. Woof, woof! Bow, wow!

The reaction to the above that is closest to my own reaction is:

a) Baby talk is condescending and unnecessary.

b) How beautiful such a learning process is!

c) Shouldn't a child know such simple words as *dog* and *woof* before sixteen months?

d) How proud a parent I would be to hear my own sixteen-month-old respond to my patient teaching by saying "Dog, dog! Woof, woof!"

e) The opportunities for expanding a young child's horizons seem exciting.

f) I cannot see myself in this picture at all.

32. A majority of the following infant-care tasks are ones that I would like to do.

   diapering
   bathing
   feeding

dressing
preparing food
watching over
amusing
playing games
repeating words
snuggling
walking
talking to
taking to doctor
burping
answering crying
stimulating through sound and sight

33.   A majority of the following toddler-care tasks are ones
      that I would like to do.

bathing
toilet training
arranging for play with other children
teaching physical coordination
teaching colors and shapes
teaching words
teaching rules
teaching to dress
correcting
watching over
playing
telling stories
reading stories
dealing with illnesses
providing stimulation
analyzing and dealing with the beginnings of aggression
roughhousing

34.   My five-year-old is playing a game with toy soldiers. I
      announce that dinner is ready. Ten minutes pass and
      Sally is still not at the table. I:

a) give another warning

b) physically compel her immediate presence at the table

c) explain why she must come—other family members are waiting, etc.

d) proceed with dinner, figuring she'll come when she's hungry

e) proceed with dinner, but will leave her supperless as a lesson in punctuality

35. I don't mind errands, driving the car around.

36. Six- to twelve-year-olds are old enough to assume some responsibility around the house.

37. Six- to twelve-year-olds are ready to learn to handle money.

38. I would give a child who was ten an allowance only for books and school needs, not for records, clothes, candy, etc.

39. In a dentist's waiting room, from available reading material, I would choose to read:

a) current *Time* or *Newsweek*

b) month-old *People* magazine

c) *Sports Illustrated*

d) *Travel and Leisure*

e) *Parents* magazine

f) *Reader's Digest*

g) *Ladies' Home Journal*

h) *Redbook*

i) pamphlet "Tips for the Small Investor"

j) pamphlet "20 Ways to Improve your Marriage"

k) pamphlet "Psychology of Toys and Play"

l) pamphlet "Low-Cost Dinner Ideas"

m) *Vogue*

n) *Cosmopolitan*

40. I would rather go to a concert than to the circus.

41. Nature hikes and bike riding excite me very little.

42. If I had an eleven-year-old who was interested only in basketball, to the exclusion of studies, family recreation, or even other sports, I would be likely to say:

    a) "Are you going to be a basketball bum all your life?"

    b) "Look, only a handful of people can play basketball professionally—you'd better get suited up for another career."

    c) "Why don't you do something cultural or intelligent for a change?"

    d) "If I play ball with you tonight, will you listen to records with me later?"

    e) "You know the discipline you're giving yourself would sure be nice applied to homework."

    f) "Practice makes perfect—you're sure to make the school team and make me proud of you."

    g) None of these—I'd accept the exclusive attention to basketball.

43. I overhear the following in a store. A father says to a man he encounters, "Gee that's a great-looking shirt, Joe," then after a minute moves on. The father's child confronts him with, "But dad, you *hate* Hawaiian shirts." The father replies, "I know, but Joe likes them, so why make him feel bad?" I think that father is being:

    a) hypocritical

    b) tactful

    c) dishonest

    d) realistic

44. The idea that a child of mine might be violent or cruel to other living things makes me angry and sad beyond belief!

45. My school-age son or daughter has won an election as class president. My first thought is:

    a) I want to phone or write our parents and in-laws.

    b) I want to tell all my friends.

    c) The family should go out to dinner to celebrate together.

    d) How wonderful if this meant a future of adult political leadership!

    e) I want to tell my child how proud I am.

    f) I must watch my child carefully for signs that he or she will become too conceited because of this victory.

46. Due to dyslexia (a correctable central language impairment) my child has not found schoolwork easy. With remedial help, he has made good progress but still has a ways to go. Close to the end of the school year, the guidance counselor suggests that he repeat first grade. I feel sure that he could catch up with his classmates before the end of next year, but am not sure he should have to struggle that hard. I feel my reaction would be to:

    a) do what the counselor advises

    b) do what my child would prefer

    c) avoid repeating a grade at all costs: challenge is good, and children rise to expectations

    d) avoid repeating a grade at all costs: how could I tell my friends?

    e) have him repeat first grade because the strain of trying to keep up with second grade work might harm his desire to learn permanently

    f) feel that the question is irrelevant: a child of mine would not be a poor student

47. My child's teacher telephones one evening to say that my child was caught cheating on a spelling exam. My response is:

a) "Most schoolchildren cheat: what's the big deal?"

b) "I hope you will give him a failing mark for the exam."

c) "Thank you for letting me know. I will do my best to deal with this."

d) "Please don't let this influence his overall grade; I guarantee it will not happen again."

e) "If this is true, it is your fault for running a classroom where such actions can occur."

f) "You must be mistaken—a child of mine would not cheat."

48.   In my preoccupation to get a lot of work done one evening, I fail to notice a pretty card my child has left for me on top of the day's mail! I only notice the card after he is asleep.

a) I wake my child to say thank you.

b) I give my child a special hug without waking him.

c) I write a thank-you note and leave it where it will be seen first thing after awakening in the morning.

49.   My seven-year-old comes shyly to ask me for a pair of Bass Weejuns. ("All the other kids have them.") This is an expensive kind of loafer and our family budget is strained this month. My reaction is:

a) I will somehow manage to buy them. I want my child to have nice things.

b) I will somehow manage to buy them so my child will not be different.

c) I will not buy them, and will have a talk with my child about conformity, status symbols.

d) I will not buy them, explaining to my child that I would like to but we cannot afford them.

50.   Late one afternoon, I receive a call from a department store. My twelve-year-old has been caught attempting to shoplift a $70 camera. At the store I am allowed to speak

privately with my child, who says tearfully that he
wanted to take pictures of good quality like several of
his friends who have expensive cameras but had been
afraid to ask me for the money. I am most likely to say to
the department-store authorities:

a) "This is a serious matter, so my child should be
taken to the police station in order to learn a real lesson
from this incident."

b) "I will buy the camera if you will let my child go
with no further punishment or humiliation."

c) "I feel partly responsible for this because my child
did not feel free to come to me to ask for something he
very much wanted."

d) This item is irrelevant to me. A child of mine would
never be in such a situation.

51. The quality and quantity of a child's television viewing
does not concern me greatly. TV is educational, and the
efforts of parent reform groups are increasing the quality
of TV programming for children continually.

52. A six- to twelve-year-old should be expected to eat
everything served at family meals. Food likes and
dislikes at this age are a way of testing parents.

53. My child has not been invited to Kevin's party.
a) I say, "Never mind. You can give a party and not
invite Kevin."

b) I say, "It's not important. You and I will do
something together."

c) I ask my child if he has any idea why he was not
invited.

d) I phone Kevin's parents to see what is at the bottom
of this!

e) I do nothing—this is solely my child's problem.

54. Sometime between the ages of six and twelve, if not

before, sex education in the home should be a subject about which adequate information is available.

55. Parents must teach children principles of safety outside the home—to avoid strangers, and so on.

56. Parents should know where six- to twelve-year-olds are at all times.

57. Most childhood illnesses can be prevented with careful health supervision.

58. Rudeness or bratty behavior among six- to twelve-year-olds should be dealt with forcefully.

59. You have always set an example of simple, stylish dress. Most of your daughter's friends, too, wear understated things—jeans, slacks, shirts. Tonight, your twelve-year-old daughter appears in a flouncy, laced-up dress she found at a street sale. ("Miss Kitty of 'Gunsmoke'!" you think, seeing her.) She intends to wear this thing to a party tonight. Knowing her attire will conflict with what's being worn by almost everyone else (as well as conflicting with all principles of taste and good sense which you have tried to impart to her) you:
    a) tell her she cannot go the party wearing *that*!
    b) give her your opinion about what you think she should wear, then leave the final decision up to her
    c) smile and let her wear whatever she wants without comment

60. A parent of a teenager should be more a pal than an authority figure.

61. It's too late to teach a teenager values—you've either done that already, or it's too late now.

62. Adolescence is rougher on the kids than the parents.

63. Parents have to expect teenagers to be sulky, moody, uncommunicative; it's part of the growing-up process.

64. Parents can still enforce whatever rules of behavior they want from teenagers in their own house.

65. It would be fun to introduce an almost-grown-up child to some of my favorite adult pastimes—tennis, boating, appreciation of classical music, or whatever things I particularly enjoy.

66. Your fifteen-year-old has taken to using profanity. He or she has been warned to stop it. Now, after a mild argument, he or she tells you, . . . "fuck off!" . . . and walks out, slamming the door. Your reaction is likely to be:

    a) Well, he's in a bad mood—so are we all sometimes.

    b) Is he ever going to get it when he walks back in!

    c) I will firmly and finally state my disapproval of profanity, but privately acknowledge I can't control it.

    d) My response to this question would depend on when, and in what frame of mind, my teenager walked back in the door.

    e) My response to this question would depend on whether this fifteen-year-old is a son or a daughter.

67. My reaction to knowing that a sixteen-year-old had written the following essay and turned it in as a class assignment

> I love girls. I love what the girls have. I am nuts about the girls that are big and fine. All the girls love something about the boys and the boys love that thing that girls got. It's so good to be with a girl in bed at night.

would probably be:

    a) shock

    b) disgust

    c) outrage

    d) concern for morals of today's generation

    e) disapproval for a teacher who would accept this kind of self-expression as schoolwork.

f) acceptance of the fact that sexual mores seem to be increasingly liberal with each generation

g) I do not know how I would react if I myself were the parent of a teenager.

68.   My teenage son or daughter leaves the car in a mess.

a) I insist the car be clean at all times.

b) I insist that the car be left clean when other family members are going to use it.

c) I take no action: it's not worth fussing about.

69a.   I find out that my eighteen-year-old daughter is sexually active.

a) I punish her.

b) I forbid her to continue such activity and restrict her movements if necessary to enforce what I say.

c) I make sure she is protected by birth control.

d) I ask her if we can talk together so that I can share my feelings on what sex should mean.

e) I ignore what I have found out. My daughter is old enough to take care of herself.

f) The question is irrelevant. A daughter of mine would not be involved in premarital sex.

69b.   I find out that my fifteen- or sixteen-year-old daughter is sexually active.

a) I punish her.

b) I forbid her to continue such activity and restrict her movements if necessary to enforce what I say.

c) I make sure she is protected by birth control.

d) I ask her if we can talk together so that I can share my feelings on what sex should mean.

e) I ignore what I have found out. My daughter is old enough to take care of herself.

f) The question is irrelevant. A daughter of mine would not be involved in premarital sex.

70.   Before doing laundry, I check pockets of jeans my

sixteen-year-old has stuffed into the laundry hamper. I find tobaccolike residue in several pockets that I am sure is pot.

a) I ignore it. Using pot is normal experimenting behavior among teens.

b) I forbid certain privileges as punishment.

c) I forbid certain privileges unless he or she promises to stop using and carrying pot.

d) I point out the risks and express my disapproval, then let him make his own decision about continued use.

e) Take no action because I personally do not disapprove of marijuana use.

f) I'm sure that by the time a child I might have was old enough to be interested in marijuana, laws will have changed, it will be legal, and this issue will have disappeared as a typical problem of adolescents.

71. The school calls. It seems that when my child was told his book report on *Catch–22* was unacceptable in English class because it was on a list of unapproved books circulated early in the year by the school, he took an unexpected course of action. He told his teacher he would re-do the assignment and review another book in order to receive a grade. But then, with the help of friends, he set up a BANNED BOOKS display outside the English office, displaying such books as *The Naked Ape, The Fixer, Slaughterhouse–5, Soul on Ice,* and *Lady Chatterly's Lover* and offering information about these books. My reaction is:

a) amusement
b) approval
c) confusion
d) distress
e) disapproval
f) shock
g) anger

72. Coming home from work an hour early one afternoon, you hear sounds from the bathroom and, thinking your sixteen-year-old son is sick, push open the bathroom door, which is slightly ajar anyway. What you see makes *you* feel sick. Your son and a friend of his break away from each other hastily, but they have clearly been engaged in a homosexual act. You:

  a) take stern action—order your son's friend out of the house and punish your son in the most severe way you can think of

  b) say, "Tom, please get your pants back on—I'd like to have a talk with you."

  c) close the door and walk away, intending to ignore the incident

  d) close the door and walk away, because you don't know what else to do

  e) close the door and walk away, intending to take no action until and unless your son comes to *you* to discuss it

  f) run for the Yellow Pages to look for a psychiatrist

  g) The question is irrelevant. A son of mine would never be in such a situation.

73. Overall, discipline during teenage years has to be approached with a certain attitude of resignation. Sometimes nothing will work, because it is a developmental task of teenagers to rebel and to use this as one way of establishing independence from parents.

74. Your teenager wants to drop out of the public high school he or she has been attending, wanting instead to attend an alternative high school which features work experience programs, nonacademic programs, and somewhat offbeat (to you) minicourses.

  Typical of the alternative high school's curriculum are courses in "Finding Inner Space" and "Creating Folk Toys from Wood."

Typical of this school's approach to traditional subjects is the "American History and Civics" course, which is based on a series of community polls the students are to conduct. Since the school is new, there is no way to evaluate how students will compare with their public-school peers in academic areas after a year or so of this (to you) "nonsense." You:

a) allow your child to make his or her own decision

b) discuss the matter with your child, make your own feelings strongly known, then allow child to decide

c) forbid your child to attend this school

d) forbid your child to attend the alternative school this semester but hold out hope of reevaluating the situation after more is known about the school

75. Your teenager will graduate from high school soon. But he has steadfastly resisted long-standing urging to apply to colleges. He wants instead to work as a soda jerk for a year "and *then* I'll think about college." Fearing that "and then" may become "never", fearing that your son or daughter will drift into a low-income, dead-end way of life, you:

a) forbid him or her to live at home if such a plan is followed, meaning what you say

b) forbid him or her to continue to live at home, hoping this strategy may startle your child into facing the realities of life (and a change of mind)

c) urge college as strongly as possible, but, after making your final statement, let your child decide what course to follow

d) accept what your new graduate wants to do, hoping that this life-style experiment will either be successful—or *short!*

e) accept your child's plan on the condition that he or she apply now for the following year's college term

Am I Sure I Want to Take This Trip?

Think of the preceding set of questions as a travelogue, as seventy-five color slides showing just a few of the tour stops in "Kid's Country." Since the only charters available are long ones, ask yourself: Is this a trip I want to take?

Was your overall response to this section of the questionnaire positive or negative? Did the situations described seem interesting to you or not?

If you feel like one nonparent who reviewed this section and said, "All these questions are incredibly boring," we'd like to stress that there is nothing wrong with that. Not everybody in the world is thrilled with baby talk and child development; not everybody is willing to give up great books for Dr. Seuss; not everybody has to! Fewer and fewer people these days insist firmly that we should all like the same things, hold the same values, and live the same way. We will only offer the obvious suggestion that if you find kids and their activities less than fascinating, you might think twice before signing on for a twenty-year cruise on the good ship *Parenthood*, because people who *do* have little choice but to ride out the waves they encounter. Sometimes the effort to do so with good grace results in what might be called emotional seasickness.

A very new idea among certain experts has it that hostility toward children is a natural and inevitable phenomenon. Judge Gertrude Bacon of Parents Anonymous has said, "Every parent is a potential child abuser." Eda LeShan in her book *How to Survive Parenthood* quotes a new father who told her, "It's the funniest thing. I never used to notice how many people murdered their babies. But when I read a newspaper now, that's all I notice."

She tells that story calmly, with understanding and acceptance, then goes on to remark, "One of the best kept secrets there is is that virtually every mother alive at some time or other will scream at, shake, or hit her baby."

We frankly don't think that has to be the case at all. Because more and more parents are admitting ambivalent or negative feelings toward their kids, it is tempting to accept such feelings as normal. We don't!

We don't think parent-child hostility is inevitable. We don't even think it has to exist in a widespread way or in a majority of cases.

We feel it does exist because *a great many mothers and fathers find themselves in a situation they neither like nor are right for.* Having signed on for a long tour in parental territory, they would now be grateful for a bail-out option or an escape clause. But it's not available, and the travel agent who sold them this Parenthood Package has disappeared; so they have little choice but to take out their disappointment on their closest traveling companions. Obviously we feel there are alternatives to such a situation.

Certainly the job of raising a child holds awesome possibilities for anger, and every parent is going to get mad. But the anger doesn't have to be a consistent feeling—*and shouldn't be;* and it doesn't have to predominate—*and shouldn't.*

In any job you do, you are generally not angry if you are interested in what you are doing and you're generally not angry if you like those around you. Where parenthood is concerned, your chances for overall happiness increase greatly if you find the tasks involved in child-raising interesting.

And it helps a lot if you like children.

Of course, this business of whether or not one "likes" chil-

dren easily gets complicated. It is complicated first of all by
the fact that virtually everybody claims to like children (or to
love children), whether they really do or not.

By way of illustration, Lisbeth Schorr, married to TV com-
mentator Daniel Schorr, has written, "My husband did a doc-
umentary on CBS on social programs for children, and the
working title for it was 'Why do we hate our children?' because that's how it really comes out in the way we treat children in a lot of contexts. And he found in talking about it that
people were terribly shocked: 'We *don't* hate our children.
We don't, we don't, we don't. Why, everybody loves children
more than anything.' And yet, we have absolutely outrageous
things happening to children at public hands . . ." Schorr
and other contributors to a recent anthology, *Speaking Out for
America's Children,* recommend direct confrontation of convincing evidence that as a society we have quite ambivalent
feelings toward children, and the asking of such tough question as, If we love children so much, why do we put thirty-
seven or thirty-eight or even forty-three of them in one single
classroom at the same time that we complain about a surplus
of teachers?

And getting to the real meaning of personal claims to love
children often involves a certain translation. "I love children" often translates to "I love *some* children." Children's
personalities, after all, are not stamped out as though by a
cookie cutter. Children are not all alike, and some are more
lovable than others. Similarly, "I like children" often should
be translated to the more accurate meaning of "I like children
sometimes" (or "I like children when they're quiet," "I like
children when they're good," etc.)

Some questionnaire items in the preceding section are
meant to help assess whether your basic feelings toward children are positive or negative.

Being able to see yourself in situations with children (such
as driving a school bus); interacting with children when you
encounter them (as in a friend's home); being willing to see

children integrated into the social world of adults; seeing children as imaginative; and having sympathy for their problems (seeing adolescence as "rougher on the kids than the adults") can all be valid indications of a basic liking for children. More trustworthy, of course, is having had actual experiences with children that you found enjoyable—and the more recent and varied these experiences have been, the more trustworthy they are (baby-sitting memories we found a little unreliable).

On the other hand, ignoring children when they are around; feeling that kids today "get away with murder"; fearing children will be "spoiled by too much attention";* believing that pocket money should allow only for needs, not personal impulses; fearing a child who wins an honor may become conceited; being able to envision oneself using sarcasm as a tool of behavior change ("Are you going to be a basketball bum all your life?")—such responses, taken together, indicate a basic indifference toward children—even envy or hostility—rather than a natural reservoir of warm and positive feelings toward them.

It is perhaps worth mentioning that we are not taking into consideration the possible effectiveness of certain of these responses. Sarcasm, for instance, can be effective in changing a child's behavior; that doesn't mean it's a good idea. We are considering, instead, the more basic issue of how difficult it will be for a parent to feel satisfied in his or her role if he or she lacks affectionate tendencies toward children.

Since parenthood is not the same game through all its innings, let's begin by considering whether you have positive feelings about infants and very young children.

Liking to pause to admire infants seemed insufficient to indicate liking infants: happy and unhappy parents alike, we found, said they paused to admire infants. This seems to be an

---

*A good number of successful parents had an interesting, virtually identical response to Item 15. "You can't spoil a child with too much attention," they wrote, "only with too many material things."

aesthetic appreciation rather than an emotional reaction, and so strongly culturally cued as to be untrustworthy.

Just how automatic the response to infants is—and just how false it can be—can be gathered from an incident related by Professor Harry Harlow. As part of a lecture he gave at a Texas university, a slide picture of an infant was shown. "The audience of college women began to *coo*," he related. "The room sounded like a seaplane taking off, 'oooooh.' . . . Now this is phony as hell. It's social pressure."

You might ask yourself if, when you pause to admire an infant, you are genuinely responding to the infant or being polite to the parents (or doing what you think is expected of you).

Liking to hold infants and small children seems to be a much better indicator of a real, affectionate feeling. Far more successful than unsuccessful parents said they felt physically drawn to infants. As might be expected, too, available professional studies view *holding* as one of the most important indices of maternalism. Pediatric researchers have noted, in fact, that a child will not develop normally without physical touching and holding during the critical period of infancy.

Dr. Lee Salk has commented, "Children who are picked up and held a great deal want to be picked up and held, and they seek out much more stimulation . . . [and] I have seen children begin to show autistic-like features in their behavior after periods of crying it out."

Adequate care of small children involves much more than just physical holding, of course. According to responses of both groups of parents, you can probably consider your own feelings about diapering, bathing, feeding, dressing and so on, to be important. If you responded honestly that you would indeed like a majority of those tasks, you have something in common with successful parents.

Of course, at this point your responses are probably imagined ones, and the reality of bathing a baby might be different from the way you picture it in your mind. For this reason we might comment very briefly on just a few tasks involved in early child care.

Watching over is worth mentioning, if only to emphasize the amount of time this takes. Typically, a child will need fairly constant watching over in infancy during sleeping as well as waking periods (to determine any habits of turning during sleep that might be dangerous, etc.) and for all waking hours during toddlerhood. It is certainly true that the at-home spouse or care-giver can be doing other things during much of this time, as long as those other things don't require total concentration or absorption. One parent made several distinctions that are worth repeating. "You can write personal letters," she said, "and you can read books as long as they're not so interesting that you mind putting them down and losing your place. You can paint a picture, or even a wall, as long as you're not standing on a ladder that will come crashing down when you rush to respond to the baby crying. You can listen to music, even loud music, as long as you position yourself somewhere between the sound of the radio and any sound the child might make so that you'll be certain to hear the latter. You can play the piano: You cannot compose a sonata."

Changing diapers for most people represents the worst maintenance task of parenthood, distressingly symbolizing the basic servitude of early parenthood both because the task is not intrinsically pleasant and because it must be repeated so often (typically, nine or ten times a day for an infant, four or five times a day for a toddler). If you indicated that you thought changing diapers could be beautiful, you might question how realistic you are being. Even among our successful parents, not one said they considered it something beautiful. And remember, they have been through it!

By the way, you and your spouse might check right now on each other's response to Item 20 in this section: If by some chance both of you indicated that you would expect the other to be responsible for this task, you should have a talk.

Some successful parents did point out that other, more enjoyable and meaningful nurturing tasks can go on at the same time that diapers are being changed: talking to the baby, holding him, and stroking him. One parent wrote, "It's a mistake to draw a line between 'meaningful nurturing tasks' and 'just maintenance' tasks. If you can arrange the baby's room or changing area so that he's always looking at something interesting while being changed, then you're providing stimulation, not just diaper service."

Whether it is approached separately or integrated with more ordinary care-giving (or both), providing stimulation for young children is a very important responsibility.

Dr. Fitzhugh Dodson cautions new parents against thinking, "A baby is just a baby. He spends most of his time sleeping. When he wakes up, he is fed. His diapers are changed. He is bathed. That's the life of a baby. He's too young to learn much." Far from being too young to learn, Dr. Dodson stresses that a baby begins to learn from the moment he or she is born.

Recent studies show that even newborn babies can discriminate visual patterns, and day-old infants can discriminate between a variety of sounds and odors. In fact, the most recent word from child-development authorities, and it's a virtual consensus, is that *a child learns more in the first two years than in all the rest of his or her life.*

A sensitive parent can be aware of a young child's potential for absorbing sense impressions but should probably not be too worried at a lack of responsiveness. The world of an infant is frustratingly inaccessible to adults, and, often, the parents' way of trying to get a hold on understanding that inner world is to compare their infant or small child to others. The only problem is that as soon as this is done, worry sets in if one's own child is not grasping at objects as consistently as is the baby next door; standing or walking as soon as your sister's child did; or responding to picture books at the age deemed appropriate by librarians, writers of children's books, or some nationwide norm. There is no right answer as to whether or when a parent should become worried about a possible lag in development: The voices of authority which say "don't worry" seem exactly balanced in number and volume by those which urge "don't take a chance." And reality demands that parents be aware that at some stage or other most children will fall behind in something!

Successful parents were pretty much inclined to allow children to progress at their own rates; they were less likely than were unsatisfied parents to push for optimum development.

Successful parents seemed tolerant of early forms of sexual curiosity and experimentation among children. Even very young children have an emergent awareness of sex. They are particularly fascinated with their own genitals, with masturbatory play, with attempts to imitate bathroom habits of the other sex. And preschoolers love to use words associated with their own processes of bodily elimination. It will probably come as no surprise that unsatisfied parents tended to disapprove of this crude streak in their children, and that the satisfied parents were more accepting.

The preschool child generally manages to present a challenge to parental authority, thus beginning a war of the wills that can be expected to last (with intermittent truces) as long as two generations live under one roof.

The opening maneuver of this battle, however, will in all likelihood seem to be a rather innocuous one—perhaps a refusal to take a nap. Or, perhaps, an inability to take a nap. Parents have to understand the activity needs of preschoolers. Dr. Fitzhugh Dodson tells a couple of stories which illustrate these needs well:

Seated across from me in a restaurant one day, I noticed a young father and mother with their little boy, who appeared to be about four years old. He was restlessly wiggling around in his seat, shifting position several times every few minutes. The father exclaimed impatiently, "Can't you sit still?" I felt like saying to the father, "No, he can't sit still. He's only four years old. And you couldn't either, at that age!"

and again

A psychologist once ran an experiment in which an hour-long movie was taken of a preschooler in action in an outside play yard. Afterwards, this movie was shown to a member of a college football team. He was instructed to go through the exact same motions for an hour that the preschooler had performed. At the end of an hour the football player was exhausted.

Parents will also find it helpful if they can understand the compelling nature (to children, anyway) of children's play. Having prepared dinner, mom or dad may find it rude if Sally doesn't want to come to dinner "now!" As someone once remarked, "Play is the child's work," and whatever combination of play and learning is going on at a given time just may seem more important to the child than adult-created schedules. We're not suggesting that schedules don't play an important role in maintaining household order—just that some degree of flexibility be allowed. (After all, if you were playing the last set of a tennis game, would you appreciate dinner being abruptly announced?) One might be tempted to view such an approach as overly permissive; perhaps, though, *flexibility* would be a more accurate term. By whatever name you choose, successful parents were inclined to it.

Many not-yet parents feel that when a child of theirs takes his first step alone, or utters her first word, or reaches some other landmark achievement of the early childhood years that the magic of that moment will cause any past or future hardships of parenthood to pale into insignificance.

According to successful parents, such a belief is purely romantic thinking, and most rejected the idea that some "magic moment" captures the meaning of parenthood or compensates for sleepless nights and other trials. "You can't get through parenthood just waiting for the magic moments that will erase all the hurt and hardships of all the non-magic hours and weeks and years," wrote one mother, "because there just aren't enough of them. You have to be able to take the whole range of moments and hours and days, some of which are magic; most of which are mundane; lots of which are frustrating; and a few of which are simply awful."

"If I had wanted magic moments," wrote another, "I'd have bought a tall hat and gone into another line of work!"

The Child from Six to Twelve

Six- to twelve-year-olds are more difficult to understand and control than preschoolers.

Somehow, they come as more of a surprise. When prospective parents set out to have a baby, they envision a *baby*— what pregnant woman in her right mind has ever explained to a friend, "We're having a six-year-old?" Yet, eventually, that is what happens.

Eda LeShan asks an interesting rhetorical question. "We all wanted babies, but did any of us want CHILDREN?" Then she tells the following story:

> My daughter and I were having lunch in a drugstore crowded with young mothers and their children. Four of the young women were very pregnant, and after my daughter had listened to them screaming at their nursery-school-age children for about fifteen minutes she asked a very perceptive and logical question: "If they hate their kids so much, why are they having more?"

What comes across as hate, of course, is apt to be frustration at expanded parental duties. Teaching a child to control impulses, to have good manners, to behave in public, to handle money, to understand potential dangers, to assume household responsibility, to cope with peer-group pressure and school competition, and to handle the temptations of an affluent society must all be added to the job description for the parent of a school-age child.

Decisions must be made as to what responsibilities around the house are reasonable, what standard of school achievement you expect, and how many hourly messages can be absorbed from the "idiot tube" without threatening permanent brain damage!

Small kindnesses can appear, but so can small cruelties. Jean de La Fontaine in his fable "Les Deux Pigeons" was speaking of this age child when he remarked of a certain boy, "A rascal of a child—that age is without pity." Monomanias may also surface: obsessions with a certain sport, a certain book, a certain color, a certain entertainment star.

Getting a child immersed in his or her peer group—the first significantly influential community of children—and the activities of that community can now begin to create logistical problems for parents who live in areas without safe public transportation.

We mentioned before that we considered the differences between urban and exurban parenthood to be worth thinking about. Although the need to own and drive a car if a family lives outside the city is not the most significant difference, it was mentioned extremely often by both satisfied and unsatisfied surburban parents. Even if both parents work, a good deal of time can be used after work hours in the car on errands and chauffeuring: dropping off coats at the cleaners and returning books to the library; picking up cookies at the bakery and your child from school or a friend's house, then delivering both child and cookies to the site of the Scout troop bake sale; getting one child from a piano lesson and another to a swim lesson (and perhaps getting a third to a rendezvous with your spouse, then getting them both to a school soccer game and yourself to a PTA meeting). Chauffeuring bothers a lot of parents. Would it bother you?

Concern for expanding your child's horizons—socially, culturally, educationally—may mean less time than ever for spouses to be alone. Or it can mean that when they are alone, more time than ever is spent in discussion of child-related matters.

Pediatricians tell us that the variety of major illnesses a child will have is greater during ages six to ten than during all other ages between birth and adulthood. Communicable diseases include measles, chicken pox, mumps, whooping cough, scarlet fever; but respiratory ailments (colds, sinus, flu) and stomach upsets outnumber all others in frequency. Children in this age group will spend about twenty-three days per school year not feeling well, and an average of seven days staying home from school.

The central concern of most six-to-twelve-year-old children and their parents is school. The pressure to do well is felt by virtually all children, whether or not parents consciously require good school performance. The idea of cheating shocks almost all parents, yet it is an increasingly common practice in schools and is probably best understood not as dishonesty or faulty moral character but a desire to please . . . guess who?

Dr. Stella Chess tells a revealing story of just how easily a good though not excellent student can become a "dishonest" one:

> Joanne is an average (in marks) third grade student. Her teacher, though, finds her a great addition to the class. She is very curious. Her questions and observations stimulate the other children's interest and participation. She is a catalyst.
>
> Her parents expect her to get A in everything just like her older brother. She gets 70s and 60s in spelling. The teacher is not concerned. She is confident that Joanne will learn to spell better as she begins to write more.

The parents have a daily ritual. Both children present their papers for inspection every evening. Brother gets the praise. Sister gets the blame.

One day Joanne's spelling mark has been changed from 60 to 80 and two of her four misspelled words have been corrected—not very skillfully.

A few days later the teacher sees her looking at her neighbor's paper. She spells all her words correctly and gets 100 . . .

Successful parents continued to show a lack of inclination to push for school success and academic achievement. They showed a willingness to let a child with learning difficulties repeat a grade in school, and a disinclination to project an ambitious response onto a child who had won an honor. (Predominant successful-parent responses to the item about a child winning an election were "to tell child how proud I am" and "the family should celebrate together.")

In questions of discipline for the six-to-twelve age group, successful parents indicated they would "deal forcefully with 'bratty' behavior" and would, on at least some occasions, spank. Though there were greatly varied opinions shown in marginal comments as to just what misbehaviors called for spanking, there was overwhelming rejection of the idea that "a child should never be spanked."

An interesting series of responses indicated successful parents' involvement with and concern over questions of their six-to twelve-year-old's popularity or peer-group acceptance. Good parents would investigate why a child was not invited to a party; they would try to prevent their children from wearing an outfit that peers would be apt to consider inappropriate.

Marginal notations of good parents indicated a strong concern for their children's peer group when setting guidelines for TV watching. While the members of the satisfied-parent group totally rejected the idea that television could be generally trusted to be valuable educationally, and while a few stated that strict limits had been set as to hours of TV per week that could be watched or specific programs that were acceptable, a great many successful parents wrote that they had relaxed guidelines for children's TV watching so that their children would not be different from their peers. Not atypically, one parent wrote, "When you know that the following day all the other kids will be talking about Baretta and Wonder Woman and the Fonz, can you really place your own kid in the position of being the only one to say 'Well, gee, I did something wholesome instead. I played checkers with my dad.'?"

A final item indicating concern for a child's peer group was the one asking whether parents would purchase a certain kind of expensive, status loafer that "all the other kids" had.

Responses to this item surprised us. We had expected successful parents to refuse to make a purchase that seemed a simple expenditure of conformity, and we expected the less-satisfied parents to be the ones who would be more inclined to gratify a child's material whims (due to, we thought, a possible wish to make up for lack of emotional involvement with the child by providing material things the child desired). The responses we received were exactly opposite to our expectations. Almost all the successful parents said they would buy their child the Bass Weejuns. About one-third said this was because they "wanted their children to have nice things"; and about two-thirds because they did not want their children to "be different." And it was the less successful parents who were more apt to reject this "status symbol."

While specific responses as to just how they would react to a child's cheating or shoplifting varied, successful parents avoided the response of "This could not happen to my child." Even though such an incident had happened to very few of the successful parents, they seemed to believe that it might.

Facing the Years of the "Terrible Teens"

Housewife Erica Tate, the heroine of Alison Lurie's novel *The War Between the Tates*, contemplates her two teenagers one morning and muses sadly,

> They had been a happy family once. . . . Jeffrey and Matilda had been beautiful, healthy babies; charming toddlers; intelligent, lively, affectionate children. There were photograph albums and folders of drawings and stories and report cards to prove it. Then last year, when Jeffrey turned fourteen and Matilda twelve, they had begun to change; to grow rude, coarse, selfish, insolent, nasty, brutish, and tall. It was as if she were keeping a boarding house in a bad dream, and the children she loved were turning into awful lodgers—lodgers whose lease could not be terminated. They were awful at home and abroad; in company and alone; in the morning, the afternoon, and the evening. . . . They were no longer versions of her children, but two young people she hardly knew. . . ."

Though there can be particular joys to seeing a child of yours acquire the independence and responsibility that is possible during the teen years; find his or her own unique patterns of interest; begin to reflect on life's larger questions in surprisingly mature terms; and even show appreciation for what his or her parents have given him or her; still there is, as Alix Shulman arrestingly portrays, a certain strangeness about the years when a child transforms into a teenager. And it is this strangeness which seems the overall reason for parents' typical uneasiness about overseeing the adolescent years.

There are other lesser reasons why this particular stage of parenthood might lack allure. By reputation, teenagers tend to be disagreeable and disobedient, whining and peremptory, selfish and narcissistic, sexually active, personally untidy, and inclined to tie up the phone for hours. And a parent knows in advance that he or she will lose the ability to control a child sometime during adolescence—and who can be expected to look forward to that?

Teenage behavior seems calculated to establish a new highwater mark of changes in values. Their values, being vastly different from ours, naturally express themselves in actions that are (from our point of view) risky, unseemly, and bizarre.

Then, too, there is the inescapable fact that teenagers hold a more privileged position in life than do adults: They have all or most of life's possibilities ahead of them, while we don't.

On some grander scale, too, this age group seems privileged, even catered to. Philippe Aries wrote, in *Centuries of Childhood,*

> It is as if, to every period of history, there corresponded a privileged age: "youth" was the privileged age of the 17th Century, childhood of the 19th, and adolescence of the 20th.

While this is indisputably true, adults once in a while wonder just what adolescents have done to deserve this privileged status. Nonetheless, they have it. Sociologists scurry around trying to find out what teenagers are thinking, marketers frenziedly wonder what they want to buy, and occasionally a writer like Charles Reich, author of *The Greening of America,* becomes fervently convinced that teenagers have come into exclusive possession of new and secret philosophies of life clearly superior to any previously known adult ones.

Clearly, being the parent of an adolescent is no dream job. It means giving up a lot, and often means putting up with behavior seemingly intended to produce conflict where none need exist. Haim Ginott warns in *Between Parent and Teenager* that a child of this age will cast off your judgment, whatever it is. He tells of overhearing a youngster in this age group ask a store clerk, "If my parents like this sweater, can I bring it back?"

Marginal comments on questionnaires by satisfied parents indicated a great many uncertainties. "Until age thirteen, you can demand accountability," wrote one parent. "Afterwards, there's less and less you can demand, and more and more you have to beg for."

Most successful parents acknowledged the need to accomplish anything you hope to by means of talk, not action. "Punishment no longer works," wrote one parent in response to the pal *vs.* authority figure question, and another in response to the marijuana question. However, there was a strong consensus among these successful parents to control behavior, through punitive action if necessary, regarding a sixteen-year-old who was sexually active.

The idea of teenagers being sexually active can be perfectly appalling to many parents: yet the reality that must be faced is that, according to a large national survey conducted in 1971 by the Johns Hopkins University School of Hygiene and Public Health, there is better than a one in four chance that a fifteen- to nineteen-year-old girl has had sexual experiences; and more recent indications are that the percentages of teenagers who are sexually active are increasing year by year.

Successful parents were far more likely than unsatisfied parents to accept the idea of teenage sexuality (again, with the exception of the item dealing with a sexually active sixteen-year-old girl, which drew strong disapproval from both groups). "Teenagers have to learn to deal with the realities of life," wrote one parent, "and for them today, sex is often one of those realities." Many of the successful parents indicated perplexity over the value system within which some teens regard sex. "How can it be treated so casually?" wrote one, but the most common marginal notation of successful parents on this topic dealt with the responsibility of parents to make sure their teenagers had received adequate sex education and birth-control information.

Singly or in combination, marginal comments of the successful parents regarding sexual behavior of their youngsters touched on most of the points stressed in a recent interview by Dr. Adele Hoffman, specialist in adolescent psychiatry at New York University School of Medicine. Dr. Hoffman's points included (1) Don't lose all hope; not every single teenager is sexually active and in fact not a few are quite traditional. (2) Try to keep things in perspective; premarital sex, after all, is premarital sex—it is not the same as killing. (3) Ask whether it is interfering with other functioning of your youngster; if it is, some action is justified. (4) Try to make sure there is no exploitative quality to any sexual relationship of your child's, for example, "buying" weekend companionship with sex. (5) Does your child's sexual behavior fit within peer-group standards? (6) Importantly, is your child, if sexually active, protected by birth control; does your child, even if not (to your knowledge) sexually active, *know* facts about birth control?

Teenage sexuality can be viewed as just the most visible sphere of behavior in which a new rule for parental discipline has to be strictly adhered to. This rule, it was generally recognized by the successful parents, could be stated simply as: Know when you can't enforce something, and if you can't enforce it, don't try. This represents a realistic pulling away from the parent's role as parent, as child-rearer. This role is now ending, and parents have no choice but to recognize this, and not cling to it. One of the satisfied-parent group wrote, "After all, the entire job of being a parent is to raise a son or daughter who will not need you." This particular parent continued, "As advice to anyone whose children are still young, or who hasn't had children yet, I would suggest that you not get addicted to being 'needed' as mom or dad—or that if you really like being 'needed' you very early in your parenthood career find something or someone other than your own kids to 'need' you."

Similarly, another parent wrote, "When you teach a child to walk, it doesn't occur to you at that moment that one day the child will *walk away*. But it happens. And that's both the worst—and the best—thing about having children. The best part of any job is seeing that it's done."

Chapter 3

Why Am I Applying for this Job?

Questionnaire 3

1. Were I to have a child, its sex would make no difference.

2. As a child, I often envied friends who had advantages I did not.

3. It is extremely important to me to receive credit for what I do.

4. It would not matter to me if a child of mine did not look like me.

5. I would do all I could to make sure a child of mine had educational and cultural advantages that would aid her or his chances to be a success.

6. I could accept it if my son or daughter wanted to be:
   a) a gardener
   b) a truck driver
   c) a ballet dancer
   d) a writer of trashy novels
   e) a priest, Roman Catholic
   f) a rabbi
   g) a priest, Eastern mystic religion
   h) a professional athlete
   i) some of the above
   j) most of the above
   k) any of the above

7. I admit I would be disappointed if a son of mine were short.

8. I have many good traits which I would like to see carried on in a child of mine.

9. I have many good traits; therefore I feel I have a responsibility to have a child so that these qualities are carried on.

10. Frankly, I think that my genes should be carried on.

11. My child would be a superior child, perhaps even brilliant.

12. My six-year-old daughter Jody is running a race with a neighbor child to see who can reach our house first, where I have lemonade ready. Jody is winning this little race. Suddenly the other child cries out, "Stop, Jody, *stop! I* want to win!" Jody stops and lets her friend win the race.

    a) I say to Jody, "That was nice of you to let your friend win."

    b) I say to Jody, "There was no reason to let your friend win just because she wanted to. You should always do your best at work or play."

    c) I say nothing at all, but serve the children their lemonade.

    d) I say nothing right now, but may ask Jody later why she gave up the race.

13. Jody is my six-year-old son rather than my six-year-old daughter. My response to the above question remains the same.

14. I'd like to have a child who would think I was the greatest.

15. One reason for having a child is that a child does give immortality to lives that are otherwise mortal.

16. If I read that it had been pretty definitely established that punishment increased competition and

assertiveness in children—that within reasonable limits the most punitive parents had the most aggressive children—I would use punishment pretty freely, as an aggressive nature would help my child excel in a competitive world.

17. Researchers comparing closely spaced children with a control group of children have found consistently *lower* IQ scores for the closely spaced children (and the highest abilities of all among only children). Knowing this, I feel I would want to separate children's births by a good number of years, or have an only child.

18. You always love your own child, just because it's yours.

19. I am happy with my field of work.

20. My progress in my field of work has been satisfactory.

21. I am not liked by some close co-workers.

22. A project at my job, completed to my satisfaction, causes me to feel very proud.

23. I have held my present job or position for more than three years.

24. At least two of my close co-workers treat me unfairly.

25. My work is boring.

26. My ideas at work are not listened to.

27. My work is meaningful.

28. I would like to quit my job.

29. I read a lot of things related to my job even when my work does not require it.

30. I enjoy talking shop with others in my line of work.

31. My job has no future.

32. I sometimes work late:
     a) because I am required to
     b) because I enjoy it
     c) both of the above
     d) neither of the above

33. People at my place of work are almost like a family.

34. I wouldn't be unhappy to imagine myself keeping my same job for many years.

35. My relationship with my spouse or partner could best be described by saying:
     a) We are very compatible and share many interests.
     b) We are both very compatible and very fond of one another.
     c) We are in love but have some incompatibilities.
     d) We are very much in love and have very few incompatibilities.
     e) We are intensely in love and have virtually no incompatibilities.

36. My spouse or partner and I love to be alone together.

37. My spouse or partner and I laugh often.

38. I can admit weakness or failure to my partner.

39. Our current relationship or marriage has lasted more than four years.

40. I occasionally envy the freedom of my single friends.

41. I often envy my single friends their freedom.

42. If something exciting happens to me, my spouse is the first one I share the news with.

43. If I get a really bad break, my spouse is the first one I want to tell.

44. Our major area of marital sharing is:
    a) sexual
    b) social
    c) financial
    d) political
    e) personal companionship

45. I would not want to see my marriage changed; I'm happy and satisfied with things the way they are.

46. My mate and I discuss potential problems before they become real ones.

47. I wish my mate were a better or different lover.

48. A really exciting sex life is incompatible with a long-term relationship.

49. Being able to foster a romantic and spontaneous sex life within a relationship is, to me:
    a) crucial
    b) very important
    c) important
    d) less important than other things.

50. I do not/would not see anything wrong with me or my partner having affairs outside of our marriage.

51. Gretchen, a pregnant friend, confides to me that she has specifically asked her obstetrician for a cesarean delivery! She explains that she does not want to risk having her vagina cut or stretched out of shape because, she has heard, that often affects postnatal sexuality (in terms of how partners "fit together."} My feeling about this is:
    a) If that is what she wants, it should be her choice—if her doctor approves, of course.
    b) Somehow Gretchen's values seem wrong: why deliberately request a dangerous birth procedure just in order to stay sexy?

52. My partner and I have sex too seldom.

53. My partner and I have sex more frequently than I would wish.

54. If my partner does something that angers me, I typically
    a) say something right away to bring it out in the open
    b) don't say anything, try not to let it bother me
    c) get upset outwardly, quarrel
    d) get upset inwardly, brood about it
    e) take a "wait and see" attitude: sometimes things improve if left alone

55. My spouse and I have discussed the pros and cons of having children.

56. Often, when an occasion arises, such as when we see children playing or encounter them with their parents, my mate and I get into a discussion about how children should be raised, treated.

57. My spouse and I do not presently agree about whether or not to have a child.

Respond to questions 35 to 57 again, in the extra spaces provided. This time respond as you imagine your mate has responded. Your mate should do the same.
Compare your responses to questions in this section. How well do you really know each other's feelings?

58. I care enough about my parents to be in touch frequently and visit whenever possible.

59. My parents impose on me too much.

60. Most of my childhood memories are happy ones.

61. I was given too much domestic responsibility as a child.

62. I would like to *be* just the kind of parent that I *had*.

63. My parents are proud of my accomplishments, what I've done with my life.

64. I would like to please my parents so much that I have made, or would make, major decisions about my own life with their feelings in mind.

65. I am more of a success in life than my mother and father.

66. I like to let my parents know when I succeed where they failed.

67. A child I would have would have the advantage of better parenting than my own parents gave me.

Questions 68–84 for women

68. Getting married was extremely important to me.

69. I secretly feared no one would want to marry me.

70. A list of other women I envy or would rather be would be very short.

71. Wives should defer to husbands in financial matters.

72. I wish I were sexier.

73. I believe that I am, if not beautiful, attractive enough to feel no real unhappiness about my appearance.

74. Boys shouldn't cry.

75. People would like me better if I were prettier.

76. I like to flirt.

77. I have at least one physical feature that bothers me greatly.

78. If I disagree with a man, I ordinarily do not say so.

79. A woman is loveliest when she is pregnant.

80. Love generally doesn't last.

81. Becoming a mother represents feminine fulfillment to me.

82. I would rather be described as "warm and loving" than as "cute and sexy."

83. Men and women should share responsibility for:
     a) income
     b) housework
     c) birth control
     d) child care
     e) none of the above
     f) some of the above
     g) all of the above

84. I would think twice about becoming pregnant if I knew in advance I would be one of those women whose feet swell two sizes during pregnancy.

Questions 68–74 for men

68. I think it demeans a man if his woman disagrees with him in front of others.

69. Sex is more exciting if the woman is not protected by birth control.

70. It's important to me that my wife be sexy.

71. With male friends *only*, I often attend sports events or watch them on TV.

72. If my wife were entertaining some friends, I would be willing to serve them coffee.

73. Affairs outside marriage are more natural for men than for women.

74. Becoming a father proves manhood.

75. I wouldn't take a daughter fishing, just a son.

76. I would hesitate to hug or kiss a son the same way I would a daughter.

77. Boys shouldn't cry.

78. I read men's magazines—*Playboy*, *Hustler*—regularly.

79. Husbands should have the final voice in family financial matters.

80. If I happened to have an affair with a well-known woman who urged me to keep the affair secret, I would probably still tell at least a few close friends.

81. There's a lot to be said for the old-fashioned family style where a woman's place is in the home.

82. Men and women should share responsibility for:
    a) income
    b) housework
    c) birth control
    d) child care
    e) none of the above
    f) some of the above
    g) all of the above

83. I would try again for a boy:
    a) if my first child were a girl
    b) if my second child were also a girl
    c) until I succeeded in having a boy
    d) none of the above

84. A woman is loveliest when she is pregnant.

85. I have a nice circle of friends.

86. Several evenings a week there are TV shows I just don't miss for any reason.

87. If I have a serious problem, I generally keep it to myself.

88. It's generally true that nobody looks up to me.

89. Often, I wish I could just sail away into the sunset.

90. I do not generally introduce myself to strangers at a social gathering.

91. I have had the same best friend (other than my spouse or partner) for a number of years.

92. I feel there is a barrier between me and other people.

93. There are several friends I can just drop in on without much notice and always feel welcome.

94. I am often lonely.

95. When I am criticized, I tend to change my behavior to correct the thing about me which has been criticized.

96. I am not comfortable in anything but conventional clothing.

97. I would rather achieve something to make others love me than achieve something of great benefit to a future generation.

98. I shrink from crises; I hate trouble.

99. In school I did pretty much what the group did.

100. It is usually a mistake to be different.

101. Leadership and individuality are very nearly the same thing.

102. If I were seeing a psychiatrist
    a) I would not hesitate to tell friends that I was.

b) I would tell friends only if I felt pretty sure they would not disapprove.

c) I would tell only those friends who I knew were in therapy themselves or who had previously seen a psychiatrist or counselor.

103. Having children is an obligation one must fulfill.

104. I've never questioned the idea that one day I'll have children.

105. A person who does not want children is not normal.

Ego at the Starting Gate

A professional gambler accompanied his wife when she visited a Saint Louis gynecologist in the spring or summer of 1970 and expressed a wish to discontinue birth control and become pregnant. "What we want to know, Doc," the husband said, "is what the odds are." The gynecologist responded by saying that most pregnancies of women of good health are carried to term; that about 81.3 percent of births are uncomplicated; that his wife's medical history and his own showed no indication of diabetes or other hereditable disease, no problems with Rh factor . . .

After a few minutes of this, the potential sire interrupted by saying, "No, no, Doc, I don't mean any of that. I mean, I know we're going to have a racehorse. What I want to know is—what are the odds that we're going to have a *winner*?"

Though that man's announced-in-advance motive for wanting a child might seem on the wrong track, it is at least straightforward and unequivocal, and, on analysis, not all that rare. Many people who want to have a child hope for a winner, even if they do not calculate the odds. For them a child represents a projection of their own sense of pride or ego.

Our minds are inclined to leap immediately to the conclusion that such a reason for wanting a child is a wrong reason. It probably is. Yet to think in terms of right and wrong reasons for wanting children is in itself less right than wrong. There are times when the worst of reasons can somehow win our sympathy. In Tennessee Williams's play *Cat on a Hot Tin Roof*, for example, Maggie has not one but a combination of seemingly awful reasons for her desperation to have a child. She wants to rebuild her shell of a marriage to her husband, Brick. She wants to satisfy Big Daddy's desire for a super grandson (a "winner") so that she and Brick will win Big Daddy's inheritance. She wants to compete with her sister-in-law, Mae. She wants a child for lots of reasons which do not happen to include wanting a child for the child itself. Yet audiences generally hope Maggie will conceive at the end of the play.

More rarely, the worst of reasons can produce the best of children. A Department of Health, Education and Welfare publication discussed the case of a Jerusalem woman who had had a child, thinking this would reform her husband, who was a thief. The man repeatedly landed in jail anyway; and the woman, due to this and other frustrations, beat the child savagely every day. The official to whose attention the case was brought interviewed the child and reported, in astonishment, that the child appeared completely normal and did not seem to mind his treatment. In fact, he seemed to understand it! The case report concluded, "Here was a woman with a frank psychosis, living under terrible conditions. Yet she had produced a healthy boy."

What is right? What is wrong?

Clearly there are no 100 percent guaranteed guidelines.

In discussing motivations for having children, we are, like the Missouri gambler, talking about the odds.

Broadly speaking, there are four major categories of motives for parenthood—egotistic, compensatory, conforming, and affectionate—and the odds are that the first three out of these four categories will cause you trouble!

Let's consider each category in detail.

Examples of clearly egotistic reasons for wanting children include:

to have a child who will look like me
to have a child who will carry on my admirable traits
to have a child who will be successful

to have someone who will carry on my name
to inherit family money or property
to have someone who will regard me as the greatest
to do something that I know I could do well
to feel the pride of creation
to keep me young in heart
to help me feel fulfilled

Typical compensatory motives are:
to make my marriage happier
to make up for my own unhappy family background
to make up for lack of satisfaction in my job
to make up for social isolation, lack of friends
to make me feel more secure about my masculinity/
femininity

Conforming motives are generally as simple as:
to be like most other people
to please my parents
to forestall social criticism

Affectionate motives include:
to have a real opportunity to make someone happy
to teach someone about all the beautiful things in life
to have the satisfaction of giving myself to someone else
to help someone grow and develop

However, ultimately these four types of motives may all be viewed as egotistic. Someone compensating for a poor marital relationship is interested in "making my marriage happier." Someone intent on avoiding raised eyebrows wants to conform to what others are doing and have a child "so that I won't be criticized." Even affectionate motives can be ego-based reasons for reproduction—wanting a child, for instance, "so that I will have the satisfaction of giving myself to someone."

Of course, not every exercise of ego, reproductive or otherwise, brings inevitable disaster. If one is driven egotistically to achieve fame, for example, a great discovery may be the byproduct of your ego needs but of great benefit to others, nonetheless. And if one wants to have a child out of the prideful certainty that one can do a good job, there is likewise the possibility of social benefit from the raising of a well-adjusted and productive human being. But the potential danger of such motives as "to help me feel fulfilled" and "to be a success for me" is that such wishes clearly place large demands on small human beings.

Egotistic reasons for having children can be based either on our conviction that we're pretty special—or on our equally strong faith that we're not. Sometimes a child is intended to extend our own impressive achievements but more often to achieve something impressive in our stead. There is for most of us something we wanted to do, but didn't; someone we wanted to become, but haven't. Maybe our children will do it for us.

When a parent exclaims excitedly, "That's my child!" at the hospital, what he may mean to say is, "That's my success!" This ego projection can handicap a child at the starting gate; if it is maintained by the parent, it can deny autonomy to a talented child's own developmental inclinations and doom the underachiever.

Ego dictates our desire that children resemble us physically; that they respond like thirsty plants in rain to the advantages with which we intend to shower them; that they run where we stumbled along life's pathways ("*Now* there is a reason for my ninth-grade unpopularity," one mother of a newborn daughter said, anticipating the satisfaction of helping her child avoid her own past mistakes); that they choose an occupation which reflects our own values; that they excel in competitions, no matter how minor; that they *win the race.*

It is ego which makes lots of people want not children, but star athletes and salutatorians, doctors and artists, executives and concertmasters, statesmen and champions.

It is ego which convinces us that no matter what our feelings are about children in general, we will delight in our "own" children. Most of us have seen this occur at one time or another. There was an accountant of our acquaintance who stiffened with distaste given the mere presence of any human being under the age of reason but who began taking his own child to social engagements while she was still in diapers. But the seemingly loving acceptance that shows on the surface here has an unstable quality. There are strings attached. Puppetlike, to maintain this parent's love, the child must continuously meet the contract terms of his conception and be a credit to his parent on the parent's own terms. "I'll love my child" is loose translation of "I love myself," and as long as the child behaves as a proper extension of that self, things may be just dandy.

As we know, not all parent-child relationships are dandy.

Attempts to channel children's free-flowing ambitions upstream in a direction the parents happen to like have been known to be strikingly unsuccessful: It is often as a direct result of knowing he is expected to be "my son the doctor" that Johnny refuses to consider med school.

And even when such experiments seem to work to the parents' satisfaction, the cost to the child is often high. Mary Astor's father, according to the actress's autobiography, "groomed me to be a star as carefully as he would have groomed a racehorse." He got his dream—a winner—but the actress herself felt cheated of normal childhood experiences, normal social and emotional development.

Perhaps we don't expect our children to succeed where we failed, but merely to follow the path of our own success, or even to take the inheritance of intelligence or talent we offer, and find their own uses for it. One Pulitzer prize–winning journalist said, "It's not that I'd want my kid to be a writer. In fact, I'd just as soon he wasn't. But I know my own abilities are pretty rare—my IQ is higher than that of 99 percent of the general population—and so I want to have a child because his potential would be great no matter *what* field he wanted to follow."

Not only does "be a success *like* me" carry the same risk for the child as "be a success *for* me," but that journalist's ego in this application can only be seen as genetic narcissism.

Oh, it's tempting to assume that if we are intelligent our children will be bright, too. They may be. But if this is so, it may be because of the surroundings we offer them.

To set out to have a child because you want a genius is very risky. There is a bell curve of human abilities, with as many potentials falling below the mean as rising above it. It is a fact that most children are average. Even the children of geniuses are usually not geniuses but of average or slightly above average ability.

There is one further point. As Isaac Asimov wryly observed, "Some geniuses are terrible parents. This nullifies the effect of the genes."

Leaders of nations and builders of better national capitals and the like often have no patience with alphabets and vaporizers and "bow wows" and "woof woofs" and actually relate very little to their children. In effect, they are not parents at all. They may think they've done their job by providing genetic material via their sperm or egg cells, but parenthood is not a biological process. *Conception* is biological; *gestation* is biological; *birth* is biological. But *parenthood* is psychological. Its building blocks are aptitudinal components, not DNA and RNA. Geniuses may be no better at it than the rest of us. In fact, they may be worse.

Questionnaire responses of successful, satisfied parents showed low ego needs, a willingness to accept a child for whatever the child might become. And since these respondents *were* parents, they weren't just making empty claims.

Virtually all rejected the notion that you can dislike or feel ambivalent toward children in general but love your own child. "If yours is the only one you love, then it's not love," one wrote. Many others said that one reason they knew they should have a child grew from experiences they'd had with other children before they themselves became parents. Although spacing children so as to give a possible advantage of basic intelligence potential was approved, there was strong resistance to structuring punitive parental behavior toward producing a high-achieving child.

The only ambiguous response to a questionnaire item designed to measure ego was seen in a mixed response to "A child would be my immortality." Almost as many successful parents wrote T as F, and marginal notes in this case weren't really clarifying; they were vague and they, too, were mixed ("Leave part of me here," wrote one; "Ridiculous!" penned someone else).

There has been very little written about the immortality wish as a possible motivation for parenthood, perhaps because the idea touches on mysticism; social scientists, therefore, don't regard it as their province and thus don't address it.

Explaining *immortality* in pragmatic terms, nonparent Stewart Mott wrote in 1973,

> The idea that children are a guarantee of "immortality" is one that has never been explained to my satisfaction. I am practical enough to think that anything of value must be earned—including immortality. And true immortality cannot be earned by so simple a means as reproduction. To my way of thinking, immortality is worth striving for if one defines it in terms of deeds; and calls to mind, as models, the poets and philosophers, scientists and scholars whose ideas and works and discoveries have survived them. To view immortality as a mere matter of biology is completely unsatisfactory.

Weight can be given to this view of immortality by thinking of those whose ideas and works have survived them: The immortality of a Galileo or a Beethoven or a Marie Curie does not rest on sons and daughters, Mott would claim.

A more contemporary illustration came to hand just as this was being written. The February 13, 1977, *New York Times* Book Review section on its front page declared, "A quarter century in the making, the definitive book on oil has finally appeared. . . . In the future, official Washington cannot plead either ignorance or confusion about how the oil industry operates." The writer of the review went on to add, however, "The one tragic footnote to the book is its author's unexpected death a few days before its release," and to combine praise for John M. Blair with appreciation for the book he had written. Few names survive centuries; but perhaps on slightly more modest levels, too, for John Blairs as well as Beethovens, immortality is deeds, not descendants.

Yet the opposite opinion—that the begetting and bearing of children per se does invest one's existence with immortality—is often stated in both essay and fiction. A 1966 article appearing in *Bride's* magazine entitled "Why Men Marry" argued that

> A man without children is not complete. . . . Children establish my place in the long chain of generations who have carried my blood from the dark caves of the past and will carry it endlessly forward into time. Children are my continuity. . . . In reproducing, I affirm my place in the system of life inhabiting the earth. The man without children has lost his place in history.

And the housewife heroine of Anne Roiphe's *Up the Sandbox* links her fourth pregnancy to the cosmos by explaining,

> We are doing what the Neanderthals, the Indians, the Babylonians and the Assyrians, the Egyptians and the Hittites, the Tartars and the Mongolians, the Indo-Europeans and the Twelve Tribes of Israel have all done. We will not be spun off the planet's surface, unlinked to our kind. . . .

Whether or not achieving immortality by having a child is possible may simply depend on how one defines immortality. If it is physical continuance, parenthood can be said to provide it.

Baby Will Make It All Better

BABY AS SEX THERAPIST

Sexually unsatisfied partners may think, "If I had a baby I wouldn't mind the lack of an exciting sexual relationship." Sexually indifferent partners may instead look forward to the fading of the sexual role in marriage once a baby is born, perhaps intuiting that the very circumstances created by the presence of an infant make this likely.

A very logical question is, Why don't spouses with problems of sexual incompatibility seek sex therapy instead? That is not only a very logical question but a very simple one; and like a lot of simple questions, it is extremely difficult to answer. At first it might seem that today's open attitude toward sex would make discussion of problems easy. While for some people this is true, some members of the American Association of Sex Educators, Counselors and Therapists estimate that perhaps only about 20 percent of married people who have sexual-adjustment problems seek counseling specifically directed toward this problem. "With the diminishing number of sexual prohibitions, almost the only sexual prohibition left is *restraint*," says an officer of AASECT. "The new sexual permissiveness now subtly stigmatizes anyone who doesn't feel he has a fully happy sex life—to the point where owning up to that fact is so threatening—humiliating—that avoidance mechanisms are apt to be sought instead."

Avoidance mechanisms such as thinking . . . *maybe a baby will make the problem go away* . . .

This particular compensatory mechanism can work, but not by making sex more satisfying; rather by making one partner not mind that things aren't working.

BABY AS SEX-ROLE REINFORCER

Compensating for shaky sex-role identity as defined by traditional views of what's masculine and feminine, assuaging feelings of not being enough of a man or enough of a woman—these, too, believe it or not, are among reasons why people have children.

Since begetting a child is a socially credible way of saying, "I'm a man," an insecure male may want fatherhood as a tool to enforce his woman's subservient position, and to enhance his own position in the community. At its extreme this motive can operate to keep the wife "barefoot and pregnant," with two results: (1) the wife's chances of becoming competitive in the job market are diminished, leaving the husband's role as breadwinner unthreatened; (2) the wife is made less accessible to and/or less attractive to other men, leaving the husband's role as romantic object less threatened as well.

Similarly, a woman who does not feel secure in her femininity may think that producing a child will be a way to hold onto a partner who might otherwise stray. Sometimes this motive can express itself in very practical and cold economic terms. Edward Pohlman, author of *The Psychology of Birth Control*, tells of a wife whose marriage was in frequent danger of breaking up who sought a fourth pregnancy to make the potential burden of child support so high that her husband could not possibly afford to leave her.

Usually, however, the motive operates more emotionally than economically. "He might leave *me* but couldn't abandon a helpless infant who would be his own child," or "He might love me more if I had his child" are thoughts which indicate not just a perception of a flawed relationship (one which the man might indeed be apt to abandon) but a deeper, underlying feeling of inadequacy as a female and the consequent fear that finding another man would be less than easy.

"There's a lot of pressure on you in this society to be feminine, yet you can never be sure you're feminine *enough*," one young woman put it. She was a college student for whom the women's movement had not quite clarified things.

But it's her sisters and brothers who are untouched by ideas of contemporary liberation who are the greater victims. Those whom family scientists call *high-masculine men* and *high-feminine women* are far more vulnerable to feelings of sex-role inadequacy.

During adolescence, high-masculine boys have been found to possess more self-confidence and greater adequacy feelings that other males. Researcher P. H. Mussen found, however, when interviewing such men in their thirties, that their self-confidence had lowered significantly and was in fact lower than that of the low-masculine males who had been their peers in high school. David Lynn comments in *The Father: His Role in Child Development,*

> It may be that the traditional masculine values, highly prized by adolescent boys, not only may be less valued in the adult world but may in fact handicap a man. The super-masculine image that produces admiration and followers in high school may not produce such with adults who value a broader spectrum of traits, many of which have a feminine component.

The disillusionment such high-masculine men may feel can easily become part of a parenthood dynamic. Competing with liberated men less successfully than he might like, he produces a child to help him feel like a man. But afterward he may instead feel less a man, since the burden of supporting an expanded family increasingly threatens feelings of masculine adequacy.

Still, the thought is often advanced that high-feminine

women and high-masculine men would be well suited for parenthood: the woman content to stay home raising the children, the man suffused with pride as he fills the breadwinner role unchallenged and with none of the sex-role confusion of the "newfangled" egalitarian partnerships to complicate things!

Evidence so far does not support this notion, however.

For example, the Bem Androgyny Scale, developed by psychologist Sandra Bem of Stanford University, has indicated that high-feminine women and high-masculine men were both somewhat less apt to be nurturing than were more "liberated" men and women.

High-masculine men are understandably not inclined to nurturance: that is "woman's work." The surprise is that, in test situations, *the high-feminine women aren't terribly nurturing either!** And the best guess made seems to be that insecure feminine feelings give rise to vanity and narcissism, which are incompatible with nurturing tendencies—and perhaps even with good basic adjustment. Psychologist A. B. Heilbrun found adolescent women who were high-feminine to be the least well adjusted.

Narcissism as a childbearing dynamic reaches its extreme in the motive of *wanting pregnancy only.*

Perceiving that society in general is truly solicitous of the pregnant woman, according her treatment that is usually re-

---

*Test situations designed to measure nurturance, the extent to which a person was willing to be responsible for or helpful toward another living creature, involved, in one such experimental setting, responsivity toward a six-week-old kitten. As expected, high-masculine men were less responsive to the kitten than other persons (only 9% of them responded to the kitten, as compared to 52% of other persons in the experiment). But as the experimenters themselves reported, "There was an unexpected result: the androgynous (low-feminine) women played with the kitten more often than the feminine women who are presumably so fond of small, cuddly things, 64% to 36%." Towards a baby in a similar test situation, the high-feminine women responded more warmly, but no more so than the androgynous or low-feminine women.

served for the most beautiful of females ("Can I call my pregnancy anything less than a long holiday?" wrote Colette), a high-feminine woman may see pregnancy almost as a magic cosmetic, one that will make her special, beautiful, and loved. She knows that she will receive gratifying attentions almost continuously from the time of the pregnancy announcement to the time of the birth announcement! It is that period of time which interests her.

But such women are often observed to become increasingly tense as the time of delivery approaches. Their motive in wanting pregnancy, after all, had no connection at all to wanting a child!

After childbirth, the heightened feelings of being special continue for a few brief days. But there comes a time when the cards and flowers stop arriving, the visitors leave, the phone rings less frequently, and the burden of making an insecure woman feel feminine is left on very tiny shoulders.

Edward Pohlman says it simply and well: "Wanting pregnancy only involves short-sightedness with tragic consequences."

"BABY, YOU SHOW THEM!"

According to Freud, having a baby is a way of competing: a man with his father and a woman with her mother. But with or without the psychoanalytic underpinnings, the motive exists.

Its most obvious form is seen in the statement of a Puerto Rican woman to interviewer Lee Rainwater, author of *And The Poor Get Children:*

> My husband's father had 15 children. We want to beat him with 16.

But to some, those are last year's rules. More and more adults from large families who remember a crowded and confused childhood with too little attention and too much sharing have a new strategy they use to compete with their own parents. "I'm not dumb like my parents; I'm not going to repeat their irresponsibility and have a lot of kids; I'm smart enough to plan my family better than they planned theirs." And thus, with a new "quality not quantity" rulebook in hand, these parents have only one or two children—but they are really playing the same old game. In effect they are saying, "I had an unhappy childhood, but my child won't"—and that is still a compensatory mechanism.

It's important to want to give a child a happy childhood, understandable to want to give a child some things you didn't have when you were young. But when competition, compensation, and even revenge are mixed in with that desire to give, then the gift becomes a little sinister, tagged as it is with the message, Be happy, kid—or else. The "or else" can move this compensatory game into a public arena: a counseling agency or child-welfare office. Psychologists have found that parents who abuse their children physically often suffer from feelings of failure, inadequacy, and isolation, and often disliked their own parents intensely.

"WITH BABY, I'M THE BOSS!"

Kitty Jensen doesn't like her job. The time clock seems an insulting reminder that somebody doesn't trust her to arrive at her desk by 9 A.M. without mechanical policing. The stenographic typing duties she sits down to at approximately 9:10 A.M. cannot by any stretch of the imagination be called stimulating. Only the last few minutes of the day hold any fun at all. She and the other stenotypists have taken to putting on their coats at 3:45, typing absent-mindedly till 3:50, then turning their typewriters off, putting the typewriter covers on and beginning in unison a loud whispered "countdown" until the buzzer sounds at 4 o'clock (at which time they race from their desks, pushing and shoving, bunching up by the exit clock, then scattering through the parking lot or past it to the bus stop). Their "quitting" fifteen minutes early is a game which the section manager, from his glass cubicle in the middle of the floor, has so far watched impassively. His point of view is that this small symbolic nose-thumbing isn't really threatening office efficiency—and may even be doing a bit to raise morale and relieve frustration on the part of the typists. Kitty Jensen isn't the only one of them who doesn't like her job.

Kitty Jensen is likely to become a mother when circumstances allow, but not at all because she sees herself as a maternal type. Lots of men and women are drawn to parenthood not because they find it intrinsically attractive, but *just because it seems better than something else.* Pregnancy offers women like Kitty a "legitimate" excuse to walk away from an unsatisfying job and try a new role. Lots of women do this every year, particularly if their jobs offer little opportunity for advancement or change.

Research by sociologist Carolyn C. Perrucci indicates that career women who consider themselves successful are less apt to become mothers than working women who consider themselves unsuccessful.

Another sociologist, Jean E. Veevers, who has extensively studied voluntary childlessness reinforced this finding. She wrote,

Several voluntarily childless wives reported that the only times they had seriously considered having children were times when they had suffered some substantial career set-back, such as failing a major examination, conducting an expensive but useless scientific experiment, or being unable to find suitable employment.

With unusual candor, one young mother revealed this kind of compensatory thinking to the New York *Times*. "Maybe if I'd been able to tell jokes or sing or ice-skate exceptionally well I'd have had a baby anyway, but the fact is I didn't seriously consider creating a child until it had sunk in that I would never be a world-famous anything. . . .''

In the traditional way of looking at things, the career woman was presumed to be compensating for the fact that she did not have a child. As Veevers points out, today's perspective is shifting; we are beginning to see the equal likelihood that the woman who has a baby may be compensating for the career she doesn't have the courage to pursue, the degree she hasn't finished, the pictures she never painted, the book she will never write.

Having a child to compensate for lack of career achievement need not imply lack of career potential. A woman may find choice and a multiplicity of opportunity as intimidating as the possibility of failure. Illustrating what might be called the "escape from freedom" dynamic, a West Coast artist wrote, "I was just about to fall into the trap (pregnancy). Being an artist, I have many doors open to me. Almost so many that I wanted to run from all of them and become a mother. It's so frightening to realize that your whole life *can* be what you want it to be . . . to have the responsibility to make it so is scary. For long moments, motherhood seemed safer."

While women are still somewhat more likely than men to have unsatisfying jobs, they have no monopoly on them. Men often face a stubborn combination of salary plateau and seniority system which impedes the upward mobility they'd hoped for. Or psychological factors, particularly in factories or large corporations, may prove frustrating. Men rarely quit their jobs in favor of full-time fatherhood, but they can look to procreation for feelings of importance or in the hope that the impersonality of their corporate life can be compensated for by intimate ties with a child. "My job doesn't offer me a chance to be outstanding, but maybe I could be outstanding as a parent," or "Nobody here at the job looks up to me. But a child of mine would think I was the greatest" are common motivational feelings for both sexes.

MARRIAGES AND BABY CARRIAGES

Has marriage lost its lustre? For most couples there's a pearl of folk wisdom within all too easy reach: Have a baby and things will get better. At least that's the way it's supposed to work. Now, having a child to improve a poor marriage might seem a questionable practice morally, even if it worked; but does it?

As early as 1939, a small study by two noted social scientists hinted that baby carriages and good marriages were often on a collision course. Ernest Burgess and Leonard Cottrell found that, while about 50 percent of couples with no children or one child reported their marriages to be happy, only 25 percent of couples with two or more children felt they had satisfactory marital adjustment.

Then, almost a generation later, a series of reports which has come to be called "The Crisis Series" more firmly indicated that childbearing was linked to husband-wife unhappiness.

The first of these reports, "Parenthood as Crisis," in 1957 reported that 83 percent of couples interviewed felt an "extensive or severe" crisis in their marriage after the birth of their first child. "Parenthood as Crisis: a Re-Study," issued by a different researcher in 1963, found that a definite majority of couples felt "crisis" after childbirth, and in 1965 "Parenthood as Crisis: A Third Study," while pulling back a little on the degree of crisis experienced, found all couples interviewed to report at least slight or moderate crisis. Naturally, anything new or different can bring crisis. But specific components of the crisis for new mothers included physical tiredness and fatigue, feeling edgy or emotionally upset, decreased contacts with persons at work, worry about loss of figure, worry about personal appearance in general, decreased sexual responsiveness, interruption of social patterns, and doubting worth as a parent. New fathers were disturbed by physical fatigue, increased money problems, additional amount of work, having to change long-range plans made before the baby's birth, decreased sexual responsiveness of wife, decreased contact with friends, and feeling edgy or emotionally upset.

At the same time the crisis studies were going on, other researchers were independently beginning to confirm the findings of those studies. Though the sample sizes and research-interview methodologies of all the following studies varied somewhat (with sample sizes ranging from less than 100 to over 4400, and interview techniques from questionnaires to in-home interviews), the similarity of conclusions is impressive enough to make it extremely difficult to question the validity of any one such study on technical grounds. In brief, these conclusions were:

In 1955 the American Sociological Review reported that desertions occurred most frequently in marriages where there were children.

In 1964 Professor Harold Feldman of Cornell, after comparing couples with children to childless couples, found that the parents had significantly less verbal communication with each other, felt less close to each other, admitted to more problems about sex than before parenthood, had lower overall marital satisfaction, and were more responsive to conflict.

In 1968 Leonard Benson, in *Fatherhood,* cited evidence that twice as many reported marital conflicts involved the parental role rather than the marital role.

In 1970 Karen S. Renee found that couples raising children were more likely to be unhappy with their marriages than childless couples.

In 1974 the Institute for Social Research found that the periods of greatest satisfaction for parents were (1) the years before they had children; (2) the years after the children left home!

In 1974 Paul C. Rosenblatt of the University of Minnesota,

studying the behavior of over four-hundred couples in public places, found, "Couples with children were observed to touch, talk, and smile less at one another."

In 1975 the International Health Foundation in Geneva declared the childless marriage to be more stable, more healthy. Dr. Pieter Van Keep, the foundation's director, said, "Young children frequently interfere with communication, and communication is vital to marital harmony."

Even experts who are reluctant to see children as crisis-related admit the potential for marital disruption after childbirth. A typical expression of this cautious attitude is made by the authors of A Problem-Solving Approach to Marriage, who state:

> We do not agree with some researchers that the changes occurring in the marital relationship following the birth of the first child are a real crisis involving severe and long-lasting upheaval in the marriage. However, we do believe that these changes are disorganizing. Loss of sleep, financial problems, decline in sexual response of the wife, and disturbance of social and recreational patterns are common complaints of new parents. . .

Whether one chooses to call the phenomenon *complaint* or *crisis*, three studies indicate it with remarkably similar graphs. As shown in the graph, newly married couples have high marital satisfaction, which decreases after the arrival of the first child, then levels off until children reach adolescence, where another decrease occurs, followed by a leveling off and a gradual increase as the children leave home.

Importantly, evidence indicates additional crisis at time of birth of a second child and later children. Professor Feldman comments, "The marital crisis experience continues for second-time parents. More effects than expected by chance replicated when couples had their second child. If anything, there appeared to be an even greater negative effect for the multipara (i.e., mother who has given birth more than once)."

Marital Satisfaction at Each Stage of Marriage

High Point
Stage 1
Early Marriage

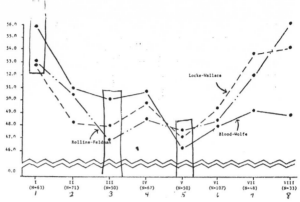

FIGURE 1. MEAN STANDARD SCORES ON MARITAL SATISFACTION AT EACH STAGE OF AN EIGHT STAGE FAMILY LIFE CYCLE MEASURED BY THREE INSTRUMENTS. SCORES ARE STANDARDIZED WITH A MEAN OF 50 AND STANDARD DEVIATION OF 10 TO FACILITATE VISUAL COMPARISONS OF TRENDS. MALE AND FEMALE SCORES ARE COMBINED.

	Stage
Low Points	1)–Newly married
	2)–Infant
Stage 3 Preschool	3)–Preschool
Stage 5 Teenage	4)–Schoolage
	5)–Teenage
	6)–Launching
	7)–Launched
	8)–Retired

Reprinted, by permission, from Boyd C. Rollins and Kenneth L. Cannon, "Marital Satisfaction Over the Family Life Cycle," in Charles R. Figley (Ed.), *"Readings in Intimate Human Relationships"* (Lafayette, Ind.: Purdue Univ. Press, 1974), pp. 124–25.

This suggestion relates to a concept recently put forth by the head of Purdue University's Marital Counseling Service, Dr. Charles Figley, as more refined than the number and spacing of children. The impact on marriage, he feels, may be best measured by child density: the concentration of children in the family, a ratio computed by dividing the number of children by the number of years of marriage.

Commenting on the crisis literature in broad overview, Dr. Figley emphasizes, "It *is* certain that children initiate role change in marriage, causing husbands and wives to assume additional responsibilities; pregnancy and the postnatal period *are* stressful times for both partners; marital morale *is* generally lower for couples with children."

But he believes there is room for hopeful interpretation of the crisis studies, at least for those couples who did not bring their babies on board a sinking marital ship—that is, who did not have their children with the specific motive in mind of saving their marriages. The trouble with a save-the-marriage baby is that saving a marriage requires skills a baby just doesn't have. Analyzing and then acting on problems that exist within the marital dyad or twosome is a must. And while an adult third party can sometimes be sensitive and observant enough to aid the process, a baby can't. Further, the baby's very presence distracts the partners themselves from analyzing and correcting problems!

The first hopeful factor Dr. Figley identifies is simply that not all couples experienced crisis, and even among those who did, perceptions of the degree of crisis varied.

Also, many couples who did report crisis—about two-thirds overall—felt initially elated about the birth itself. The fact that couples first feel thrilled, lucky, happy, wonderful involves in part a sense of relief that the months of uncertainty and worry (will the birth be normal? will the baby be all right?) are over. For the woman particularly there is a sense of accomplishment at having given birth. It is, of course, possible that prideful and exuberant postnatal behavior can carry some component of living up to expectations. If one happens to be unhappy or dubious about the birth now that it has finally occurred, this is the least acceptable moment to reveal such feelings. But these factors are probably insignificant beside the more profound reality that the new-parent couple has together created a new family member and thus a new family structure that is filled with unlimited promise and potential. The simple existence of hope, happiness, and optimism at this point can offer a sound basis for cooperative and effective efforts to work together to adjust to any stressful elements in their expanded family situation.

This possibility is also suggested by Feldman, who believes he has often observed a "baby honeymoon" in the initial postnatal period. He is not sure that real perceptions of crisis set in, in fact, until four to six weeks after birth. Just as in a marital honeymoon, during this period tolerance for inconvenience may be greatest. What will later prove frustrating is now disarmingly novel. If feelings of closeness between husband and wife can be fostered now, they may grow strong enough to postpone or minimize crisis effects later.

Even if responsibilities do threaten to assume crisis proportions, Figley stresses that if spouses can work together toward adjustment, then the crisis they face can be an opportunity for growth, not merely a destructive and disruptive phenomenon. "Climbing a mountain can be a crisis too," Figley advises, "but if there is determination to succeed, and if couples hold hands and pull together on the ascent, then overcoming the struggle can leave them better off than had they not attempted it." This is not true, of course, if problems are insurmountable—if, in choosing a mountain, one chooses beyond one's climbing capabilities—but for many couples the crisis of struggle does lessen after a period of time, particularly when the child reaches school age.

Finally, if either spouse has strong nurturant capabilities and a strong desire to experience parenthood, then, even though a decline in marital satisfaction may occur, the presence of another sphere of potential satisfaction (being a mother or father) can offer at least the reward of needing to be needed.

Even with these hopeful thoughts in mind, however, if your responses to items 35 through 57 on the questionnaire indicated a lack of communication within your marriage, envy of single friends, or other evidence of basic relationship dissatisfaction, you should face the possibility that you consciously or unconsciously are hoping that a baby will improve your marriage. And the chances are that a baby cannot do that.

Follow the Leader!

Motives based on a desire to conform constitute another category of reasons for reproduction. It is usual for couples to tend to have children within a very few years of when their friends do. One study cited by Betty Rollin has found an absolute correlation between a woman's number of children and that of her three closest friends.

Sometimes we want to conform to parents' wishes. Far from feeling hostile toward our own parents or competitive with them, we may be moved by love or loyalty to give them the grandchild they have always expected from us. Chip McGrath wrote a moving and articulate explanation of such feelings which read, in part:

> After we had been married for a few years without producing any children, my mother became blunt. She offered a $1,000 reward. "Boy or girl," she said, "it doesn't matter." I don't remember feeling pressured by my parents, and I was never really tempted by the thousand bucks—yet in deciding to have Sarah I was partly acting as a son. All things considered, I am

close to my parents and, in a curious way, dependent on them for certain kinds of approval; I am probably most dependent, in fact, when I am most critical of my parents and the things they tend to approve. For a long time I was suspicious of babies and the mentality that valued them, yet when I finally changed my mind I remember feeling something like the secret pride a child feels when he's done the right thing and pleased his mother and father. . . .

A much-reported technique of would-be grandparents is the "casual" conveying of news of other births in the family. One woman described the effect of her mother's letter saying, "Your cousin Elaine and her husband Jim are expecting a baby in March" in the following way:

> Not only did my mom's letter seem to discuss *only* the coming birth, to the exclusion of any of my own activities about which I'd recently written her, but it seemed to awaken my close ties with Elaine when I was little. Then, I yearned to do everything Elaine did—whether it was going to summer camp, taking swimming lessons at the Y, getting a sewing machine, or making straight As two semesters in a row. I found myself thinking it was time *I* had a baby *too.*

But sometimes in following the leader we're not copying the cousins or keeping up with the Jones's birth announcements but conforming to something at least one step removed. Maybe we're obeying authority figures who represent social norms or responding to even more diffuse expectations of the culture in general.

Most people have children. It is more comfortable to be like most people than to be different. Therefore, it's very easy to drift into parenthood because the expectation to do so is so universal, whereas one is seldom handed an invitation to consider not becoming a parent.

Our earliest role models are parents. From toddlerhood on, we hear, from visitors and relatives, confident predictions about our future ("When you grow up and have children of your own . . .") often enough that we easily come to view parenthood as inevitable.

Often the first books we read as children showed women primarily as mothers. Even today, one popular "liberated" children's book intended to emphasize careers for women is called *Mommies at Work* (rather than "Women at Work.") Educator Claire Paisner Doubrovsky writes, "In grade 10, when students are subjected to such topics as 'Finding Life's Purpose in Raising Children' we witness the school reinforcing all the social pressures which propel young women toward early motherhood."

Media images of mothers are quite lovely. The mother in the Clairol commercial, the mother in the Geritol ad, and even the mother in Planned Parenthood's public service announcement might all be sisters to a Raphael madonna. In these images, the mother role looks serene and fulfilling. And since these images so often are found amidst what is essentially a sales medium (commercially sponsored television, magazines), a strong case could be made that motherhood is being subtly sold, too.

The expectation that one will have children is presented even by casual acquaintances. Such people "are a lot more nervy and direct than longtime friends are," according to one young woman who wrote a lengthy letter to the National Organization for Non-Parents.

"Good friends are generally too polite to pressure you much," she explained. "But some less-than-good friends have gone through elaborate campaigns to try to get us to have a child. One week, they will dwell on our selfishness. If that doesn't seem to affect us, the next week they will tell us how wonderful children are and what wonderful experiences we are missing. The following week, they may spend several evenings describing how lonely we're going to be when we're old. The next step may be to try flattery—to tell us we should have children because we would be such good parents. It just *doesn't stop.* It's not that we lack sales resistance. It's just that the continual pressure can become a strain."

When pressure turns to accusation, as it sometimes does, the strain on a nonparent couple increases. "No kids? What's wrong with you?" can be a painful question to deal with, even if one has inner faith that nothing at all is wrong. "It's not normal not to want to be a parent" is a similarly powerful accusation. If one buys the presumption behind these pressures to bear, that is, that a person without children is not normal, then one may have a child *not from a wish to have a child, but from a desire to be seen as normal.* Often, couples have a child not from their own choice but from society's.

Satisfied parents differed sharply with unhappy parents in their responses to questionnaire items on motives for having children. Among unhappy parents egotistic and compensatory motives were indicated in some combination by almost 100 percent of respondents!

Satisfied parents, on the other hand, were remarkably free from indications of egotistic or compensatory motives. They had not had children to expand their own feelings of importance; they had virtually never hoped to compensate for an unhappy job, sex life, or marriage. Satisfied parents did frequently reveal some conformity to social expectation. This was most noticeable in indications that such parents accepted wanting children as normal and viewed not wanting children as not normal. Some satisfied-parent respondents drew a distinction between believing this prior to their own parenthood and believing it presently. "I assume we're still to be answering these questions by looking back to how we felt when we didn't have kids," wrote one, typically. "Then I'd have said anybody who didn't want children was strange and abnormal. Today I don't believe that's necessarily true, though." But similar to more than a few others was the comment, "Nobody ever knows what life is all about till they have kids. That's what I thought before we had kids. That's what I still think."

It seems worth commenting on the fact that, while several

lists of Wrong Reasons for having children have been circulated widely (Planned Parenthood's list has even been dramatized for television in a public service ad), there has been virtual silence on the subject of Right Reasons. Though we pointed out earlier that to speak of right and wrong reasons at all is to use a handy but imprecise shorthand for types of reasons that should more precisely be called functional and dysfunctional, or promising and unpromising, we too have clearly been discussing reasons for parenthood that seem far more wrong than right, more unpromising than hopeful.

There is an explanation for the negative approach. Wrong reasons are simply more visible to people looking at the subject. One psychiatrist explained, "Philosophers don't draw up lists of reasons for reproduction; counselors do. Who do counselors see? Couples in trouble. Why are they in trouble? Because they had children for the wrong reasons.

"Somewhere out there," he continued, "there are couples—a minority maybe, but they're certainly there—who had children for reasons that are right or at least workable. But it's in part a matter of speculation as to what their reasons were, because they're not coming to the clinics." Psychologist and counselor Carl Faber, asked by Betty Rollin and Paul Ehrlich to find a "right reason" for parenthood for their 1971 television program aired in Los Angeles, "Should You Have a Baby?" had trouble coming up with one!

Are there "right" reasons for parenthood? If so, what are they?

It might be useful at the start to point out the obvious fact that "wrong" motivations can exist in greater or lesser degree, singly or in combination. An egotistic motive can appear as a rather mild and benign feeling that it would be nice to have a child who'd be a credit to me as well as a frantic, consuming feeling that my child must bring me credit—that being the child's sole intended purpose.

Compensatory motives (say, to compensate for an unsatisfying marriage) can vary, too. There is a difference between wanting a third person around to better balance the family boat and grasping at the idea of a child as a lifesaver when the craft has already overturned.

Conforming motives can exist all along a continuum, from rationally arrived at decisions to neurotic needs.

It might be useful, also, to make a subtle distinction between *reason* and *motive*. *Motive* implies a specific psychological dynamic that springs from an individual's personality, and which may or may not be rational. *Reason* by semantic implication should mean a dynamic which could meet some external test of rationality. Once, of course, there were good and valid reasons to have children. Over the sweep of humankind's first few millenia, survival of the species was a reason. Prior to industrialization, survival of the agrarian economic unit was a reason (as expressed in the Indian saying, Every new mouth to feed brings two hands to work). National strength and old-age security were also once reasons—as, in its way, was the absence of birth control, which made childbearing the more or less inevitable result of sexual activity. But whichever term is used, the question, "Are there any *right* ones?" still begs an answer.

ALTRUISM AND AFFECTION

Certain reasons or motives which seem to indicate affectionate feelings should be worth taking seriously and respecting. These involve a *basic nurturing attitude* whereby personal gratification results from giving, not receiving; and a desire to express this nurturing tendency in relationship to children.

Specific motives which might fit within this general description include:

to be able to teach children things I like or really know about
to have a real opportunity to make someone happy

to take care of someone
to give myself devotedly to someone who needs me
to help someone grow and develop
to experience more fully my love for children

We respect the above reasons, as does nearly everyone we've talked to. That is not to say that even these reasons are unchallengeable, however.

Though to make someone happy, to give oneself to someone else, to help someone grow and develop seem as unimpeachable as any human wish could be, it is still possible to wonder, Do you have to have a child in order to make someone happy or to give yourself to? Though it might seem skeptical to some to raise the point, we would probably be remiss not to mention that, at last count, world population slightly exceeded 3.1 billion. There is probably someone already born who could benefit from a little of the nurturance and affection that such prospective parents have to give.

Certain other reasons for wanting children have a definitely altruistic overtone; these include:

to contribute a worthwhile human being to society
to give the world someone who may change the world for
the better

Such reasons are clearly preferable to those like "to save my marriage" or "to make me feel feminine," but they also invite a skeptical query. If you are capable of producing someone who could change the world for the better, then perhaps *you* are someone who could change the world for the better. Along this line, Nigel Balchin, recalling the Parable of the Talents in which a man hid his talent in the ground, wrote, "Nowadays he would not bury it. He would simply expend it on raising children"—with the result, one imagines, that each generation may simply pass on its own failed talents and unfulfilled responsibilities to the next.

LIFE IS WORTH SHARING

A third genre of right reasons reflect a basic *satisfaction with life* prior to parenthood. Examples would be

to show someone all the beautiful things in life
to share my own values and delights in life

and could, along with the affectionate and altruistic reasons, be considered a very hopeful preparental frame of mind. Dr. Carl Faber considers it of utmost importance that prospective parents feel they are willing to bring a child into the world *given the way they feel about the world*. "Based on an individual perspective, parenthood means one of two things," he explains. "It means you are either bestowing upon, or condeming a child to, *existence*—life. Obviously, you should give life to a child based upon your own perception that life is worth something—rather than feel 'Well, things are rotten but they may improve,' or 'My own life didn't work but who knows? maybe my child's will.' "

FULLER EXPERIENCE OF LOVE FOR CHILDREN

"To experience more fully my love for children" seems to stand out from all the rest, even within this category, as perhaps the closest thing to a full right reason to have a child. Its important implication is that the person holding such a motive is already experiencing his or her love for children, and has thus resolved that complicated question of what "loving children" really means. The child contemplated by the man or woman giving this reason for wanting one is not contemplated as a child apart from other children but will instead share love that is already felt for other children.

The hopeful promise of this motive was borne out by feelings of satisfied parents, who overwhelmingly rejected the notion that you can fail to like children in general but like your own. All but a few successful parents responding to this questionnaire indicated that prior to their own parenthood they had had rewarding experiences with children in a variety of ways, whether by taking part in a Big Brothers or Big Sisters program; teaching or counseling; or simply being a good friend to other peoples' children. Such responses seem to give credence to a claim of genuinely liking children and thus being able to have largely altruistic or affectionate reasons for wanting one's own child.

Oh, it would be true enough that one could "experience love for children more fully" by adopting: but to expect or insist that any of these motives be 100 percent altruistic or "right" would be to forget that motives come in a human package of behavior. It would be more than a little silly to pretend that human beings very often act in ideal ways. Saints, we suppose, do. But for most of us, our reasons for wanting children are pretty much like our reasons for wanting anything else. They are a mixture of generosity and selfishness, ego and compassion, good and evil, curiosity and conformity and pride; biological impulse, blind faith, and wishful thinking.

And if those of us who want children can't expect to put our reasons into clear-cut categories or even neat columns of right and wrong, we can at least try to identify major elements within our mix of feelings. And we should try to avoid the obviously bad, the clearly risky or questionable.

As Simone de Beauvoir has summarized, "Children are not substitutes for one's disappointed love, they are not substitutes for one's thwarted ideal in life, they are not mere material to fill out an empty existence. They are neither playthings, nor tools for the fulfillment of parental needs or ungratified ambitions. They are responsibilities and opportunities and obligations."

The thought and introspection any one of us needs to determine the reasons for wanting children do not constitute the easiest of tasks. But to do so will ultimately be less difficult than struggling through years of parenting hampered at every step by long-standing complexities in our emotional background that we never sorted out, motives that we never understood.

Evaluating Reasons for Nonparenthood

Having tried to examine right and wrong reasons for having children, it might be worth at least idly turning the microscope in another direction and asking whether there are, similarly, right and wrong reasons for *not* having children.

Certainly, ego can as easily keep one away from parenthood as propel one toward it. Narcissism or a desire for personal indulgence can be conscious reasons for avoiding reproduction. A nonparent may be attempting compensation for an unhappy childhood in his own way: perhaps by giving himself all the material luxuries he envied others for when he was young. Conformity? That, too, can operate. Nonparents may want to conform to a life-style they view as new, exciting, sophisticated—and perhaps just a little variant or deviant, vaguely naughty or immoral.

Nonetheless, viewed functionally or pragmatically, these "wrong" reasons are not wrong in the same sense as are the comparable reasons for *having* children.

Societies define right and wrong according to social impact or general harm. Thus, injuring a person is more wrong than stealing from him, because life, not property, is harmed; but injuring someone is less wrong than killing him, because the harm is temporary not permanent.

From this same functional or pragmatic viewpoint, nonparenthood cannot be "wrong" since it carries no social impact, causes no general harm.

Put another way, not having children is a personal decision only, affecting only the individuals involved. But having children is both a personal and a social decision, since the presence of a child affects not only his or her parents but also places demands on the community as a whole as well.

Every American baby costs taxpayers in general a good amount of money—over $500 per year in government personnel expenditures alone, according to a 1972 study; and an abandoned child's support may easily cost the general populace $73,000 per year if the child becomes a "boarder baby" at a public institution (this figure from a report in the March 6, 1977 *New York Times* Sunday magazine). But if a couple with good parenting capabilities fails to have a child, whom have they harmed or affected by their decision? They have only narrowed their own potential areas of fulfillment. They have not touched society.

Thus there can no more be "wrong" reasons for childlessness than, say, wrong reasons for ceramics or bowling, ski parties or French lessons.

One can want to learn French for all the wrong reasons: for ego and status rather than for love of language; to conform; to compensate for past failures. Yet the effect is still socially benign. The same is true of childlessness, at least in terms of our world now.

Things do, of course, have a way of changing.

At some future time society as we know it may be quite different, as may social needs. Zero population growth and even negative population growth may be achieved. Societies may hunger for more births. At such a time it may suddenly become clear to everyone that a man or a woman who has the capability to be a good parent and who does not want children is avoiding a vital responsibility, is selfishly refusing to contribute to the general good, and is in other words behaving in a manner that is personally and socially and morally wrong!

At such a time, certainly, if such time comes, an impressive, carefully reasoned—and probably long—list of "Wrong Reasons for *Non*-Parenthood" can be expected to appear.

Chapter 4

What's Really in This for Me?

Questionnaire 4

1. I envision my child as a robust and healthy baby.
2. My child would look like me, be like me.
3. Children allow creativity to those of us who can't be artists.
4. My child would be physically perfect, and bright.
5. I can't imagine a child of mine as being badly behaved or having annoying habits.
6. There are problems that are solely your child's, even at early ages.
7. Children are by nature disruptive.
8. Children make life more complicated.
9. The joys of children ultimately outweigh any complications.
10. A child of mine would not be a "TV child."
11. There's a lot of truth in the old saying, Children bring constant cares, but uncertain comforts.
12. I believe my mate would be less apt to leave me if we had a child.
13. A child would mean my spouse and I would have a happier relationship.

14. A child gives a man and woman something significant to share.

15. Our sex life would be as good as ever after the birth of a child.

16. Responsibilities of parenthood don't have to interfere with a career.

17. Having a child would make us more mature, responsible.

18. We'll spend holidays together when the children are grown.

19. Though my mate and I may not share child-care tasks equally on any given day with every given task, we will share responsibility for child care fully.

20. It seems to me that people without children are generally happier than parents.

21. Girls are easier to raise than boys.

22. Christmas is for children.

23. Children give parents a chance to rediscover the child in themselves.

24. There are no bad children, only bad parents.

25. Humankind's best hope is always the next generation.

26. Parenthood has a way of making most people develop resources they never knew they had.

27. The nice thing about parents and children is that they love each other without having to earn each other's love.

28. Parents can get through tough times with sheer grit and determination.

29. Parenthood is largely fun.

30. People with children are less apt to be lonely in later life.

31. Since my interests in leisure activities differ somewhat from those of my mate, it is not unusual for us to spend an evening in some independent way.

32. Having a child inevitably means certain life-style changes which it is both impossible and futile to try to predict.

33. No other work can be as meaningful as parenthood.

34. Nothing else can be as personally rewarding as parenthood.

35. Children may be a financial strain but we'll manage.

36. We'll go out just as often.

37. We will see to it that parenthood does not disrupt our lives significantly.

What's Really in This for Me?

Sociologists lay the blame for much human unhappiness directly at the door of something called *discrepancy of expectations*. This term, applied to parenthood, simply means there are apt to be differences between what you think will happen and what is really going to happen.

Brought down to specifics, this could mean: (a) you expect a law student and get a flower child; (b) you expect a ballerina and get the neighborhood's only aspiring ten-year-old go-go dancer; (c) you expect a leader of men and get one—but one who organizes something called The Pagans instead of a sandlot baseball team; (d) all of these.

Parents surely hope their children will be like them in major ways. Once, this tended to happen. When children grew up on isolated farms with only their parents (no competing role models from TV or peer groups) and one generation took up the activities of the preceding generation, this happened a lot, in fact. Once, Will Rogers, Jr., could say about his father, "His heritage to his children wasn't words, or possessions, but an unspoken treasure, the treasure of his example as a man and a father. More than anything I have, I'm trying to pass that on to my own children. . . ." and there seemed something universal in that statement.

Now, in crowded urban environments, parents' role examples carry less impact. From a fairly early age the bulk of a child's time can be spent not with his parents but with a peer group whose values are apt to be far more influential. The potential impact of the child's exposure to electronic media should not be underestimated, either. A mother we know said of her six-year-old, "Heaven knows what this one will turn into: already I feel I hardly know her."

How realistic is it to expect that a child will be like her or his mother or father? A possible indication comes from a survey conducted in 1974 by Dr. Toni Falbo at North Carolina's Center for Creative Leadership, in which she asked several hundred students: "In terms of making you the person you are today, who was the most influential person in your life?" Answers revealed that a much higher percentage of only children (40%) chose parents than did first borns (3%), middle borns (2%), or last borns (7%). Believing that a child you have will be like you could be courting the discrepancy of expectations Dr. Wright speaks of—and consequent disappointment.

According to marriage counselor Dr. David Knox, an even more basic expectation that prospective parents almost universally hold, is that their child will be physically perfect. Our own interviews with prospective parents lead us to agree. People contemplating parenthood are optimists in this way. They are generally in good health; good health care is something this nation offers; so they naturally envision a child who will be robust and healthy, strong and calm. No one focuses on colic or fever, birth defects or delayed development.

Fortunately, most children are born with normal physical and mental characteristics. But our questionnaire responses showed a sharp contrast between unsatisfied parents (who had assumed they would have a physically perfect child) and successful parents (who hadn't counted on it)! One of the successful parents wrote, "Expect illness—mumps, coughs, flu, measles." Another wrote, "Hope for health, but read up on asthma."

It at least seems worth reflecting on the chances for a child who will not be the physical ideal we envision. For a child, like a spouse, has to be taken for better or worse, has to be loved whether strong or weak or bright or not. Prospective parents have to be prepared to love and care for the child they get, not the one they expected.

Given the incidence of a few of the more common handicaps of early childhood such as hyperactivity (15%, according to a 1974 California senate survey), birth defects (1 in 18 children, or about 5%, has a serious birth defect), diabetes or related endocrine disease (3%), asthma or other chronic upper respiratory problem (10%), and nonsevere learning disabilities (6%), generally reliable sources such as government agencies indicate that a prospective parent faces about one chance in three to have a child with at least one of these problems.

Child psychiatrist Charles R. Shaw has reported further that a study made on a large group of nonhandicapped children revealed some disruptive behavior in at least one out of five "normal" children. This is not to say that this was constantly present in these children; in fact, in many it was transient, occurring only in a short period of time during the entire childhood. The point is, these can be signs of deep disturbance, yet they also commonly occur in physically perfect youngsters. As listed in Dr. Shaw's book, *When Your Child Needs Help*, these symptoms include:

Temper tantrums. Tantrums severe enough to be considered more than simple outbursts of anger were seen in over half the boys and one-third of the girls.

Fears and worries. Found in almost half of normal children of both sexes, these varied in severity and in content. Commonly, they were nonrational (e.g., fear of the dark rather than fear of auto traffic) and marked by excessive concern about death around age eight.

Oversensitiveness. Seen in one-third of the boys and half of the girls, the parents' complaint was usually that the child was too easily hurt, too finicky, too quick to cry or to withdraw, to be moody or to pout.

Nightmares. In about one-quarter of the children, bad

dreams were consistent enough to be considered a serious disturbance.

Nail biting. A chronic habit for one-quarter of the children.

Lying. Characteristic of one-quarter of the boys, slightly fewer girls. (There is of course a continuum from the occasional lie to a situation of chronic lying, and beyond that, an inability to distinguish truth from untruth.

Bed wetting. Can be seen as a matter of age. All young children do it, and then, at various ages, give it up. At three years, one-quarter of normal children still wet the bed; at five years, one out of ten still does so (and even at fourteen years, one out of fifteen).

Thumb sucking, poor appetite, and destructive impulses were among other symptoms sometimes found in "normal" children.

The Comfortable Cliché

Such feelings as "girls are easier to raise than boys," "Christmas is for children," "children give parents a chance to rediscover the child in themselves," "having a child will make us more mature," "humankind's best hope is the next generation," and the like are perhaps not so much genuine *expectations* as an indication of the degree to which a lot of us have absorbed cultural clichés about parenthood and children. While none of these statements is wholly false, neither are they very true. Girls are easier to raise than boys—if you raise girls to be more passive. Christmas is for children—if that's the way you look at Christmas. Parenthood does make you more mature—if you consciously work toward mature responses to it.

The point is that unquestioningly internalizing such simple beliefs can keep parents from doing some much-needed thinking. Statements such as the above were generally rejected as false by satisfied parents in our group. Those same parents responded more favorably to "Children bring constant cares, but uncertain comforts," "Children are by nature disruptive," "Children make life more complicated," and "People without children are happier than parents," a list of tougher, more realistic statements.

Just for consistency, by the way, with no thought yet of scoring, you might check to see whether you gave identical, or different, responses to "It seems to me people without children are generally happier than parents" and "A child would mean my spouse and I would have a happier relationship."

Logically, one of those statements should be true and one false, unless you are consciously predicting the effect of children for you and your spouse to be different than it is for other people.

"We'll Go Out Just as Often"

"Before we had children, Cal and I used to go to dinner and a film whenever we felt like it. We just walked out the door. It seems incredible to remember how easy it was. Now, dinner out or any other evening event requires just about as much preparation as the Normandy landing!" wrote a young mother of two.

Responses to this questionnaire item again showed sharp contrasts between expectations of happy and unhappy parents. The unhappy parents remembered assuming they would go out just as often. The satisfied parents almost always knew they wouldn't!

("You go out either *more*, or *less*," wrote one father. "We started going out two nights a week so as to have some time alone, whereas before we'd always stayed home. So you go out, either more, or less; but you do *not* go out 'just as often!'")

Of course, changes in a couple's social patterns after a child's birth aren't adequately measured by just the number of evenings out. Parents who had adjusted well and enjoyed parenthood named other dimensions to this question. One was spontaneity. "You learn to value spontaneity much more," wrote one woman. "You learn to value it so much you find yourself plotting and planning and arranging for it! Maybe you get the kids to friends' houses for an evening so that you and husband can be free to do something 'on the spur of the moment.' Is this spontaneity? It is, if you can maintain the illusion.''

Also mentioned was a change in the kind of recreational activities couples chose after they had children. Intuitively, one might easily enough imagine that parenthood often requires social life to fit within traditionally acceptable patterns. Sometimes, former lively indulgences have to be dropped and replaced with more wholesome pursuits. In all but the most tolerant and sophisticated (and generally urban) communities, drinking and dancing till dawn can call into serious question one's fitness as a model for one's own young.

Budget constraints often dictate a change from active to vicarious enjoyment of cultural and sports activities. "Often, now," explained one father, "we simply have to hear about the concerts second-hand from friends, or be content to read the reviews instead of seeing the plays." Watching sports events on television rather than at a stadium was mentioned by others.

Finally, successful parents pointed out that many recreational choices must be made with children in mind. The phrase "good for the children" seemed to appear constantly in marginal notations of both parent groups, but the unsatisfied parents used the phrase in a context of some resentment, the happier parents in a spirit of willingness to take part in activities that were of intrinsic interest only to children, or activities that would aid children's development or expand their horizons.

Successful parents also realized the need to plan many social activities in conjunction with parents of their children's friends, (particularly when children are younger) and to help a child develop his or her own social life by becoming directly involved in it whenever necessary. One woman wrote, "A word of advice to new parents is this. Children's parties may not be thrilling to you, but you should take your thrill instead from your child's pleasure. Learn to see things as your child sees them. That way, you can learn to love the circus, pin-the-tail-on-the-donkey, paper party hats, skate boards, and maybe even a few of the less dumb TV shows.''

When Children Can Bring Closeness

The myth is that children can bring couples closer and, in fact, sometimes children do bring couples together.

But it doesn't always happen and it certainly can't be counted on to happen. Crisis is in fact a more usual result of childbirth than is closeness. But a more closely woven marital bond does at times follow parenthood.

Ironically, a child seems most likely to add happiness to marriage when that is not the purpose for which he or she was intended. Putting into plain words what philosophers and poets have said, the pursuit of any form of happiness is apt to be a counterproductive effort: The more aggressively happiness is pursued, the more elusive it becomes. Where children are concerned, counseling psychologist Dr. Herbert Robbins explains simply, "It's precisely the couples who intend a child to cement a marital bond who find out that cement can *sink* as well as bind.''

When children do bring happiness to a given marriage, it is usually as an addition to preexisting contentment and closeness. This generalization does carry an unexpected qualification, though: a child can often add happiness to preexisting happiness *if* the preexisting happiness is not too great! Several researchers, including Harold Feldman, have noted that *the closest marital union can be most susceptible to the shock of change.* A husband and wife used to intimacy and privacy and quiet hours alone can find the time and attention that must be given to a child a disappointment or a threat. The prior, intense, romantic quality of the marriage must now give way to responsibilities perceived as intrinsically unromantic and undesirable. To be happier as parents than they were before, a couple must be ready to move on to another phase of marriage, and intensely close couples usually *aren't*.

But given a basically sound and cooperative marriage, a child can bring added unity. Specifically, what characterizes the marriage to which a child can bring improvement?

According to professional observation, the couple most likely to benefit from the kind of change a child brings is likely to have a marriage that is less than vibrant, but far from devitalized. It is a satisfactory marriage, and insofar as satisfactory unions can be seen as successful ones, it could also be called a good or successful marriage (thus, importantly, there are no compensatory motives operating); still it is not characterized by starry-eyed absorption of the partners with one another.

The partners of such a marriage tend to function with notable *independence*. This is not independence in the sense of alienation or apartness, however. While each partner pursues separate interests and perhaps to some extent even a separate social life, there exist good communication and enough shared interests to provide what several sociologists term *couple identity*. The marriage is generally of at least several years' duration; and companionability is a more valued component of the marriage than romance or sexuality.

One sociologist described the impact of a child on such a marriage with the following analogy:

> It's somewhat as though, prior to parenthood, the husband and wife had been involved in the "parallel play" of the four-year-old. They were not unaware of each other; indeed they were watching each other closely and learning from each other's activities by observation, and by both non-verbal and verbal communications. Each was *primarily* interested in his own playthings, however. Suddenly, it is as though someone brings in a new toy that interests them both; sharing it, they become closer than they were before.

Our sample of successful parents often indicated that their preparenthood relationship had much in common with the kind of marriage just described. Companionability was valued over sexuality. While refusing to indicate "I wish my partner were a better or different lover," they had a tendency to agree with the statement, "A really exciting sex life is incompatible with a long-term relationship." A value judgment underlying that view of successful parents might be reflected in their responses to Item 49. Here, asked whether a "spontaneous and romantic" sex life was crucial, very important, important or less important than other things, successful parents tended to divide their responses between the last two options. Less satisfied parents divided their responses between the first two. Uniformly, there was vehement disapproval among successful parents of the idea that a woman might choose a method of childbirth out of concern for future sexuality.

Another indicator that seemed extremely important was *agreement on issues relating to parenthood and child-raising.* Successful parents had contemplated the idea of having children and had hypothetically discussed how they felt children should be treated and raised. Marginal notes also indicated agreement on size of family and birth spacing. Agreement on subjects related to parenting was not only uniformly the case within our sample, but has been a consistent finding among other studies which have investigated the transition to parenthood. (Feldman makes the specific comparative point that agreement on issues of parenthood is more closely related to marital satisfaction than is agreement on matters pertaining to a wife's career.) Several consortium consultants agreed at one meeting that possibly the most significant factor in predicting successful adjustment to initial stages of parenting (assuming the basically companionate marriage we have described) was a situation in which the partners' degree of desire for a child was almost identical.

Other professionals also point out that whether or not couples can adjust well to parenthood depends in great part on their *realistic advance assessment of the nature of the adjustment*. It seems this principle can even at times apply if the adjustment is problematic enough to be called a crisis. "Partly," Dr. Figley advises, "the baby crisis is a crisis because it's a surprise."

The importance of realistic expectations is borne out by the happy and successful parents who responded to this questionnaire, for they had generally approached parenthood in a fairly tough-minded way.

One couple, for instance, indicated that they had predicted very accurately the changes that would be likely to occur in their relationship if they had a child. They wrote, "We made a list of what we thought we would have to give up in order to have a child. Then we went over that list and asked ourselves if we were willing to give those things up.

"We also made a list of things that we thought would go wrong. Then we asked ourselves if we could face those things." The wife added, "I even told Charles, who hates to see people out of control and liked me because I was so calm, 'There'll be times when not only will the baby be screaming but I'll be screaming. Maybe you'll walk in the door and I won't talk to you or kiss you but I'll yell at you because the baby's been yelling at me. Now you've got to make up your mind to face that because if you turn around and walk out the door, it's going to be all over.' "

A surprising number of those parents who felt happy with their parenthood experiences even recalled anticipating that there would be some effect on their sex life if they had a child. One explained, "I supposed sex would diminish from what I'd seen with my own parents. We like to think we're so different from our own parents but really people are pretty much alike. Anyway, I remember, when I was growing up, thinking that my parents didn't seem to be very sexually involved. Yet I knew they must have been at one time or they wouldn't have gotten married. So I figured that maybe the difference between the way they must have been at first and the way they were then, when I was noticing them, had something to do with their being older. Or something to do with being married longer. Or something to do with me."

For many couples the thought of a change in their sexual expression is an especially troubling aspect of looking ahead to parenthood.

Is There Sex After Childbirth?

Scarily enough, Dr. Richard Udry informs us that "as the fetus matures, it comes physically between the parents, makes their lovemaking awkward, and reduces their interest in sexual relations with one another." (The scariness to some will be a matter of emphasis: i.e. "reduces their interest in sexual relations *with one another.*") Were that not enough, the most optimistic of the general crisis studies was unequivocal on the matter of sex, stating plainly, "There is a significant reduction in desire for both husbands and wives after the birth of a child." Dr. Michael Carrera, vice president of the American Association of Sex Educators, Counselors, and Therapists and a practicing therapist himself, acknowledges that "this is what new parents really want to talk about—the change."

One could view the depressed libido that seems highly expectable in a physiological way (glandular change), a psychological way (role change), or a psychoanalytical way (image change). But it is possible to forego the analysis and move toward an acceptance, that is, to realistically acknowledge the likelihood of a postnatal change in sex life.

Dr. Carrera suggests that much of the decrease in sexuality has a lot to do with the felt need to adjust to a new person in the house and is thus perhaps not much different from the more temporary adjustments couples must make if they are sharing quarters with visitors. Practical coping behavior (such as seeing to the baby's anticipated physical needs before beginning lovemaking) may have an impact on spontaneity but can increase enjoyment of the act itself by removing both potential distractions and the worry about them. (One mother commented, "If you're reasonably sure the baby is attended to for the time being and you won't need to hear a sudden cry—you might as well get used to closing your bedroom door *now*.")

Some successful parents felt that sexuality did not so much decrease after childbirth as *change*. Wives often indicated that husbands became more affectionate and solicitous during pregnancy, and that this carried over into increased tenderness when lovemaking resumed later. A more mature quality to the sex act was mentioned by a few. One woman felt "there was more of a sense of gravity to lovemaking after we had a child; if sex was less spontaneous or less frequent, it seemed more meaningful. Because we knew then what our bodies could do." Some viewed the change in marital sexuality as only temporary: "It improves after a while," wrote one woman. "After all, new roles have made you new people. You have to get to know each other again." Finally, a perspective offered by one successful parent that might prove helpful to many is this: "Couples who really want children," she wrote, "should view this whole business of intimate changes as part of what a baby 'costs'—*and is worth!*"

Sexual Desire, Pregnancy, and Childbirth

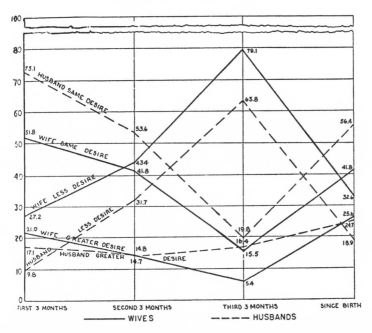

Figure 1. Percentages of husbands and wives rating sexual desire in three periods of pregnancy and since birth, as compared with desire before pregnancy. (Total responses: first three months, 209 husbands and 211 wives; second three months, 210 husbands and 211 wives; third three months, 206 husbands and 207 wives; since birth, 203 husbands and 206 wives). Reprinted, with permission, from Daniel Hobbs, "Transition to Parenthood," *Journal of Marriage and the Family*, No. 30, 1968. Copyrighted 1968 by the National Council on Family Relations.

Kids and Careers

Having a child doesn't have to interfere with a career? Well, technically, it doesn't we suppose, any more than marriage has to interfere with bachelorhood, given some very odd circumstances. One could, if so inclined, take a child soon after birth to live with another family who would raise him or her, as was a widespread practice in eighteenth-century France.

Practically speaking, of course, children *do* interfere with careers of working parents, particularly working mothers (this problem in most families exists far less for the father), and women with both children and a career can give almost daily examples of just how the interference works.

Recently, an agent for a major talent company told of ushering a top rock star into her office at noon, instructing her secretary not to interrupt them until their catered lunch arrived at one o'clock. In the meantime a management contract would be discussed and approved, thus giving Sandra the biggest client of her twelve-year career. Not to be disturbed was important, Sandra emphasized. This performer liked—indeed, insisted on—such special little deferences. Just as the contracts were being brought out, however, there was an urgent buzzing of Sandra's intercom. "Your son lost his money and missed his bus and is calling from a phone booth," the secretary informed her. During the frantic few minutes that followed, learning that her husband had already left for lunch and could not be reached, Sandra faced the choice of taking a taxi to personally rescue her confused and frightened seven-year-old or continuing the most important negotiation of her career.

A working *woman* is not the same as a working *mother.* A working woman can work late without phoning the sitter, accept travel assignments without arranging for Aunt Alice to visit, plan a winter vacation without checking to see when the school semester break is, and ask for a raise with a new wardrobe in mind, not the increased costs of orthodontistry and piano lessons.

A working mother, however, has two jobs—one of which she is paid for. The other, unsalaried one is no less demanding, though. "A working mother is always facing another shift," commented one. "She's always moonlighting."

A working woman begins to understand the nature of the conflict as soon as she becomes a mother. Only the mother can give birth—and fathers cannot breast-feed. And even excluding the more obvious and specific conflict-inducing situations such as children in phone booths, mothers of infants who return to work often report a subtle psychological pull that is its own kind of job interruption.

Typically, one woman insurance executive explained, "I'm still making the same salary, I'm still considered one of the most promising women in my company, my job is still important to me: but I'm less alert to opportunities for initiative or advancement. There's a brake on somewhere. I don't go to talk to a partner about a new policy idea because I don't want to get involved in a really interesting exploration of it that would keep me at the office late."

No wonder a prominent sociologist has called motherhood "the principal barrier to occupational commitment and success for women." Evidence of this could come from many quarters. One example is that in a recent year among women who were Woodrow Wilson fellows, dropout rates of mothers exceeded those of nonmothers by an average of 18 percent (in the areas of humanities, social sciences and physical sciences).

If perfect day-care existed perhaps the statistics would be different. But finding even adequate day-care is a problem. The concept of day-care has been so much publicized that there is a general notion that it is readily available. In reality there are only 700,000 day-care spaces in the entire United States to accommodate more than 5.6 million working mothers with children of preschool age. Further, facilities vary widely in quality and are clustered mainly in urban areas. Licensing standards are often not observed and officials privately admit reluctance to close substandard centers if doing so would leave no day-care at all available in the area.

Common problems for the mother whose child is in day-care are lack of flexible hours and lack of interaction with staff. Usual problems for the children are lack of personal attention and small insensitivities (e.g., forcing a shy child into activities he or she can't cope with). One day-care director blames much of this on the low salaries day-care personnel are paid. "As a general rule," she explains, "a parent pays about $25-$30 per week per child for out-of-home, group day-care. Now for that money it is unrealistic to expect excellence. I guarantee you you'll have more luck seeing Europe on $5 a day than finding quality day-care at that price."

Noted pediatrician and author Dr. Stella Chess advises flatly, "If you want good day care, *I would plan for it before I planned a child.*"

The future for quality day-care looks so unpromising, in fact, that one wonders if it will not be one factor in a move away from the entire day-care concept.

Twenty mothers recently interviewed by Jean Simmons at the University of Michigan had, prior to having a child, held enjoyable and profitable professional positions. Now, all were staying home. Some stressed the benefit to the child that can come from continuous caretaking ("I make her happiest," one mother said); others simply found staying home with a small child more enjoyable for the time being than continuing their careers.

We have been asking if parenthood interferes with a career: it does; but in the view of some it not only *does—it should*. One psychiatrist's opinion is that "busy people shouldn't have children unless they're willing to give up something they're doing now." One nonparent gives his reason for not having children: "My activities are very fulfilling and demanding. A child would have to be 'crowded in.' But a child should mean being willing to devote *personal* time to parenthood—it should mean some sacrifice of self or other interests." One sociologist wonders if the "do both" syndrome for women may not be replaced by the "forced choice."

Speaking almost exactly to this question, actress Joanne Woodward told Gene Shalit in an interview,

> I do not believe, being a prime example of one, in being a working mother. If you're going to work, *work*. If you're going to be a mother, that is an exciting career if you feel equipped to do it. If not, you shouldn't have children. If I had it to do over again, I would make a choice one way or the other. My career has suffered because of my children, and my children have suffered because of my career, and that's not fair. I don't know one person who does both successfully, and I know a lot of working mothers.

Today, one hears young women contemplating motherhood and disparaging the idea of having a child that somebody else will raise or having a child only to deliver it to some church basement every morning. Further, one hears talk of choosing between motherhood and a career so often that it's obvious some kind of disillusionment with the child-career combination has set in. Perhaps it's the pendulum effect regarding women's roles at work again. Or perhaps it's a new, increased valuation of motherhood, which would be unsurprising given lower birth rates. At any rate, our concept of what constitutes a "successful woman," having undergone great shifts in recent years, may be about to shift again.

CHILD-CARE EXPECTATIONS:

"OF COURSE I'LL HELP," HE SAID

"A childless egalitarian household is easy," said one new mother still in the shock of transition. "You both work outside the home, and sharing comes almost naturally when you get home. But almost all husbands I know resist infant care. When one father told our consciousness-raising group, 'You've never heard of a paternal instinct, have you?' everybody laughed."

Her opinion is borne out by at least one important survey. Lois W. Hoffman of the University of Michigan, investigating "Effects of the First Child on Woman's Role" in personal interviews with a cross-section of 1569 married women, found that:

Mothers report less household help from their husbands than nonmothers even within employment categories: thus, an unemployed mother receives less spouse help than a childless woman who is not working; an employed mother receives less help than a childless wife who is employed.

Many couples, prior to parenthood, pledge something approximating 50-50 sharing. But intentions may not ripen into actions.

One father said, "My own father never had very much to do with me, and I was determined to be different. I said I would share everything to do with the baby. I tried. But I was annoyed with the crying, uninterested in playing, and really put off by the nasty jobs! I found myself creating yard work or imagined repairs just to avoid taking my turn with the baby. . . . "

Women report that getting a husband to help with a child can become an ongoing job in itself. Many report serious backsliding from prenatal promises. Many say they finally decide it is simpler to do the work themselves than risk continual tension from attempted promise-enforcement.

At least one authority suggests that getting fathers to share in child care fully may not be worth the effort often required. Sara D. Gilbert, author of *What's a Father For?*, while acknowledging the vital importance of a father's early involvement with a child, suggests to fathers:

> No matter how important early involvement may be for you and your child, you may not be cut out for infant care. You may be terrified beyond all reason that you will drop the baby. You may have to gulp to keep down your lunch at the sight of a dirty diaper. You may not be able to sit still long enough for a baby to finish a bottle. Your nerves may scream every time the baby does.
>
> If you can't keep your negative feelings under control, the baby will sense your attitude and your distaste. . . .

And that response of course, defeats one major purpose of father child-care, which is father-child closeness.

Hopeful notes are that when fathers do manage to participate in child care with genuine willingness, they gain a much deeper appreciation for the being they helped to produce than they would have believed possible. For some, a kind of tolerance threshold is crossed if they persist at tasks ("After the sixth or eighth bath, I began to enjoy it. . . . ").

Also, some fathers make up for their reluctance to participate in infant care when the child is old enough for outings. Perhaps there is nothing wrong with one parent assuming primary responsibility for one phase of child development, the other parent for another phase. But it is worth emphasizing the virtual consensus of contemporary feeling that fathers should be parents, too, that they should make some commitment to sharing child-raising tasks and be sincere in their efforts to fulfill that commitment.

We will mention that not many among our successful parents had expected to share. "My husband had his career outside," one woman wrote. "The children were my career. But of course," she added, "things were different then."

"THE KIDS WILL TAKE CARE OF ME"

Several factors point to this assumption being a little unrealistic. The increasing mobility of our population makes close ties between generations difficult. And with the uncertainty of our economic future, children born today, even if they would like to help parents financially, may have a difficult enough struggle just maintaining their own financial independence. At least one gerontologist has in fact documented that more money passes from senior citizens to their grown children than the other way around.

This may be a reason why the Institute for Social Research study previously mentioned found older, child-free couples to be at least as content in their later life as couples who had children. In fact, the older men who had never had children were more content than the men who'd become fathers.

"Save money, not kids" for your old age, advises one counselor.

Fewer than 20 percent of our successful parents recalled ever having had a strong expectation of old-age support or protection against loneliness as part of their thinking before they had children. And many strongly disapproved. "It's not right to think kids owe you anything when they're grown. They didn't ask you to have them. They're kids—not insurance policies," wrote one man.

Still, if this is something you feel a strong expectation or desire for, along with cautioning against it, we will pass along the information that here, as in a few other instances, only children seem to exhibit closer ties with their parents. Norma Cutts and Nicholas Moseley in their book *The Only Child* found only children more likely than sibling groups to be responsive to their parents' needs in later years.

Chapter 5

Could I Be a Nurse, a Judge, a Teacher?

Questionnaire 5

1. I melt when I see a small, helpless animal.

2. I often find myself listening without hearing.

3. I can't imagine myself ignoring a crying child, someone hurt.

4. I'd rather be a host or hostess than a guest.

5. People who are very emotional irritate me.

6. For a three-year-old, I would buy slip-on shoes rather than ones that had to be tied.

7. Friends find me sympathetic.

8. I am comptroller and a partner of a mid-sized, urban insurance agency employing about twenty agents at any one time and four or five trainees. I met one trainee briefly before his active selling began and subsequently heard he was having trouble in the field. Calculating his commission three months later, however, I notice he had finally made an impressively large corporate sale.

    a) I call him to congratulate him.

    b) I write a brief note of congratulation and slip it into his pay envelope.

    c) I do neither (a) nor (b) because I don't know him well enough to know whether he might feel self-conscious about my implied knowledge of his earlier difficulty.

d) I do neither (a) nor (b) because it seems too personal, too much like coddling and therefore inappropriate in a business situation.

e) I do neither (a) nor (b) but will keep an eye on his future progress and perhaps motivate his further success at some time in the future by suggesting to my partners that he receive a small promotion.

9. I'm good about visiting sick friends.

10. When someone is upset, I pride myself on being able to do or say the comforting thing.

11. If I had been reading to an elderly person for a week who only smiled and nodded at the end of our hour together and never directly said thank you, I would discontinue this particular charitable practice.

12. This morning I had planned to serve a huge mushroom omelette to guests for Sunday brunch. I have other food in the house but the omelette is my specialty. Learning that one guest has a serious cholesterol problem,

a) I change the menu completely.

b) I make the omelette for everyone else but make something different for this one guest.

c) Since this omelette is so delicious and just about the only thing I make, I figure a small portion won't hurt him that much.

d) I somewhat guiltily proceed to make the omelette, but make a mental note to cook with fewer eggs whenever he visits from now on.

13. I like to touch—to hug my friends to show happiness, to stroke a dog's fur, to fondle soft fabrics.

14. Strength and gentleness are incompatible.

15. Today I have on my mind
a) someone who'd be interested in something I just read

    b) someone to whom I'd like to send a note or card or simple gift.

    c) both of these.

    d) neither of these.

16. My spouse has been told by our doctor to eat less meat, but hates most meatless dishes. I will

    a) discuss the situation and insist that he or she learn to like new things.

    b) gradually serve less meat (small strips of meat in Oriental sauce instead of a roast) and experiment with meat substitutes without saying anything.

    c) neither of these: I am my spouse's husband or wife, not keeper.

17. I'm the kind of person who would talk to plants if I thought it would help them grow.

18. I have agreed to keep a friend's two small cats while the friend is on vacation. My friend says, "It's really all right to change their litter box every three days or so, and since I'll be gone only five days you really need only change it once," then adds, "but they really like it if the litter box is changed daily."

    In all likelihood:

    a) I will change the litter box only once

    b) I would change it daily only if my own fastidiousness called for it

    c) I will change the box daily because the cats themselves prefer it

19. The sort of person who continually goes around doing favors and small kindnesses for others is very likely to be motivated by weakness or insecurity or both.

20. I believe in equitable relationships between self and others, between the self and the world around you. Give what you get is a good rule.

21. When I say no, I feel guilty.

22. In a discussion I can be firm about conveying my point of view.

23. What I do and what I say tend to be the same thing.

24. I have a hard time telling people I think they've done a bad job or done something wrong.

25. I could never be cruel, even if it meant being kind in the long run.

26. I worry a good deal about whether other people like me.

27. It has crossed my mind, when reading or hearing about widespread cheating among students, how difficult it must be for a teacher or monitor to actually confront and accuse a student so engaged.

28. It would be a lot of fun to catch someone cheating on an exam!

29. I have always hated regulations!

30. It's hard for me to set limits when my spouse is making a lot of demands on me and my time.

31. My own parents' discipline was:
    a) generally fair
    b) generally strict, but fair
    c) generally strict, at times unfair
    d) generally harsh, often unfair

32. One of the most important things children should learn is when to *dis*obey authorities.

33. "Let a child's first lesson be discipline, and his second what you will," said Benjamin Franklin. I agree.

34. I like to feel powerful; to be captain, not crew.

35. At my job, I am in charge of the Xerox machine. A co-worker who is also my friend is Xeroxing personal letters, breaking a rule which I had just emphasized at a

department meeting that morning. There is a small line behind him.

a) I ask him to stop doing personal Xeroxing, and I ask him in front of the others in line so that they will hear and get the point too.

b) I take him aside and remind him of department policy.

c) I pretend not to notice, for now anyway.

36. A new office boy typed something for me the wrong way, not according to instructions I gave him. Since I can get it done faster by retyping it myself, I retype it myself.

37. Discipline and punishment are the same thing.

38. Spanking a child means
a) the parent has failed
b) a good parent: spare the rod and spoil the child
c) if the parent is a conscientious one, the spanking is only in case of real physical danger.
d) I am not sure.

39. I have at least one personal indulgence (smoking, drinking) that is a little out of control.

40. The U.S. Marines have the right idea about discipline.

41. Discipline and forgiveness are generally incompatible.

42. I manage Archie's Hot Dog Stand. One young employee is always late, but with beguiling excuses. He's a nice guy and really needs the job, and I personally don't care if he arrives late, but the owner wants a policy enforced of three late nights in a row obligating me to fire an employee. After three nights in a row of being late, I offer him one more chance. The next night he again is almost one-half hour late.

a) I tell him to turn in his uniform.

b) I ask him why he was late.

c) I pretend not to notice—I simply give up!

43. My child brings home a report card with all Cs even though he or she is capable of better work. I issue an order: restricted evenings out until I see all Bs. At the end of the next grading period, my child hesitantly shows me six Bs and two Cs. My response is:

    a) I issued an order and will stick to the letter of it. Continued restrictions until I see all Bs.

    b) If my child has tried hard, I would relent.

    c) I would remove some or most, not all, restrictions.

    d) Maybe my requirement was a little too harsh. We'll discuss it.

44. Spanking a six-year-old is appropriate and/or necessary in the following situations:

putting self or others in danger

injuring pets

destroying property

spilling contents of kitchen cannisters

spilling one glass of milk

spilling several glasses of milk after being warned
    following first spill

threatening another child

saying "I hate you" to a parent

making noise when other family members are resting

lying

walking outside with no clothes on

    a) all of the above

    b) some of the above

    c) none of the above

45. I'm always willing to give directions when someone asks.

46. People often bring their problems to me.

47. I've been told that I bring out the best in people.

48. Children sometimes get crushes on me.

49. I can make my ideas sound interesting.

50. Stupidity irks me.

51. I would enjoy showing someone from out-of-town around my town or city.

52. If a friend's daughter came to me with a question about masturbation, I would:
    a) refer her to her own parents
    b) answer the question
    c) provide an appropriate book
    d) call the local school district to see why health and sex education are not being adequately taught

53. Since I have some camping experience, I've been asked to teach twenty Sierra Club members about camping on different terrains, different altitudes, and so on. I can teach these evening lessons any way I want. My preference is:
    a) lecture and discuss on all aspects to all twenty new campers at one or more meetings
    b) divide into small groups, assigning each to research one aspect of camping before the first meeting
    c) call a meeting at which I provide pamphlets and am available for questions

54. I have to take several items to a friend who is ill. My four-year-old is playing quietly. The friend lives only minutes away and my child would be safe if I left her here.
    a) I say I'll be right back and leave child at home.
    b) I explain where I'm going but leave child at home.
    c) I explain where I'm going and ask if child wants to go.

d) I take the child with me.

e) I ask the child's help in gathering the items I am to take and explain why we are going on this errand.

55. "You grew inside mommy's body" is a better explanation for any age child who asks "Where did I come from?" than "The stork brought you."

56. Values can be taught best by example.

57. A good philosophy of teaching is Praise success, ignore failure.

58. Teaching is the job of the schools.

59. My eight-year-old child has weak ankles. All her close friends go ice skating. She has gone with them but doesn't keep up too well and often falls. Last time she gave her forehead a really nasty bruise. This morning she's getting ready to be picked up to go to the rink as usual.

a) Fearing for her safety, I do not let her go.

b) Knowing how much this means to her, I let her go.

60. The most important thing to teach a six-year-old is:

a) the alphabet and how to read

b) courtesy

c) use of a children's library card for expanded horizons in reading

d) kindness

61. If a neighbor's child wanted to "help" me cook, I'd politely discourage the idea because of the mess it would make.

62. Helping my teenager with homework, I explain that MacArthur could have prevented a divided Korea after World War II. The next day, my teenager explains that his teacher, during class discussion, had called on him in class to discuss a related area; my son had expressed

what I'd told him the night before; the teacher said that
such a view was wrong. My child has brought home a
source book of readings in history which seems to prove
or at least strongly indicate that the teacher is right and I
am wrong. My response is:

    a) I am right; the teacher is wrong.

    b) Well, it seems I was wrong; I'll admit it.

    c) That's the way I learned history in school; history
seems to change in the way it's looked at in schools.

    d) I am afraid my child will never ask me for help with
homework again or trust my answers related to
homework.

63. If psychiatrists are so smart, they should just tell people
Here's what your problem is, here's what you've got to
do, and so forth instead of just saying hmmm and asking
lots of subtle questions.

64. For teachers, I think getting to know the students is just
as important as their firm knowledge of the subject
matter they're teaching.

65. I have promised each of my children that they can
always count on my complete support if their claim is
right and just. Now my younger son has taken my older
son's picture puzzle without asking. I hear Ben, who is
seven, say to six-year-old Peter, "You've got to give it
back because it's mine and you didn't ask and if you
don't I'll hit you." At this moment I have no choice but
to support Ben's right to have his property back since it
was taken without permission, but I shall find another
occasion soon to reprimand him for this threat.

66. I've often served as go-between for friends who are
quarreling with each other.

67. I'm good at dealing tactfully with landlords, salespeople.

68. My spouse and his/her sibling are in conflict about where

their mother will stay while she visits in town next week. Each suggests she stay at the *other's* house. My response is:

a) My first loyalty is to my spouse; I side with him or her.

b) I invite spouse's brother or sister over to discuss the matter.

c) I suggest deciding simply on the basis of who has more room and can thus more easily provide hospitality.

d) I'll pay for a hotel room for her.

69. My child is playing with another child at a playground. Their conversation is a continual childish quarrel: "I want to swing." "No, *I* want to swing, you push." "I pushed all yesterday, it's *my* turn." "No, you didn't," and so on. I observe this for a little while and it doesn't stop. I am most apt to:

a) observe but do nothing; children must work things out for themselves

b) since my child can usually be counted on to be honest about whose turn it is, I make the other child let my child swing

c) suggest tossing a coin

d) impose a time limit to end the arguing, telling both children that if they cannot resolve the matter themselves in a few more minutes they obviously don't really want to play and must both go home

e) I don't know what I would do.

70. The only way to handle disputes is to bring the people in conflict face to face.

71. Quarrels among small children usually arise over matters of property.

72. Sibling rivalry is inevitable. The best parent can't prevent it.

73. I shy away from talking over differences of opinion with my spouse.

74. Sometimes a cooling down period helps mediation.

75. When there are angry feelings in the air, I feel like running and hiding.

76. Walking down a street, I see two boys about ten years old struggling with a baseball bat. They're so involved in the struggle they don't even seem aware that I'm approaching them on the sidewalk. As I come next to them, one boy almost gets a whack on the head; to prevent this I grab the bat impulsively, saying "Hey, watch it." Suddenly I'm somehow in charge of the situation. The smaller boy says to me, "It's my bat, mister." The other boy smiles and says, "Aw, it's not really his" and starts to talk very persuasively, telling a convincing story about how the bat had been taken from him by his brother and only loaned to the smaller boy. I try to get the smaller boy to respond to this but he just hangs his head down and insists once more, "It's my bat, really."

    a) I give the bat to the smaller boy.

    b) I give the bat to the boy who told the persuasive story.

    c) I suggest they share it and not fight over it.

    d) I would play with them for a while until I could judge the matter better.

77. It is generally better to let children play out their arguments and conflicts than to enforce an uneasy truce.

78. An effective way to get siblings to get along is:

    a) to give a cooperative task like doing dishes

    b) to ask the older one to dress the younger one

    c) be careful to give all toys to both children to eliminate or minimize possessiveness

d) to be careful to distribute praise equally to minimize rivalry

e) to let each win half the time

f) none of the above can be counted on

79. My nine-year-old son and three friends have stopped by our apartment just before dinnertime, after a dress rehearsal for a school assembly to be given tomorrow morning in which my son has the lead. They are discussing the play they will put on, and my son's three friends seem to be making disparaging remarks about my son's performance (first joking, then mean). My son is silent for a while, then bursts out, "You know what the trouble with you is? You're all just *jealous* because you weren't good enough to get a big part." Frankly, I think my son is right. He is quite talented and this isn't the first time I've seen other children resent the easy way he can get the limelight.

a) I will talk to my son later about the wisdom of not being so frank about his obvious superiority.

b) I will tell him to be proud of his superiority—that he did the right thing in confronting the other children with the fact of their destructive envy.

c) I will suggest he offer to help other youngsters with singing or reading lines before the next school assembly.

d) I will call the parents of the other children to discuss the matter.

e) I don't know what I would do.

80. My eight-and-a-half-year-old daughter is jealous of her new baby brother. Soon after he was brought home from the hospital, she began to wet the bed nightly. I believe the best way to react is:

a) to discuss it with her

b) to understand how jealous and hurt she feels and give her more attention

    c) to ignore the behavior—it will stop sooner or later if it does not result in more attention

    d) to punish her for this practice, since it is obviously deliberate and something she can control if she wants to

    e) to take her to our pediatrician or family doctor for a talk

81. Sometimes kids just have to fight; adults shouldn't interfere.

82. If my child got to be known as the peace-maker among a group of children, I would be afraid that he or she lacked sufficient self-assertion.

83. Often I am too hurried to chat with neighbors or co-workers.

84. I push myself, am always on the go.

85. I always see to it that my work is carefully planned and organized.

86. I very often feel behind, not caught up with things.

87. I like juggling a number of interests.

88. I remember the small details so many others forget.

89. I wish I could find time for the important things—things I really want to do.

90. I tend to bite off more than I can chew.

91. I envy people who are easygoing, relaxed.

92. Physical environment around the house can have a lot to do with whether a family feels organized: convenient placement of telephone or often-used items; enough space so that things can be put in a proper place and easily found; and so on.

93. In school I prided myself on my ability to make

acceptable grades and at the same time be involved with a few after-school activities and a pretty good social life.

94. My spouse thinks I'm in a dither most of the time.

95. I am in a city to make six sales calls, each of which should take about one hour. Should I make arrangements for overnight accommodations so that I won't feel under pressure to rush the appointments through? Or shall I make sure to finish all calls today so that I can move on to another city late tonight? I would decide to finish all calls today.

96. The idea of being a committee chairperson, responsible for coordinating everybody's schedules and assigned responsibilities, is definitely unappealing to me.

Nurse. Must be genuinely interested in caring for other people and must be willing to devote full time to such care. Rarely does a good nurse simply "put in time." Must be both physically and emotionally stable to withstand the strain of caring for others constantly. Must be sympathetic yet remain calm in face of pain, wound, disfigurement, or other body trauma, as an overly emotional response could prevent effective treatment. Must be prepared to do any task required by patient need according to institutional policy. . . .

Judge. Arbitrates, advises, and administers justice in court of law. Establishes rules of procedure on questions for which standard procedures have not been established by prior law . . . listens to presentation of cases, rules on admissibility of evidence, and settles disputes between opposing parties. . . . Should be unswayed by emotionality or effectiveness of argument and attentive only to underlying evidence. . . .

Teacher. Fosters intellectual and academic development of individuals. Plans method and content of instruction, adapting these to meet individual differences in learning abilities. Helps individual on to next stage of learning, having from past knowledge and experience identified that next stage. Diagnoses disabilities among students and develops remedial instruction. Copes quickly and effectively with threats to good teaching which can arise from the processes of inter-student socialization.

[from occupational pamphlets]

Practitioners of the above occupations must have certain skills and abilities that are part of a parent's profession as well. The questionnaire items you've just completed should help assess your potential ability to nurture, to discipline, to teach and aid development, to mediate, and to organize.

The Care and Feeding Principle: "Nurse, it Hurts . . ."

Doctors may analyze and operate, describe or study, prescribe or diagnose or treat. But it tends to be nurses who actually deliver the treatment. Nurses are often the ones who foster well-being and healing and growth through appropriate care.

The nurturing process requires more than delivering the bare requisites of care perfunctorily or automatically. *Attentiveness* is required (a nurse has to be alert enough to sense when something is wrong, when "something hurts,"), as is a sympathetic or solicitous attitude.

Anyone who has ever been a patient in a hospital remembers the difference between the nurse who just handed you the Darvon saying "Here, take this," and the one who knew you'd take the spansules more readily if they were accompanied by a conversation; the difference between the nurse who wheeled the refreshment cart through the ward as quickly as possible, and the one who bothered to ask how you were and remembered that you preferred apple juice to orange juice.

Such small touches are not irrelevant pampering. Studies have shown that patients' recovery rates are influenced by such psychological factors as feeling cared about, not merely cared for, by someone genuinely interested in their recovery.

Successful parents tended to be *nurturers* (often in strong contrast to the less successful parents). The words *nurse* and *nurture* both originally came from a Latin verb meaning "to nourish" or "to feed." And though the meaning of nurturance has broadened, it still means to feed—in real and symbolic ways.

Based on the successful-parent responses, a personality with nurturing potential is one willing to give more than he gets—to give instead of getting. Such a person, given a choice, would rather be a host or hostess than a guest. He responds to something helpless, something crying, and someone hurt.

Responses of these parents indicated willingness to put the nurturing principle into operation regardless of reward or gratitude expressed in return even in the face of unappreciative or distinctly rejecting response (as, in the case of plants or pets who can't communicate appreciation, or the case of someone whose diet is modified for their benefit without their even being aware of it). A moment's thought would reveal what an important element this could be in satisfaction felt by a parent in his or her role, since children are not generally noted for freely flowing expressions of gratitude for all that parents give them.

A majority of the satisfied-parent group indicated they frequently had other people on their minds. Gestures of friendship were standard behaviors for them.

"This isn't always a big deal," one woman wrote. "If we're invited out to dinner, I don't call FTD and send a dozen roses. But I'm apt to take some biscuit dough so that whoever is going to the trouble to fix a company dinner that night can have an easy breakfast the next morning. Or if I know someone who's going through a real struggle—like one of my friends who's just gone back to school—I'll look for a funny card to give them." Someone else wrote, "I travel sometimes and there's often a little time to kill in airport shops. I pick up a good number of souvenirs, especially food. And since last Christmas when my wife's best friend Jeanne got a coffee mill, I'll pick up a pound of an unusual blend of coffee beans if I'm someplace like Georgetown or Ghirardelli Square." Habits of giving small gifts within the family were frequently mentioned.

Satisfied parents were apt to indicate that they were tactile people. Women in particular were apt to note in margins, "I'm a toucher!" or "I love to hold things." And one father wrote, "I like to pat my dog on the head when he brings me a stick, or roughhouse with him if the ground isn't wet outside. And I like gardening because plants have such interesting textures. And I like to be the one to take care of Timmy when he's sick because he's at a stage where he thinks he's 'too big' to be hugged by his dad, but when he's sick he doesn't feel that way." The idea that nurturing is heightened if nurturers aren't afraid to be physical is confirmed by several studies of early child care. In institutional situations it has been observed that no matter how adequate their diet, babies who were not held and fondled failed to grow. This is something that nurses are taught about—and something *nurturers* may just naturally know. And while it might seem safe to automatically assume that all parents would naturally be physically affectionate toward their children, an essay appeared in a recent *Readers' Digest* entitled "Did You Hug Your Child Today?" addressing the regrettable fact that a lot of parents *don't*.

A hug, of course, can also be seen as an affectionate gesture. Sending a note saying "nice job" is in this sense a nurturing act. In response to Item 8, most of the satisfied parents indicated they would send an encouraging note, whereas fewer than a fifth of the less satisfied parents indicated they would do so. This was consistent with the overall pattern for the nurturing questionnaire items 1 through 20 in this section. Almost three-fourths of the satisfied parents' responses indicated nurturing tendencies throughout this section; only about 20 percent of less satisfied parents indicated these tendencies consistently.

". . . And Gladly Teach"

Some of the skills a parent needs (ability to nurture, ability to teach), as well as some of the traits from which these abilities spring (selflessness, patience), exhibit themselves in the performance of an exercise in empathy that sounds simple but doesn't come easily to everyone: *the ability to put oneself in another's place.*

Teaching involves such an exercise, for teaching is almost always a personal process.

Except for those rather awful situations wherein a college professor in front of a microphone delivers a fifty-minute lecture on "Implications of the Eurodollar for Western Economies" to a large auditorium of indifferent students, a teacher must possess many more resources than mere knowledge of subject matter. Certainly, so must a parent.

A parent is always in possession of "subject matter" he or she wants to impart to a child. But even if the subject matter is as basic as a lesson in how to tie shoes, much more is involved beyond a diagrammatic explanation of what happens to the right shoelace and the left one when shoes are to be tied.

More than a dozen steps and stages are in fact involved:

1) *Exposure* to the task. ("Come and sit on daddy's lap and watch him tie his shoes.")

2) *Assessment* of readiness for the task. (By assessment of

manual dexterity in similar situations — e.g., ability to grasp, move and control pencil or crayon)

3) *Explanation* of the task. (Accompanied by demonstration)

4) *Supervision* of a child's first effort to duplicate the task demonstrated.

5) *Reinforcement* of correct behavior (successful accomplishment of task) through praise or encouragement.

6) *Analysis* of incorrect behavior, unsuccessful efforts to perform the task. ("No, you can't start the bow until the knot is tied. . . . ")

7) *Correcting* inaccurate teaching from other sources. ("I know Susie does it differently from the way we practiced, but she's right-handed and you're left-handed.")

8) *Patience* overseeing repeated tries at the task.

9) *Creating* novel learning situations where task can be practiced. ("Can you tie Dolly's shoe for her the way I just tied your shoe for you?")

10) *Exploiting* happenstance learning situations ("See how that little boy is tying his shoe? He's making it easier by putting his foot on the park bench first; that way he doesn't have to stoop down to see what he's doing.")

11) *Understanding* attempts to postpone or avoid performance of the task. ("I can't tie my shoes this morning because the shoes are lost.")

12) *Recognizing* when techniques being used to teach any task aren't working.

13) *Deciding* whether (11) and (12) are due to lack of readiness for the task or need for change in teaching techniques or teaching psychology.

14) *Revising* method of explanation of task, if and as necessary, and beginning again at Step (3).

The teacher-parent should know—by practice if not by name—about the principles of positive and negative reinforcement of behaviors. To praise success will reinforce a behavior positively. Ignoring failure will negatively reinforce behavior, but it won't accomplish teaching. This requires not ignoring failure but analyzing it.

Exactly the same principles of teaching apply when a parent is concerned with imparting something more complex to a child—say, the exercise of kindness. There are infinitely more of these abstract lessons than the easily definable tie-your-shoes ones.

Though both the multiplicity and immediacy of specific tasks to be taught can make such tasks seem more numerous on a parent's teaching agenda, they are never more important than value-oriented teaching. None of the satisfied parents saw teaching of the alphabet or reading skills as more important than teaching courtesy or kindness. Authoritative opinion would here agree that *even for very young children, the most important kinds of learning are social, not academic or task-oriented.* And social learning is going on continually, whether the parent is aware of it or not. Even very young children are quickly absorbing the value system which surrounds them.

Are values taught by example?

Yes and no. More than half the successful parents either rejected or modified by marginal notation the statement that "Values can be taught only by example." Most successful parents seemed to feel this statement was too facile a generalization. ("There's more to it than that," one wrote.) An overall feeling was that example alone was not enough, that *explained examples* were needed.

This would seem to tell us that the more abstract teaching tasks, too, can be broken down into steps and stages: *explaining* an act of kindness when you perform it; *requesting* a child's help with that act; *assessing* the child's readiness to re-peat a similar act at his or her own level; *reinforcing* lessons in kindness when the environment presents these; *dealing with* contradictory learning input from other sources that would in-terfere with absorption of the parent's good example; and so on. In this last regard, one parent wrote, "What if you're teaching kindness to animals in your home and your child vis-its Tommy, who throws the family kittens around the living room? There are endless examples. You've got to be alert, an-tennae always out, to see what examples *other* than yours your child is receiving!"

This takes us back to the basic prerequisite of teaching: be-ing able to put yourself in another's place. An effective teach-er understands that any lesson begins not with what he or she knows but with where the student is. By way of illustration, a little diagram explaining the interpersonal dynamics of a counseling situation may be useful.

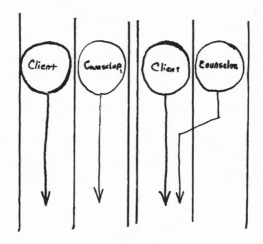

Illustration by Anthony Ravielli from *The Shape of Intelligence* by H. Chandler Elliott, Copyright © 1969 Anthony Ravielli, re-printed with permission of Charles Scribner's Sons.

In everyday situations, each person listens or speaks from his own point of view, but a counselor must see and understand what is going on from the client's viewpoint. A parent has to be able to make that crossover, too! If the parent is unable to, many chances for teaching and communicating to a child will be lost.

Therefore, an important predictor of your teaching ability exists if you listen sympathetically to others, if others come to you with problems or even "just to talk." A good teacher is first of all a good listener. Whether or not you are aware of giving specific help or advice, if people come to you repeatedly to discuss personal matters, you are making the crossover illustrated above: You're teaching them something.

A few suggestions obviously grow from this concept, the most basic one being that a teacher does not so much *teach* as *create conditions favorable to learning* from the student's point of view. This is comparable to the way counseling and therapy operate; a counselor usually does not solve problems of a client by direct instructions to "Leave your spouse!" or "Change your job!" but instead gradually leads the client to appropriate actions based on his or her own insights.

Successful parents indicated an understanding of this by agreeing with the statement that "Knowing students is as important as knowing subject matter"; by preferring small-group assignments among students to other teaching methods; and by indicating they would involve a child directly in a charitable errand.

Satisfied parents also tended to accept the idea that teaching occurs *when a child is ready to learn*, even if this should not seem the most convenient moment from the teacher's point of view for a particular lesson. A child's "Where did I come from?" question might provide a case in point. Satisfied parents unanimously indicated a willingness to give an honest lesson on that subject at any age.

In a related area satisfied parents generally agreed to let a child go ahead with a desired learning experience in ice skating, even though from the parent's point of view some risk was involved. Marginal notations, such as "You don't learn without taking some chances" and "Kids learn nothing if you protect them too much" were made in explanation of this response.

Satisfied parents were more likely than unsatisfied parents to admit "It seems I was wrong" in response to Item 62, and they seemed to fully comprehend the implication of this item. "There comes a time when kids learn more in school than you did," a few parents wrote.

On a somewhat broader scale, where parents and children are concerned, the same unwritten law of learning will eventually operate. That is, students tend at some point to pass up their teachers. And if this means that a parent-as-teacher has lost his role it also means that he has done his job.

Spare the Rod?

The first thing we know about discipline is that it requires the ability to set rules and *be firm about them*!

The second thing we know about discipline is that it requires being able to set rules and *be flexible about them*!

This tricky business makes sense only if one views discipline not as being synonymous with punishment, but as intimately related to teaching: in fact, as a teaching technique useful in correcting inappropriate behavior. Viewed that way, the catch-22 of firmness-flexibility suddenly unclasps. A good teacher, even a firm one, will decide when any teaching technique *isn't working*—and be flexible enough to change methods.

It is also important for the parent who wants to be a good disciplinarian to recognize when a disciplinary action is working, in spite of a dearth of specific evidence of working that had been expected. If, for example, disciplinary action was intended to help bring about *all* Bs on a child's report card and instead brought about *mostly* Bs, successful parents overwhelmingly indicated that such an increase in performance should merit a decrease of discipline. As more than one successful parent pointed out, maintaining the "letter of the law" in this case would fail to further the teaching function (and be likely to make the child discouraged and resentful).

The parent who can discipline well should be consistent about his or her own behavior (words and deeds being close cousins if not identical twins) and have a good measure of self-discipline.

It is possible, we suppose, for a child to understand why he can have only two cookies before dinner if mom and dad can have up to six Scotches; why he must go to bed at precisely 9:15 P.M. if mom and dad allow themselves a flexible schedule; and why he should not smoke if mom and dad do—but it does make things a little more difficult.

Even more important to good discipline is an independent parental personality. The parent who worries a good deal about being liked is apt to have trouble with discipline. If a parent is too dependent on her or his child for feeling loved and valued, then the parent's "no's" will be undermined by guilt and fear of rejection and will waver when they should stand firm. For a study-hall monitor, this quality is needed to confront a cheating student. Far more emotionally threatening for a parent, this quality of independence is needed to withstand pleas, protestations, remonstrances, accusations, and even an occasional "I hate you."

We were interested to note that while over a third of successful parents indicated an inability to rely on their own firmness or consistency in support of their value judgments (indicating T in response to statements such as "I could never be cruel even in order to be kind"), there was almost always one parent who did have a capacity for firmness—and it was almost always dad. We are aware, of course, that this scheme of things is not supposed to work. Still it seemed only one example of a good number in which satisfied parents' parenting abilities complemented one another: what one parent lacked, the other supplied.

At the other extreme, a parent's effort to maintain reasonable discipline will not survive a tendency to be too firm out of a need to feel personal power. In this area of danger, clear differences emerged between satisfied and unsatisfied parents—the latter were far more apt to like the idea of catching someone cheating; to acknowledge "liking to feel powerful"; and to agree with Ben Franklin's statement: "Let a child's first lesson be discipline, and his second what you will."

Some balance between the two personality tendencies is crucial. Both the overdependent parent and the power-needing one can absolutely be counted on to sabotage potential ability to reasonably decide which misbehaviors call for discipline and which do not; on a continuum of misdeeds running from the most innocuous (putting toys or books in wrong places) to the most serious (pushing a playmate into a busy street while playing); the overdependent parent will be unable to punish for any behavior at all; and the power-hungry mom or dad will be found not sparing the rod for even the mildest infraction of rules.

Neither extreme can possibly teach a child to recognize when authority is being exercised appropriately and when it is being used unfairly or unjustly. To the child of the "power" parent, all authority is unfair, and from the viewpoint of the child of an overdependent parent, there is simply no such thing as authority!

Since the disciplinary responsibility of parents encompasses the functions of both judge and jury, the need for the scales of justice to somehow reach a balance within a parent's own personality—or at least within the parental partnership—is unarguably great for good child development.

Will the Court Please Come to Order?
Dealing with Disputes

Judge-and-jury functions must also be performed by parents when disputes have to be mediated. A child has to be helped to recognize when a claim he or she is making is valid; and when, even if it is valid, his or her way of making the claim (as with threats) is unwise.

Disputes besides those over property are involved, even for young children (unless, of course, the time and attention of parents and other authority figures are viewed as property). Property disputes, in fact, are simple to solve—at least compared to every other kind of dispute that can be expected to show up in family court! A suggestion to divide time with toys or accept comparable substitute play or reading materials will generally work; tossing a coin to see who has the first turn on a swing is pretty quickly accepted by children as a fair compromise.

But a more diffuse sense of "my turn first" characterizes children. It is their way of assuring themselves that *they matter*. "If I really matter, mom will let me go first," runs their reasoning; or, conversely, "If she lets me go first, then I really matter." The strength of this inner reasoning process and its obvious tie to a child's feelings of self-worth obviously put a Handle With Care label on this particular package of parental responsibility. And these things do have to be "handled." Letting kids fight it out is asking for a very long fight, lasting until a child's identity is secure and ending not one minute sooner!

Children have to be guided in establishing their own security, with diminishing levels of "me first"-ness that will gradually be replaced by a sense of justice. But they must be shown that sense of justice by adult, reasoned judgment. If a child reaches this state quickly, as a few do, and becomes a mediator among others, parents should be proud rather than fear their son or daughter lacks self-assertion. "Really self-confident people do less asserting than popular belief would have us imagine," wrote one member of the satisfied-parent group in response to this questionnaire item.

Even disputes arising from conflicting psychological "me-first" claims among children can be managed without a Ph.D. in child psychiatry, fifty years of experience as a playground supervisor, or a lengthy career as a union contract negotiator *if* (and the *if* is an important one) *they occur outside the home.* As long as a child feels first in his or her own home, he can gradually adjust to being not-first in a variety of outside situations. (If you are reading this paragraph to mean that such conflicts are more easily mediated by parents of an only child, you are quite correct.)

According to both our parent groups, and according to the weight of professional opinion, it is inside the home, between siblings, that the most baffling and frightening conflicts occur.

Sibling rivalry may not quite be, as Dr. James Dobson once called it, "as inevitable and natural as breathing, eating, and sleeping," but American Psychological Association psychologists interviewed at the 1976 annual meeting of the APA do define it as "a universal phenomenon." Its eruptions can provide the most serious challenges both to parents' satisfaction and to children's development.

With siblings, both parent groups indicated that mediation was continually needed.

"Symptoms of sibling rivalry (on the part of the older child) generally have the characteristics of negativism and regression,'' the child-development experts inform us in a statement both irreproachably true and notably unhelpful.

When eight-year-old Barbara begins to wet the bed after her brother's birth, she is really having a dispute with her brother—and one that calls for quick mediation since it is very deep and serious. Barbara is quarreling with her brother's very existence, challenging it with desperate me-first! stratagems: "He wets the bed, he's first, he matters. When I wet the bed, I was first, I mattered. I'll wet the bed again and then they won't need him!" Her behavior calls for delicate execution of psychology, not punishment. But just what applied psychology would be appropriate? Unfortunately, no specific answer can be counted on to be right, here or in other sibling situations.

To his credit, Dr. Allan Fromme is one of a growing but still small number of authorities who takes sibling rivalry seriously. (For examples of just how casually fraternal friction is considered by many professionals, you might check the index of a nearby book on child care. Watch it go from *sharing* and *shyness* to *sleep* and *spanking*. Or consider an optimistic approach from one child-care book: "When she [the mother] sees him [older child] advancing on the baby with a grim look on his face and a weapon in his hand, she must jump and grab him and tell him firmly that he mustn't hurt the baby.'')

In Dr. Fromme's book on child care, originally published as *The Parent's Handbook*, he spends a good many pages explaining no fewer than sixteen things that should be done by parents if sibling rivalry is to be controlled.

His are excellent suggestions; they are better done than not. But our satisfied parents of more than one child had often—by happy accident or aptitude or intuition—done many of the things Fromme advises. Their consensus of opinion was that the suggestions can't be counted on to be very effective!

The skepticism displayed by even the most satisfied parents when they were asked to respond to these suggestions reveals better than anything else we know of just how awesome a challenge in-home rivalry presents to parents. Certainly it makes sense, as Fromme suggests, to space your children ("I'd say at least 20 years apart," wrote one parent in the margin.) and he is in fact not the only authority to point out that the closer in age children are, the more intense the rivalry. Certainly it is wise to explain to an older child that a new baby is coming and prepare him or her for what that would mean. ("Just as I would do all I could to prepare my wife for the arrival of a second wife," the same parent wrote.) It really does seem a hopeful plan of using psychology to "dedicate the homecoming from the hospital to the firstborn, not the baby." Et cetera.

But nothing can quite change the fact, for the older child, that she or he has lost unique status in the family, and in the world.

Even satisfied parents almost unanimously felt that in-home mediating skills were most debilitating. More than a few said that, while they did not regret the experience of parenthood, given their parenthood career to begin again, they would have only one child.

"Sibling conflicts are not totally solved even by the most calculated 'fairness,'" wrote one mother. "And the years of trying to deal with the children's quarrels have removed a lot of the pride we would have taken in their individual accomplishments. As individuals, they are happy and well-adjusted and healthy. But making them friends is the one area where we feel a strong sense of failure. I doubt that they will ever be friends."

"I am gentle in my advice to young people I know who aren't parents yet," wrote another mother from the satisfied-parent group. "I suggest they might think it over pretty carefully before they have a child. I am much more firm if a young couple who is happy with *one* child tells me they're planning a second. I tell them to stop while they're ahead."

Getting It All Together

Though mediation skills were felt by many to be the most difficult job challenge within the parent role, there is one other set of skills that might not be far behind in importance:

> A *Manager* [according to the occupational handbooks] has an overall view of systems and procedures within which priorities are set and details executed. . . . A manager hires and fires personnel for performance of specific tasks for which they are suited; sets priorities for overall smooth functioning of organization. . . . A manager need not be proficient at each task itself but at getting tasks performed by others.

A good parent does have certain things in common with a good manager. A parent must coordinate activities so that each family member gets where she or he should and accomplishes what she or he is supposed to.

Setting priorities? That certainly matters in home as well as business management. It's no good to tell the baby-sitter little things like what the children's favorite color pajamas are, whether they can stay up to watch "Wild Kingdom," where the chocolate milk is, where the dirty glasses go, and where the extra lightbulbs are, yet neglect to leave the police emergency number or the number where the parents can be reached.

Hiring and firing goes on, too. Family services which are delegated to out-of-home institutions must be periodically reevaluated, and perhaps Laundry X replaced by Laundry Y, a family day-care center by a federally sponsored one, or even a public school decided against in favor of a private one. As sociologist Jessie Bernard has pointed out, one important effect of the trend toward dual-career families is that parents actually do *less* parenting themselves: they instead decide *what agencies will do it for them!*

Perhaps the ability to organize and manage well is not so important as other skills dealt with in this section. Certainly differences between responses of satisfied and unsatisfied parents were less clear-cut here than anywhere else, and children have been known to emerge beautifully from households "in a dither." Still, parents' own peace of mind can be threatened by too much confusion.

As sociologist Jean Veevers calmly counseled in stunning understatement, "The cohabitation of adults and children necessitates a formidable restructuring of the daily round of adult activities." Thus perhaps a nonparent who is always behind and presently past the limits of realistic commitment should think twice before adding the managerial duties of parenthood to her or his present problems of personal management.

There are a few other sets of skills that parents have in common with other professions, too.

> A *psychologist* . . . evaluates adequacy of individual's present methods of self-perception and social interaction . . . helps individual formulate realistic future personal changes . . . follows up results of counseling to determine reliability and validity of treatment. . . .

> *Chauffeur* . . . drives private car as ordered by owner or other passengers and performs other miscellaneous duties. Assists passengers to enter and leave car and holds umbrella in wet weather. . . .

And perhaps others too numerous to document, such as:

Veterinarian (when the family pet gets sick).

Social Director (when a birthday party is two weeks off).

Diplomat (when a marshmallow soup prepared to "make you feel better" could instead prolong your stomach flu for twenty-four hours).

Employment/Investment Counselor: when a twelve-year-old needs a part-time summer job that will bring in enough money to pay for an art course (because the twelve-year-old is talented in art) but will not require enough hours to interfere with the French course she must repeat in summer school (because this same twelve-year-old is terrible in languages). . . .

Assembly-line worker (when thirty sandwiches must be made for a play-group graduation picnic).

But workers in each of these occupations are generally not required to have the skills needed by practitioners of all the *other* ones; or, if so, they generally do not have to exercise these skills simultaneously, continuously, over a long period of time, or on the very same day.

A fourth-grade English teacher doesn't really have to worry about how well her students write paragraphs once they reach fifth grade.

A judge doesn't have to comfort a disappointed defendant after deciding against his case.

A nurse needn't follow career problems of her patients once they leave the hospital and go back to the office.

It is the comprehensive performance of diverse roles that seems to be the remarkable requirement of parenthood, and when managed well, it is this profession's most remarkable achievement.

Chapter 6

What If I Plan a Picnic and It Rains?

Questionnaire 6

1. I could respond in a controlled manner to the following situations:

    a) while driving to the other side of town to an important appointment, every traffic light is red.

    b) I am unfairly accused by a shopper of knocking his packages from his arms when it was really his fault.

    c) At a doctor's or dentist's office, I am made to wait for over one hour past the scheduled appointment time.

    d) All of the above.

    e) None of the above.

2. I could respond in a controlled manner to the following situations:

    a) At 7:15 A.M. on a winter morning, it is my turn to drive carpool for the children and I have five stops to make before 8 A.M. and the car will not start, my spouse is away, and I have no jumper cables nor does there seem to be anyone around who can help me.

    b) Milk spills in a narrow space between counters. Getting it out before it sours requires cutting a sponge into thin strips and painstakingly manipulating the sponge strips with barbeque tongs.

    c) I am unfairly accused of failing to control my child in a playground dispute.

    d) I must wait for one hour past appointment time at the pediatrician's office, which is filled with noise and impatient children.

e) All of the above.

f) None of the above.

3. People who are not on time to meet me show lack of respect for my time.

4. There is usually an explanation for tardiness on the part of my friends or associates.

5. I become very upset when things do not go smoothly.

6. The details of life annoy me.

7. I don't mind going over the same material several times if it will help people understand better what it is I am trying to say.

8. I phone a department store to ask for information about an advertised item. First the store's lines are busy. Then there is no answer. Following that, I am transferred to two wrong departments. After the third transfer of my call:

   a) I figure, "Well, sooner or later I'll get the right department."

   b) I amuse myself by composing a mental essay on the subject Nothing Works Anymore.

   c) I take out my irritation on the person now on the other end of the line.

   d) I demand to complain to the manager's office.

   e) I hang up in irritation and will be in a bad mood for about an hour.

9. I enjoy doing some slow, painstaking tasks well.

10. I am not fond of indecisive people.

11. Waiting in line drives me crazy.

12. A three-year-old child who starts to cry merely because he has been startled should be firmly scolded.

13. Sometime within the past twenty-four hours I have had a hearty laugh.

14. I consider myself to have a great deal of personal dignity.

15. I require absolute silence to concentrate on work that is important to me.

16. I require relative silence, or lack of distraction, to read with enjoyment.

17. If a child of mine several times interrupted my reading of the morning or evening newspaper, I would generally be:
    a) greatly upset
    b) moderately upset
    c) only a little upset
    d) not upset at all

18. My friends are diverse in occupation and opinion, rather than all of a type.

19. When I see young people on the street in Krishna robes, I think, "What a waste of time!"

20. It is important to me to begin the day calmly, wash my face and have coffee before anything is required of me.

21. A place for everything and everything in its place could describe my home most of the time.

22. I hate it when plans are upset, things go wrong.

23. I can switch gears from concentrated activity to relaxation or from one type of activity to another without much trouble.

24. Someone who can see all sides of a question is too wishy-washy for my taste.

25. I am a perfectionist; I like things just so.

26. I like to think of different or unusual things to do for recreation or entertainment.

27. Good parents should always have a united front with children; differences confuse a child.

28. I always have a job or an outside-the-house activity.

29. I have at least a slight distrust of modern technology.

30. I cannot stand being alone.

31. I have at least one hobby or recreational interest that I take very seriously. .

32. I imagine that if I were the parent of a young child who was playing quietly in his room at the end of the day,
       a) I'd think to myself, "Terrific. He's quiet. I can have some free time."
       b) I'd think, "He's playing. I'll go play with him."
       c) I'd think, "He's probably playing happily. I'll just quickly check to be sure."

33. If I can feel like one of the group, that's generally sufficient to make me content.

34. I am greatly concerned with the impression I make on others.

35. My feelings about myself come significantly from inside me rather than all from external sources, other people.

36. I'm very influenced by expert opinion.

37. You have bought for your child a traditional tricycle, the kind you used to have. But it now turns out that virtually all the other children in the entire neighborhood have something called Big Wheels instead of a tricycle. Big Wheels is a low-slung, plastic monstrosity (to you) with wheels the size of those on

farm tractors that make (to your ears) an absolutely awful racket.

a) You return the traditional tricycle and get your child a Big Wheels.

b) You make the exchange only if some developmental sales point is offered to you by a neighbor, such as that the pedals are designed so as to give children's legs more exercise than a traditional trike.

c) You make the exchange only if your child is deeply unhappy to be the only kid in the neighborhood with an old-fashioned trike.

d) You will get a Big Wheels under no circumstances whatsoever.

38. Following is a list of toys:
Easy Bake Oven
Crissy Doll
Chatter Telephone
Tyke Bike
Mouse Trap Game
Johnny Lightning Car and Tracks
Barbie Doll
Play Family School
Big Wheels
Hot Wheels
Knowing that these are the Top Ten all-time best-selling manufactured toys for children, the reaction closest to your reaction would be:

a) I would seriously investigate and likely buy most or all of these, figuring "The proof of the pudding. . . ." These toys must offer something if kids like them so much.

b) I would buy few if any of these ten toys on principle as a rejection of advertising hype, conformity, and popular taste.

39. I do not/would not hesitate to seek professional help for serious personal problems.

40. When I am unhappy, I try to determine why and to correct the situation.

41. Love between my spouse and me has not changed at all since we met.

42. I feel sure my mate and I will be together always.

43. I feel that my marriage or current relationship has somewhat curtailed my personal growth and personal achievements.

44. I believe that (43) above is a necessary result of living with someone and do not find this a distressing situation.

45. The family that prays together, stays together, is as true today as a hundred years ago.

46. I can't imagine ever apologizing to a child.

47. Unfortunately, today, the wrong kind of people are having children.

48. A child unwanted by either partner is an unwanted child, period.

49. I have considered the possibility of not having children.

50. I've never been one to feel I had all the answers.

51. It's probably true that economic problems could threaten my present job, my future employment, my comfortable existence.

52. Parents don't raise their children these days, the world around you does.

53. Research has found that restrictions on the amount of living space limits fertility. At a lecture-discussion, you

hear others reflecting on whether living space for American families should be restricted in order to help control population. The response closest to your own is:

a) how un-American!

b) People should have as much space and as many kids as they can afford.

c) Population and space are certainly problems; I'd like to take part in such a discussion.

d) If I have a child I'm sure such discussions will be frequent and commonplace within my child's lifetime.

54. I have sometimes felt that I have so many inadequacies as a marital partner that I must make conscious efforts to fill this role better.

55. The principle of togetherness can see a family through most storms that contemporary life sends to buffet the home.

56. A man can be forgiven many faults of character if he is a good provider for his own family.

57. Given sufficient leisure time, I would prefer to:

a) develop a favorite skill rather than do volunteer work

b) prefer volunteer work to developing a skill or talent

c) both are important, I'd find some way to do both.

58. I belong to a community improvement association.

59. I am involved with a personal service project (such as visits to the elderly, volunteer reading programs for schoolchildren).

60. I am leaving home or work with $20, with which my spouse and I plan our usual Friday evening out. A neighbor or co-worker asks for a $20 loan to pay for emergency road service for his car.

a) I loan him or her the $20.

b) I explain why I cannot loan the money.

c) I call my spouse to discuss the matter.

d) I loan $10, figuring that my spouse and I can have a hamburger instead of a restaurant dinner.

61. My spouse and I are planning our first real evening out in a month or more. My response to the above question remains the same.

62. I would be willing to adopt a child if I could not have my own.

63. I would be willing to adopt a child instead of having my own.

64. The current world situation—politically, ecologically—really makes me think twice about having children.

65. I feel little responsibility to improve the world for the next generation.

66. I am bored by discussions of what life will be like in the year 2000.

67. On television a news report tells of a famine-stricken area where food supplies are so limited that only children and adults who have lost more than 20 percent of their body weight can be fed. I feel:

a) slightly upset, but then this sort of thing happens so frequently that one almost gets used to seeing it on the news

b) moderately upset, feel I'd like to do something if I could

c) greatly upset: something must be done!

68. I am leaving on a quick trip to the shopping center and a neighbor or co-worker asks me to purchase a short list of items since I am going anyway.

a) I agree, with an attitude of Of course, why not?

b) I agree, with an attitude of I certainly hope this doesn't happen too often.

c) I agree, with the spoken or unspoken assumption that he will do the same thing for me another time.

d) I do not agree.

69. *Mainstreaming* is a process of classroom assignment according to which children with mild physical or mental handicaps (poor vision, weak limbs, mild dyslexia) are brought into the "mainstream" of the normal classroom so that they may share the educational experiences of nonhandicapped children. My reaction to the idea of mainstreaming is:

(a) If my own child were slightly handicapped, I would want him or her in a normal classroom; however, if my child were normal I'd be reluctant to see other handicapped children placed in my own child's normal learning environment.

(b) If my child were slightly handicapped, I would want him or her in a special classroom; however, if my child were normal I'd be agreeable to mildly handicapped children placed in my own child's normal classroom.

(c) I would approve of mainstreaming both for my child and others.

(d) I would disapprove of mainstreaming both for my child and others.

70. I have taken my child shopping at a department store to buy a shirt or sweater, and told him he may make his own selection. However, so eager is he to choose wisely and well that it has taken him almost half an hour to narrow the selections down to two or three. The reaction which is closest to the way I would probably react is:

(a) It's good that he's conscientious and intent on choosing so carefully!

(b) I really have a lot of other things I'd rather be doing!

(c) This learning experience has really gone on long enough; he's had the experience of narrowing possible selections down to a few; now I'm going to make the final choice so that we can get out of here.

71. My daughter wants me to play ball with her and her friends on a Saturday. Given the following plans of my own, I would refuse her:

    a) a pro ball game for which I've had tickets for a long time

    b) work on project for my job because the income is needed

    c) time alone with spouse

    d) help with a Stop Shopping Center Development petition drive I'd promised to take part in

    e) all of these except (a)

    f) some of these including (d)

    g) none of these

72. Martha Weinman Lear tells the following story in *The Child Worshippers:*

> From Brooklyn, word comes of a courageous loner who quit the PTA because the girls refused to broaden their horizons. . . . "I told them we couldn't help ourselves unless we helped others," she said. "I told them, we need a new school. Ten blocks away they need a new school, too. Now why don't we think about this and examine our needs and theirs and see where it is really needed more? And they jumped on me and yelled, *"What do you mean, needed more? Our children come first!"*

    a) I can easily imagine myself in the place of that loner.

b) I would be one of those who felt our children come first.

73. I would rather be a brilliant but unstable worker than a steady and dependable one.

74. Even if I seldom admit it, my ambition is to become a great or famous person.

75. I characteristically have mood swings from elation to depression.

76. There are a lot of jobs I'd like to try.

77. What I'm doing with my life seems worthwhile.

78. One thing that definitely appeals to me about having a child is that it would be a totally new experience, something different to experience.

79. Somebody who lives most of his or her life in one place is really missing out.

80. I like to move on if a job stops being challenging or interesting to me.

81. If I had had more training, schooling, or relevant background, I would have progressed much further in my field by now.

82. Five years from now I have a specific career goal in mind.

83. I would like to seriously study arts or languages or similar subjects.

84. I would like further training in my field of work.

85. I suspect I have talents which lie outside my field of work which are undeveloped.

86. It means a lot to me to develop any talents I have.

87. It would never occur to me to go to the Cannes Film Festival.

88. If someone I knew went to such a festival, I would
    a) be so envious I couldn't stand to hear about it
    b) become interested in taking such a trip myself
    c) be only slightly envious if at all, but want to hear about it
    d) be neither envious nor interested in hearing about it

89. I am rarely home on evenings or weekends.

90. I love to go out on the spur of the moment.

91. I think it accurate to say that I have a few interesting, minor vices.

92. I want to do many things I've not yet done, have many experiences I've not yet had.

93. To travel the world is something I truly want to do.

94. I am more content than restless.

95. I find the idea of visit to Disneyland
    a) genuinely appealing
    b) of moderate interest
    c) something I might do once out of curiosity if circumstances made it easy
    d) quite uninteresting
    e) absolutely repellent

96. I often feel that difficulties are piling up so high that I cannot overcome them.

97. I cannot imagine the word *idiot* said lovingly between spouses.

98. I can see the humor in most situations.

99. Sometimes if you can manage to really internalize a hopeful old cliché like It's always darkest before the dawn, or Laugh, and the world laughs with you, you can save a bundle on psychiatrist's bills.

100. This is not a safe world to bring children into.

101. I feel that life has never really tested me.

102. Even bad breaks or bad judgment can usually be viewed as learning experiences.

103. If the person closest to me stopped loving me, I could still carry on.

104. If a child of mine broke out with measles on New Year's Eve and my spouse and I had to stay home from a party we'd looked forward to very much, it would probably not occur to me to make a game out of counting the measles spots.

The Sources of Frustration

Questionnaire 6 is meant to help you assess whether you have certain traits which many successful parents have: patience, flexibility, independence, practicality, generosity, stability, an optimistic outlook, and a sense of humor.

Psychologically speaking, the first of these, patience, involves (1) tolerance for repetitious or routine activities; (2) ability to defer personal gratifications; (3) adaptation to circumstances perceived as undesirable or nonrational; and (4) tolerance for frustration.

Parentally speaking, patience involves (1) tolerance for routine and repeated activities (say, picking up toys, and wiping up spills, and responding to your child's constant repetition of the same question; (2) ability to defer personal gratifications (like postponing going out to dinner until the children finish college); (3) adaptation to the nonrational behavior of children (as in the case of the father who emerged from his infant daughter's bedroom in perplexity, saying, "Dolores is going to have everything in the world, all the advantages we can give her. She can go the the college of her choice. So why is she crying?") and (4) tolerance for frustration.

Nearly every kind of frustration ever discovered is intensified when you have children.

Frustration is simply what happens when your normal progress toward some goal is blocked by some circumstance. A classic psychology-textbook example of the process runs something like this: You plan a picnic (goal); it rains (block); you are frustrated.

Even within this simple example it is possible to see how

the resulting frustration could be more simply dealt with by the childless, who would simply stay home and listen to records. But given children and a rainy day in this situation, the children's disappointment must be dealt with, an alternate plan for their activities hastily constructed; assurances that there will be other picnics offered, comfort given for the postponement of their own picnic-related achievements (the Frisbee competence Sally has developed, the chicken salad with granola Ken had looked forward to serving his friends), and so on.

On a day-to-day basis, children can prove frustrating to small goals parents could otherwise easily accomplish for themselves. Mom would like to have her coffee leisurely, but children must be dressed; Dad would like to relax, but children need to be taken to lessons; both spouses would like to lower the family electric bill, but children leave the door open when the air conditioning is on.

And even minor frustrations seem less tolerable when they are repeated. Do you, for instance, experience noticeable frustration when every traffic light is red? Any parent can tell you there are mornings when every glass of juice is spilled, evenings when every ten minutes brings an interruption.

Can you see yourself responding well to such minor frustrating situations?

And what of more major frustrations?

A table from Leonard Carmichael's *Introduction to Psychology* might provide an opportunity for us to expand, with a third column, an illustration of how responses to more major sources of frustration can prove *particularly* frustrating to parents.

In the following examples some personal goal deeper than the desire for an uninterrupted cup of coffee is being blocked. The nonparent will often be freer to cope with the frustration source than a parent. The parent's need for positive character traits (such as patience) to deal with the frustration will often be greater.

Source of Frustration	Nature of Frustrated Feeling	How Frustrated Feeling is Intensified for Parent
Social Ferment	The person is upset by economic change, threat of nuclear war, etc.	Changing economic climate threatens ability to support family; family responsibilities prevent full investigation of and response to issues of social change
Social Constraints	The person must observe group standards regarding sex, aggression	Pressure to provide good example intensifies perceived need to conform rather than act individualistically
The Need to Achieve	Getting ahead is a social value, but many persons are unsuccessful	There is fear of losing children's respect if parent is less successful than parents of children's peers
The Body Image	The person is less than satisfied with physical self	At time of increasing dissatisfaction with physical self (middle age), contrast to youthfulness of young adult children is painful

"My Time Is Your Time"

If frustration is to be avoided, patience often has to work hand in hand with another quality: *generosity* or *selflessness.*

Suppose, for example, that a parent takes his child to a department store to buy a shirt. The parent has told the child that the child can make his own selection—but the process takes ten minutes, then fifteen, then twenty-five. A parent who values his time, has better things to do than wait around, will find himself frustrated. Certainly there is an efficient way out of this situation—the parent could simply make the selection for the child. But this would only postpone the child's development of ability to compare items, think about their relative merits, ask questions, relate directly to the salesperson, and so forth.

There are many such situations in which parents must be willing to consider their own goals and priorities as of less value than those which serve some need of their children. Even though the personal goal abandoned here may be a very small one (the use of an hour or so of time in some personal way), the cumulative effect of many such situations upon a very self-directed personality can be severe enough to cause either dissatisfaction with the parental role or ambivalent feelings toward one's child.

People who are highly self-oriented or self-directed might view this trait of selflessness skeptically. They might see people willing to give up their time to others as patsies or low-esteem losers. But lack of high personal priorities for use of time and money seemed to characterize satisfied parents. Far more often than the dissatisfied parents, their responses indicated a willingness to extend themselves to do a favor for a friend, to wait without complaint while a child made a slow purchasing decision, and to loan $20 to a friend in need.

Satisfied parents also indicated selflessness in other ways: preferring to do volunteer work instead of developing a personal skill or talent; indicating both an involvement with specific personal-service projects and a feeling of responsibility to and for others beyond one's own self and family. That is, they were not only inclined to put aside their self-interests for the sake of a child's needs, but to evaluate needs of self, spouse, and child in the context of wider social needs.

The World Is My Family

Just as many children have a "me first!" attitude, many parents operate according to a my family first! frame of reference. The phenomenon is too usual to need argument and might seem too logical to be questioned. Evidently, however, some of the best and most satisfied parents do not have that attitude.

They showed concern for the future and stronger sympathy for a far-away, famine-stricken population than did the dissatisfied parents (dividing their responses on this item between "I'd do something if I could" and "something must be done," whereas the less successful parents were predominantly only "slightly upset").

Satisfied parents' responses indicated that for more than half of them a compelling reason to disappoint a child who wanted to play was a prior promise to help with a community petition drive. Fewer than a quarter of the less-satisfied parents checked that particular response. One of the successful parents wrote on her answer sheet, "When I started to read this question, I got ready to mark 'none of these' because what could be more important than sharing an afternoon of play when your child specifically asked you to? But you hit on something that would make me disappoint my own child. If something were going on that would affect the community environment my child has to live in, then that would be more important. Staying home would mean you'd play with your child. Helping stop a shopping center might save a nice park or wooded area where your child and a lot of others could play for years." Several parents, explaining their (d) response to Item 71, wrote, "I'd feel better if I could have checked (c) specifically, but you get so your kids are more important than the two of you." Less-satisfied parents were more apt to comment marginally that, for them, the (c) response was the most compelling one—time alone with spouse.

We had presumed that, given the high value generally attached to education, even successful parents would be intolerant of disadvantaged children being present in their own child's normal learning environment. But in response to Item 69 a slight majority of successful parents indicated that they would not mind the "mainstreaming" of mildly disabled children into their normal child's classroom. Specific responses to this question from both groups of parents broke down as:

	Unsatisfied parents	Satisfied parents
Own child mainstreamed, yes; other child, no	68%	35%
Own child mainstreamed, yes; other child, yes	22%	52%
Own child mainstreamed, no; other child, no	10%	11%
Own child mainstreamed, no; other child, yes		2%

A good number of marginal notations indicated these responses to be more than hypothetical. One parent wrote, "This has happened frequently in several of our children's classrooms. We never minded." Another wrote, "It would sure help *my* child learn to care about other kids. Normal kids don't often enough know how lucky they are."

Kenneth Keniston of the Carnegie Council on Child Development has written of the tendency American parents have "to try to separate our own children from other people's children." Seconding him, child-development specialist Elizabeth Wickenden has written, "Every child should be a community concern, not solely the concern of a single mother."

The successful parents in this sample did not seem much inclined to separate their own children from others and did seem able to view overall needs of a community of children.

More successful than unsuccessful parents indicated a willingness to adopt: 77 percent of unsatisfied parents and over 90 percent of satisfied parents responded positively to the idea of adopting a child if unable to have their own; and, strikingly, on the question of adopting a child instead of trying to have their own, 60 percent of successful parents still responded positively. Fewer than 10 percent of less-successful parents so indicated, however.

Responses to Item 72 showed further confirmation of altruistic feeling among the successful parents, 80 percent of whom indentified with the loner in Martha Weinman Lear's story as opposed to only 44 percent of less-successful parents. One woman's comment on this item is worth quoting.

How often do we hear "my children first." It's natural, I suppose. I feel it myself. But it's something I try to fight. How much kindness we shut ourself off from doing because something, or someone, isn't "mine." We pass a car parked with its lights on and walk by. It's not our car. We see an animal near the road and don't stop. It's not our dog. We see someone in an apartment corridor fumbling with a lock and wonder if he's breaking in. But it's not our apartment. This very quickly gets around to not going to the aid of somebody calling for help; and all just because "it's not my car, it's not my dog, it's not my child, *it's not my business.* . .''

Another said, "I wish we could get rid of the possessive pronouns *my* and *our* in speaking of children," by way of introducing this poem by Carl Sandburg, which she said was a favorite of hers:

> There is one man in the world,
> and his name is All Men.
> There is one woman in the world,
> and her name is All Women.
> There is one child in the world,
> and its name is All Children.

"It Is 7:10 P.M. and Time For Your Bath!"

Flexibility is part of what psychologists call *coping behavior*—adapting to meet unexpected or changing circumstances, adjusting to departure from established order, being open-minded, seeing different points of view, understanding conflicting needs.

Flexibility can be viewed as another way to cope with, or prevent, frustration.

As we have already discussed, it seems helpful if a parent can be flexible in her or his approach to teaching his children and flexible in her or his approach to discipline. Actually it helps to be flexible in approach to child-rearing in general, because the most carefully thought out method for any situation simply may not work and will have to be abandoned. To be less than flexible, warned one successful parent in a marginal note, means you are taking a "Battlefield" approach to parenthood, never abandoning any position even for strategic reasons, with likely casualties.

Many of our satisfied parents also gave the obvious advice that, to remain satisfied, they had learned to be flexible about their own lives, not just about their approach to child-raising: "Otherwise," wrote one, "you can't stay in the same house."

Some of the clearest differences to emerge between parents who felt happy with their role and those who didn't were seen in the questionnaire items relating to flexibility. The unhappy parents revealed a high need for order in their personal environment (they liked things just so; they liked quiet and lack of distractions). More satisfied parents evidently either lacked this need or overcame it.

One example of this that showed up among fathers was the degree of distress unsatisfied fathers felt if they were unable to read their evening or morning newspaper without interruption: 88 percent of them indicated they would feel great distress if their reading were interrupted. Virtually none of the more satisfied fathers so indicated.* One father wrote, "You just have to learn to put the paper down. I learned that kids are spontaneous and changing and newsprint is cold, and that the same paragraphs would be there even if I didn't get to them till 11 P.M. Usually, that is. Once or twice the kids tore it up for papier-mâché." By contrast, one of the less-satisfied fathers wrote, "The children's baths begin at 7:10 P.M. at our house, which is exactly the time I walk in the door and sit down with my newspaper."

Overwhelmingly, dissatisfied parents minded when things went wrong, and satisfied parents didn't (85% of the former

*There were no such clear differences among mothers. Virtually no mothers in either group indicated they'd be upset if their reading of the newspaper were interrupted by a child's need. Evidently the privilege of reading the newspaper in peace is pretty exclusively the birthright of the American *male.*

group gave a T response to Item 22, as opposed to only 12% of the latter group).

"If you mind things going wrong, you're of course going to go crazy," one of the satisfied mothers told us in an interview. She told the following story:

> Since we didn't have off-limits areas, we lost the everything-in-its-place battle early. But when the children were small one area that was close to sacrosanct was the kitchen. The kids weren't to be there unless an adult was too. That's because our food budget was pretty tight and we didn't want any scatter-the-cereal or empty-the-canisters games or any risk of wasting food. If a lamp broke in the living room, that was relatively OK because we didn't *have* to replace it. Food being our major expenditure was something else again. But one morning I tasted my orange juice and spit. My act was quickly followed by other family members as they picked up *their* glasses. Everybody spit except George, who was six then and asked innocently, "Did you like the way I seasoned the orange juice?" He had heard me discussing *seasoning* the night before and had put salt and pepper into the orange juice. Now, frozen orange juice seemed more a luxury then, and we rationed it pretty carefully and I *loved it.* But what can you do? I just shrugged and said, "Oh well, tomato juice can have salt and pepper, so why can't orange juice? It will be an interesting experiment to drink it this way but we'll vote on how it tastes afterwards and if most of us don't like it then *we won't season the orange juice again!*"

While we consider that story to be an inspiring story of a flexible attitude, flexibility in larger ways is needed, too.

Parents need to be able to shift gears of their total organism sometimes, not just their taste buds. Sometimes a quiet, intense talk with a neighbor or a spouse must be instantly scuttled because of a sudden yell from the playroom; sometimes the hilarity of an evening party must be abandoned because your child appears in the center of the scene crying. About this latter instance, one woman wrote, "You may hear the end of a delicious story a guest was telling later, of course—but you won't ever hear it in quite the same way. You just have to not mind.''

Juggling child care and an at-home career demands a lot of flexibility and gear-shifting, too. One young writer recalled, ''In the midst of trying to deal with one child who had slipped in the bathtub and another who had *pushed* him, the telephone rang and the voice of John Kenneth Galbraith said, 'You've been calling for several days, and I've got five minutes now for the telephone interview you said you wanted. So ask me whatever you want to.' ''

Tolerance for ideas not your own can be a useful tool of flexibility, too. ''Knowing a little about psychology,'' one father wrote, ''I decided to be very tolerant of *any* idea Jenny brought home—and she like any teenager came home often talking about astrology or mysticism or Sun-Moon. I try to find some aspect of it to which I can honestly reply, 'Well, that makes some sense.' Things are fine so far. I wonder if I rejected those ideas as I'm initially inclined to, though, if I'd have a typical rebel on my hands. . . .''

Parents whose own circle of friends includes a diversity of opinion may be better able to accept teenagers whose values or ideas often veer off at right angles from parents'.

Satisfied parents were more likely than unsatisfied parents to indicate a tolerance for diversity of ideas. Satisfied parents were less apt to think of themselves as possessing a great deal of personal dignity. ''When you have a little one who's crawling around on all fours, exploring, your impulse should be to get down on all fours and join him! Dignity has very little place in raising children!''

On another level, respondents who indicated lack of flexibility may interpret any departure from the order they've established as an affront to their dignity or integrity. Certainly a T response to Item 14 (''I consider myself to have a great deal of personal dignity'') was consistent with an overall dearth of flexibility.

"I'm Somebody Besides Mommy"

Earlier we said that a parent too emotionally dependent upon his or her child would have trouble administering reasoned discipline. Such an emotionally dependent parent will have other problems, too. One of our successful parents told this story:

> When I was a kid, I had a friend who seemed to hate her mom. She would very often, in my presence, say to her mother, "Boy, are you dumb," and her mother would always cry. It seemed she didn't have anybody else around to contradict her child's unkind opinion. I remember thinking to myself even then that if a child of mine ever said something like that to me I wanted to be able to say back, "So I'm dumb? So that's what you think. But lots of other people I know *know better!*"

What the woman who told this story intended to express was the need for a parent to have some identity source other than the parental role. For a parent (and we are speaking mainly of mothers) to have a balance of roles to complement the domestic one is far more than just a good idea; it seems essential to feelings of confidence and independence, and even to psychological survival.

A mother shouldn't feel pressured into leaving an at-home role while her child is still young. But once the need for watching over a child is gone, a too-intense scrutiny can replace it.

And a mother needn't feel pressured into a competitive career or a demanding job. Our successful mothers' outside-of-home interests varied widely and seemed seriously career-oriented in only a few cases. *But they did have outside-the-home interests* which aided their feelings of independence from not only their children but from other surrounding judgments and influences, whether those of neighbors, experts, advertisers, or manufacturers of Big Wheels. One mother said, "I only work on Wednesdays, because I basically enjoy being home. But I work both to give myself a feeling of importance, and to keep my child from getting an exaggerated sense of *his* importance due to my continual presence. When I walk out the door, the message he hears from me is, 'You're important to me. But on Wednesdays I go to work with other people who are important too.' "

No Illusions, Please!

Practicality involves seeing things the way they really are even if, at times, this is difficult or unpleasant and being able to view yourself the way you really are even if, at times, you are wrong or inadequate. Not incidentally, it involves being able to admit that all relationships, even the best, are flawed.

Someone who claims that "love between my spouse and me has not changed at all since we met" is fooling himself—even if he and his spouse have been married two weeks and were married on sight! Such a claim could be viewed as innocent romanticism were it not for the fact that romanticism, involving as it does some denial of reality, is seldom innocent in its implications. We simply cannot bronze a relationship as we can baby shoes, hoping to preserve a time of peak emotion. This attempts to deny the impact that time and experience have on all human beings and that is, in fact, the essence of living.

The danger of struggling against all evidence to deny the reality of change in a marital relationship is that it can forecast similar attempts to deny changes which occur past the point of some "perfect" moment of parenthood. (Have you heard of people who cannot acknowledge that their children have grown up?) This task is so difficult that only parents with lots of experience in denying reality seem able to manage it. But clinging to unreal or impractical beliefs does not seem compatible with successful parenting.

Similarly unrealistic is a belief that, in today's complex world, secularism can be held at bay and religion (traditionally, throughout history, a stabilizing force for the family) can be counted on to keep families together.

While only a minority of both parent groups accepted such extreme statements of unreality, the cost to personal growth of both marriage and parenthood was more often acknowledged by successful parents than by unsuccessful parents. And such practical tendencies as being able to admit inadequacy, acknowledge need for help, and define what influences you can realistically bring to bear on your child and what influences you cannot were also more characteristic of successful parents.

The Quest for Experience

We appreciate the time and freedom to pursue potential talents (even if they should prove to be only minor skills). We treasure the freedom to pick up and disappear for a weekend or a month or even a year, to sleep odd hours, to breakfast at 3 A.M or 3 P.M., to hang out the "DO NOT DISTURB" sign, to slam a door and be alone, or alone together, to indulge in foolish extravagances, to get out of bed early in the morning on a sudden whim and go horseback riding in the park before work, to become embroiled in a political campaign or a fund-raising drive, to devote endless hours to intensive research that might lead somewhere—or nowhere, to have champagne with dinner for no special reason at all, to tease and love anywhere, at any hour, anytime we please . . . without the nagging guilt that a child is being neglected. . . ."

Gael Greene, writing of the wondrousness of marriage without children, exemplifies several values typical of the childless-by-choice:
  a romantic concept of marriage
  the pursuit of self-exploration and self-development
  freedom from routine
and what might be called *whimsy*, a yearning for personal indulgence of "foolish extravagance."

Sociologist Jean Veevers gathers several characteristics of the childfree under a more generally descriptive phrase of a "quest for experience." Veevers has found among childfree individuals a consistent value on having new experiences, seeing new places, feeling new sensations, accomplishing new goals, meeting new people, traveling to new places, coping with new personal challenges.

Successful parents, we indicated, had a capacity for flexibility, but not quite this kind, based as it seems to be on a certain restlessness, a taste for freedom and continual novelty.

The determinedly childfree, according to all evidence, have a distinct wanderlust; they perceive one of the major advantages of them not having children to be the enjoyment of longer, more frequent and more far-ranging trips than they could otherwise manage. Veevers has reported from interviews, "Several wives spoke of the possibility of saving enough money to (with their spouse) stop work for six months or a year to travel around the world, *and had saved enough money and made enough arrangements to make such plans seem possible.*" (emphasis mine)

The emphasis supplied is perhaps significant. For, as one psychologist remarked at a recent conference. "Almost everybody gives some lip service to wanting an adventurous life. Almost everybody talks at one time or another of sailing off around the world. But when a childfree couple talks like that they seem to mean it—in fact, they're apt to be looking at boats!''

Oddly, the high value such a couple places on experience can prompt an occasional interest in pregnancy and childbearing as something else it *might* be fun to try. This interest is closer to idle wondering than intense desire; it's not far removed from the kind of impulse which can harmlessly commit a childfree couple to a six-day wine tour or a six-month political campaign—but it is a wholly unacceptable reason to have a child. The long-term consequences of such curiosity about childbearing could seriously interfere with such a couple's overall freedom to meet the future with giant strides. It could trap them in the here-and-now. And the chances are they wouldn't like it.

Successful parents exhibit a far different personal profile. They show generally greater stability. They *do* seem content with the present.

Characteristically, they do not nor did they ever have a burning ambition to take by storm Broadway, Wall Street, Madison Avenue, or whatever other fortresses of achievement lie behind heavy barricades of competition. They are not generally out to preempt existing possibilities for *Time's* next Person-of-the-Year cover.

Nor is their taste for personal adventure particularly keen. During the course of this survey, we watched more than one middle-aged couple with great equanimity send their young adult children off on trips to Spain, Scandinavia, Israel—when the parents themselves had never visited those places!

They are moved less by the spur of the moment than by the pace of the calendar—are willing to plan more modest adventures lengthily, long in advance—taking some satisfaction both in the advance planning of the event and the ceremonious replaying afterward. When other people, including their own children, return from a situation foreign to the experience of these parents, there is a mild (perhaps the word is *polite*) curiosity, but little envy.

About half (40 to 45%) of both parent groups indicated that prior to having children they had strong drives for achievement and experience. The difference was, given postparental modification of those drives and dreams, satisfied parents adjusted to modified goals of experience, unsatisfied parents didn't.

The difference can be clearly seen in responses of two members of each group to Item 93.

"We used to love to travel," wrote one couple,

> but after we had children we concentrated on making a home. And our home was so pleasant we didn't have the impulse to go to distant cities anymore. It wasn't so important to see Paris in the spring and things like that. Our life was our children. Their joys were our joys. And we found that you can discover everything the world holds in one neighborhood.

"I used to enjoy ballooning," one mother wrote,

> and it was and still is kind of dangerous. And when Janet was three months old, and I was supposed to go up with my partner on a demonstration flight, I realized with a shock that I just wasn't going to do it. I called the sponsors of the flight and said, somewhat dramatically as I recall, that I couldn't risk leaving my little girl an orphan. I realized that for her sake I had to start *living safely*. My feet have been firmly on the ground ever since.

And "We used to love to travel." Said a parent in the less-satisfied group.

> And frankly we'd assumed that we still would after we had children, because money wasn't much of a problem. Turned

out there was a problem, though—time. Even though I make a lot of money, I get only the same two weeks vacation that everybody else does (take off longer and somebody will try to move in on your job by the time you get back!) and when your kids want to go on a camping trip or see the Grand Canyon or pack up the station wagon for a tour of the U.S. *like all the other kids are doing* you feel like a monster saying "Sorry, kids, but Mom and I haven't seen the cathedrals and canals of Venice lately . . ." Your vacations turn into catastrophes of traffic and crowded campsites and mosquito bites that everybody else seems to think is just fine. One fellow actually told me that the fun is supposed to come afterwards, when you laugh with the other parents over all the things that went wrong!

Another parent wrote simply, "Disneyland gave me an ulcer."

For parents, the responsibilities of family life generally dictate that job security is more important than experimenting with other talents, fostering ambitions for greatness, or, with cavalier abuse of the need to spend time with children, devoting endless hours to research that might lead somewhere—or nowhere."

For parents, the responsibility to plan travel that is good for the children transcends cliché. Children do, in fact, need recreational experiences appropriate to their age, interests, developmental readiness, and peer standards. Camping is good for children; it is something most children want to do, and they can't really set up a campsite along a canal in Venice. Disneyland may or may not be good for children, but it is somewhere most children want to go, (and would you really have the nerve to be the only parent on the block whose child had never seen the Enchanted Castle?)

For parents, the responsibility to provide their children with a richly adequate preparation for adult life may mean that their own desire to "study arts, languages . . ." becomes suddenly far less important than providing art or language lessons for their children. Parents manage visits to museums and attendance at art lectures, certainly. But desires for personal growth and personal enrichment that have any scope at all wait. No parent can fully embrace and pursue an interest in Renaissance art if his child is ready to learn about fingerpaints and primary colors. If mom has not begun to study law before Johnny is born, the fact is mom generally waits until Johnny grows up.

Such considerations touch on the very essence of parenthood: for parenthood consists of fostering the growth of others by the giving (and giving up) of resources that could otherwise be given to oneself.

Do you feel equal to that challenge?

The Need for Laughter

While "It's always darkest before the dawn," "Laugh, and the world laughs with you," and other cheerful thoughts are easily detected as overstatements, the need for parents to maintain an optimistic outlook and a sense of humor should be obvious: If a case of measles visits on New Year's Eve, what is there to do but count the spots?

Chapter 7

What Does My Score Mean?

Design of the Scoring Method

Had we set out to construct an aptitude test for taxi drivers, we would have interviewed a sample of excellent taxi drivers: those who had outstanding records of safety and competence and who liked their work. We might have found these successful taxi drivers to have the following characteristics:

(1) good vision and reflexes
(2) physical stamina
(3) tolerance for traffic
(4) ability to talk easily to people
(5) left-handedness

Next, we would have interviewed some *less* happy and successful drivers. We might have found the unsatisfied drivers far less likely to have the above characteristics. So far, so good. Logically, we might then think you could evaluate *your* chances for being suited to taxi driving according to those five criteria, the basic reason being that if your personal profile closely resembles the personal profiles of good taxi drivers, then you're apt to be a good taxi driver, too.

But perhaps that approach would not be quite sufficient. Something could still be wrong with the plan.

Chances are, before evaluating your taxi-driving potential, we would also want to talk to policemen, traffic commissioners, retired drivers, and a sample of people who travel regularly by cab. This would broaden the perspective by giving us some expert opinion. Perhaps with the help of that expert opinion, we would have to conclude that item (5) above was incidental—perhaps an accident of our sample but according to authorities *not reliably related* to success in driving a cab! We would then modify our measuring instrument so that you, as a prospective cab driver, would not be penalized if you happened to be right-handed.

Thus we would have combined two *validating procedures* in order to help insure that the final implications of our Taxi Driver Aptitude Test emerged as valid and reliable as possible.

That is in essence how we have approached the construction and scoring of this parenthood aptitude questionnaire.

Scoring for all items has been *generally* determined by responses of successful parents to this questionnaire. If your overall responses reveal that you have much in common—feelings about self, present personal resources, attitudes and beliefs—with parents who have been happy in their role, then it seems reasonable to believe that you may also find parenthood rewarding. If, on the other hand, most questionnaire items reveal you to be different from the sample of successful parents, and perhaps to have a lot in common with parents who are *un*satisfied, then there would seem reason to believe the opposite.

Scoring has not only been generally determined but weighted according to this principle, and the weighting has been built into the questionnaire in two ways.

Sometimes a high point value is assigned to a question that proved a particularly important discriminator between the two groups of parents. For example, a false response to "My mate and I do not presently agree on whether or not to have children" will be worth a lot of points.

In other cases, a questionnaire item which might seem to be important might carry only one point. For example, though we discussed how important it was to be able to provide financial support and care for a child, having enough money to pay for maternity care and childbirth is worth only 1 point. Here, however, the overall issue of ability to provide for your child's care will gradually accumulate a number of points when all aspects of financial resources are taken into consideration, not merely dollars saved ("I have $2000 in savings"). More diffuse income considerations ("I have enough income to live comfortably," "My future economic situation looks pretty secure"), attitudes about money ("I don't believe in stocks and savings but in living for today"), habits of spending ("I do not bother to comparison shop") and financial independence ("I sometimes rely on my parents' loans to solve budget problems") are actually more important.

If a questionnaire item has no point value at all, chances are this item, while perhaps are interesting one for you to face and reflect on, failed to differentiate between satisfied and unsatisfied parents. For example, the questionnaire item "Parents should teach school-age, children rules of safety to follow outside the home: avoid strangers, and so on," while worth thinking about is unscored since virtually every parent, no matter how satisfied or unsatisfied, responded identically.

As you might guess from our taxi driver analogy, we have also tried to validate the scoring of each questionnaire item with a logical process. Thus, in addition to comparing the questionnaire responses of the two parent populations, we also gathered expert opinion.

Often the authoritative opinion reinforced the implications of parents' responses. A good example is the item regarding agreement between spouses on the matter of having a child. Not only was there a far greater chance that the unhappy parents had disagreed initially while the happier parents had found themselves in accord on the matter of childbearing, but virtually all experts and researchers confirmed the importance of marital consensus on childbearing. In a few cases, however, if the weight of expert opinion dismissed as unreliable or unimportant a case of differences between the two parent groups, the expert opinion was allowed to override the parent-group indications. An example of this relates to the successful parents' relatively greater willingness to buy their children an expensive, status-laden brand of loafer. This could be compared to left-handedness of taxi drivers in that, logically, one's willingness to buy material items should have no bearing on how good a parent you can be.

One further point is that, in general, questionnaire items which reflect your actual behavior will be worth more than items involving a projected attitude or imagined situation. For example, an item such as "I can't imagine myself ignoring a crying child" will carry less weight than one such as "There is one child who is my special friend." The latter question reflects reality, not just an imagined response to a child.

Checklist for Consistency

We know you did not cheat. But a few checks against unintentionally overestimating your willingness or ability to adjust to parenting have been built into the questionnaire. So before getting to the actual adding up of numbers, let's briefly do what we can to make sure that the numbers you'll be tallying are the correct ones. If you have answered all items with consistency, certain responses of yours should "check out" and be compatible with certain other responses.

Here are two examples.

Compare your responses to Items 1-2 and 1-44. Your responses to these items should be different, since one reads, "I have a pretty clear idea of where I'm going in life" and the other. "I've never really thought about what my primary life goals are." Excluding the fairly slim possibility that you gained or lost your direction in life during the minutes that elapsed between your contemplation of the above items, if your responses are not different, you should change one or the other to accurately reflect your feelings.

Compare your responses to Items 6-1 and 6-2. Though your responses to these two items should be alike, might you have said you would not mind waiting one hour in a pediatrician's office with your child, and still have said you would indeed mind waiting the same period of time at your own doctor's office? If so, consider changing your response to one or the other item (unless you are truly convinced you would willingly endure for a child what you could not patiently put up with for yourself), and revise your score accordingly.

Please continue this procedure with the following checklist of items before computing your final score:

Compare Items 3-100 and 6-33. "It is usually a mistake to be different," and "Being one of the group is generally sufficient to make me feel content." Your responses to these two items should be alike.

Compare Items 1-6 and 6-77. "What I'm doing in life matters" and "What I'm doing with my life seems worthwhile." Your responses to these two items should be alike.

Compare Items 1-29 and 6-93. "I would love to travel extensively" and "To travel the world is something I truly want to do." Your responses to these two items should be alike.

Compare Items 2-9 and 3-18. "It's not necessary to like children in general to be able to love your own child" and "You always love your own child, just because it's yours." Your responses to these two items should be alike.

Compare Items 4-13 and 4-20. "A child would make my marriage happier" and "I believe people without children are generally happier than parents." Your responses to these two items should be different—unless you have a definite reason for viewing your marriage as apart from the norm or your own experience as exempt from the general impression you have of other people who've had children.

Compare Items 5-26 and 6-34. "I worry a great deal about whether other people like me" and "I am greatly concerned with the impression I make on others." Your responses to these two items should be alike.

Compare Items 3-46 and 3-54. If you responded *true* to "My mate and I discuss potential problems before they become real ones," you should have responded to 3-54, "If my partner does something that angers me, I typically . . . " by marking (a): "say something right away, bring it out in the open."

Compare Items 3-46 and 5-73. "My mate and I discuss potential problems before they become real ones" and "I shy away from talking over differences of opinion with my spouse." Your responses to these two items should be different.

Compare Items 6-7 and 5-50. "I don't mind going over the same material several times if it will help someone understand" and "Stupidity irks me." Your responses to these two items should be different.

Compare Items 5-75 and 3-98. "Angry feelings in the air make me feel like running and hiding" and "I shrink from crises, I hate trouble." Your responses to these two items should be alike.

Finally, check your response to Item 3-1, "Were I to have a child its sex would make no difference." Your response should be the same as your response to Item 3-13, "If Jody were my son instead of my daughter . . . " and different from your response to Item 3-74, "Boys shouldn't cry."

Calculating Your Score

Questionnaire 1

Item #/Response/Points

1.	F	2		22.	F	1
2.	T	6		23.	T	1
3.	F	1		24.	F	1
4.	T	2		25.	T	2
5.	F	1		26.	T	1
6.	T	10		27.	T	2
7.	T	2		28.	F	1
8.	F	3		29.	F	2
9.	T	1		30.	T	1
10.	(a)	1		31.	F	1

11. (a) 0 (b) 10
    (c) 15 (d) 20

12. (a) 2 (b) 4 (c) 6

13.	T	1		32.	T	3
14.	F	1		33.	F	1
15.	T	1		34.	F	2
16.	F	2		35.	Unscored	
17.	Unscored			36.	T	2
18.	T	2		37.	F	1
19.	T	2		38.	F	2
20.	F	2		39.	Unscored	
21.	F	2		40.	Unscored	
				41.	F	2
				42.	F	1
				43.	(h)	4

44. F 6   45. T 4

Highest score possible this section __109__
My score ____

Questionnaire 2

1. F 1	25. T 1
2. T 10	26. (a) 2 (b) 3 (c) 4
3. T 10	(d) 1
4. (c) 2	27. T 1
5. F 2	28. (c) 1
6. T 1	29. F 1
7. T 1	30. (f) 3 (g) −3
8. T 15	31. (e) 3 (f) −3
9. F 10	32. T 2
10. T 1	33. T 2
11. (a) 1	34.
12. F 3	35. T 1
13. T 1	36. T 1
14. T 1	37. T 1
15. F 1	38. F 1
16. Unscored	39. (e) 1 (k) 2
17. T 1	40. Unscored
18. F 2	41. Unscored
19. Unscored	42. (d) or (e) 3
20. (b) 1	43. Unscored
21. Unscored	44. Unscored
22. (a) or (d) 1	45. (c) or (e) 3; (f) −3
23. T 1	46. (a) (b) (e) 3; (d) −1
24. T 1	(f) −3

47. (c) 2 (e) −2
48. (b) or (c) 1
49. Unscored
50. (b) or (c) 1; (a) or (d) −1
51. Unscored
52. Unscored
53. (c) 1
54. T 1
55. Unscored
56. Unscored
57. Unscored
58. T 1
59. (b) 2
60. F 1
61. Unscored
62. T 3
63. T 2
64. Unscored
65. Unscored
66. (d) 2
67. (f) 3
68. Unscored
69. (b) (d) 2; (f) −2
70. (d) 1 (f) −1
71. (a) (b) (c) (d) (e) 2; (f) (g) −2
72. (g) −2
73. T 3
74. (b) (c) 3
75. (c) (d) (e) 3

Highest score possible this section __135__

My score ____

Questionnaire 3

1. T 2
2. F 1
3. F 2
4. T 1
5. T 1
6. (k) 3
7. F 1
8. Unscored
9. F 1
10. F 2
11. F 1
12. (c)(d) 2
13. T 2
14. Unscored
15. Unscored
16. F 2
17. Unscored
18. F 2
19. T 2
20. T 1
21. F 1
22. T 1

23. T 2
24. F 1
25. F 1
26. F 1
27. T 1
28. F 1
29. T 2
30. T 2
31. F 1
32. (b) (c) 1
33. T 2
34. T 1
35. (b) 2
36. Unscored
37. T 1
38. T 1
39. T 3
40. F 1
41. F 2
42. T 1
43. T 2
44. (e) 2
45. Unscored
46. T 1
47. F 2
48. F 1
49. (d) 2
50. Unscored
51. (b) 1
52. F 1
53. F 1
54. (a) 1
55. T 20

56. T 20
57. T 20

After checking your second set of responses to 35–57 (how you thought your spouse would respond) against how he or she actually did respond, subtract *full* point value from *your* score for each response of your spouse that you anticipated incorrectly.

(35.) (b) 2
(36.) Unscored
(37.) T 1
(38.) T 1
(39.) T 3
(40.) F 1
(41.) F 2
(42.) T 1
(43.) T 2
(44.) (e) 2
(45.) Unscored
(46.) T 1
(47.) F 2

(48.)	F	1
(49.)	(d)	2
(50.)	Unscored	
(51.)	(b)	1
(52.)	F	1
(53.)	F	1
(54.)	(a)	1
(55.)	T	20
(56.)	T	20
(57.)	T	20

58.	T	1
59.	F	1
60.	T	1
61.	F	1
62.	T	1
63.	T	1
64.	F	1
65.	Unscored	
66.	F	1
67.	F	3

For Men

68.	F	1
69.	F	2
70.	F	1
71.	F	1
72.	T	2
73.	F	1
74.	F	5
75.	F	1
76.	F	1

77.	F	1
78.	Unscored	
79.	F	1
80.	F	1
81.	F	1
82.	(g)	5
83.	(d)	10
84.	F	1

For Women

68.	F	1
69.	F	1
70.	T	2
71.	F	1
72.	F	1
73.	T	1
74.	F	1
75.	F	2
76.	Unscored	
77.	F	1
78.	F	1
79.	F	2
80.	F	1
81.	F	5
82.	T	5
83.	(g)	5
84.	F	5

85.	T	1
86.	F	1
87.	F	2

88.	F	2	97.	F	2
89.	F	2	98.	F	1
90.	F	2	99.	F	1
91.	T	2	100.	F	1
92.	F	2	101.	T	1
93.	F	2	102.	(a)	3
94.	F	2	103.	F	2
95.	F	2	104.	F	2
96.	F	1	105.	F	2

Highest possible score this section   211

My score_____

Questionnaire 4

1.	Unscored		18.	Unscored	
2.	F	1	19.	Unscored	
3.	T	3	20.	Unscored	
4.	F	3	21.	Unscored	
5.	F	3	22.	Unscored	
6.	F	3	23.	Unscored	
7.	T	2	24.	Unscored	
8.	T	2	25.	Unscored	
9.	T	2	26.	Unscored	
10.	Unscored		27.	F	3
11.	T	5	28.	F	3
12.	F	5	29.	F	10
13.	F	5	30.	F	4
14.	Unscored		31.	T	5
15.	F	4	32.	F	20
16.	F	4	33.	T	5
17.	F	2	34.	F	2

35. Unscored
36. F 2

37. F 2

Highest score possible this section ___100___

My score_____

Questionnaire 5

1. T 2
2. F 2
3. T 1
4. T 2
5. F 1
6. F 2
7. T 1
8. (a) (b) 2; (c) (d) 1
9. T 1
10. T 1
11. F 1
12. (a) 1
13. T 1
14. F 1
15. (a) (b) 1; (c) 2
16. (b) 2
17. T 1
18. (c) 1
19. F 1
20. F 5
21. F 1
22. T 1
23. T 1
24. F 1

25. F 1
26. F 1
27. Unscored
28. F 1
29. F 1
30. F 1
31. (a) (b) 1
32. T 1
33. F 1
34. F 3
35. (a) 2
36. F 1
37. F 2
38. (c) 1
39. F 1
40. F 1
41. F 1
42. (a) 1
43. (b) 1 (c) 2
44. Unscored
45. T 1
46. T 2
47. T 1
48. T 1

49.	T	1	73.	F	1
50.	F	2	74.	T	1
51.	T	1	75.	F	5
52.	(b)	2	76.	(d)	1
53.	(b)	2	77.	F	1
54.	(e)	2	78.	(f)	2
55.	T	1	79.	(a) (c)	2
56.	T	2	80.	(a) (b) (e)	2
57.	F	1	81.	F	1
58.	F	2	82.	F	1
59.	(b)	1	83.	F	1
60.	(b) 1 (d)	2	84.	F	1
61.	F	1	85.	T	1
62.	(b) (c)	1	86.	F	1
63.	F	1	87.	T	1
64.	T	1	88.	T	2
65.	F	5	89.	F	2
66.	T	1	90.	F	1
67.	T	1	91.	F	1
68.	(b) 1 (c)	5	92.	T	1
69.	(c)	1	93.	T	1
70.	F	5	94.	F	1
71.	F	5	95.	F	1
72.	T	1	96.	F	1

Highest score possible this section   143

My score _____

Questionnaire 6

1. (a) (b) (c) 1; (d) 3   3. F 1
2. (a) (b) (c) (d) 1; (e) 4   4. T 1

5. F 1
6. F 1
7. T 1
8. (d) 1; (a) or (b) 2
9. T 1
10. F 1
11. F 1
12. F 1
13. T 1
14. F 1
15. F 1
16. F 2
17. (c) 1 (d) 2
18. T 2
19. F 1
20. F 1
21. F 1
22. F 2
23. T 2
24. F 1
25. F 1
26. T 1
27. F 1
28. T 15
29. T 4
30. F 15
31. T 5
32. (a) (c) 2
33. F 15
34. F 10
35. T 5
36. F 2
37. Unscored

38. Unscored
39. T 2
40. T 2
41. F 2
42. F 1
43. T 5
44. T 5
45. F 1
46. F 1
47. Unscored
48. T 5
49. T 5
50. T 2
51. T 1
52. Unscored
53. (c) (d) 2
54. T 1
55. F 1
56. F 1
57. (c) 1 (b) 2
58. T 1
59. T 2
60. (c) (d) 1; (a) 2
61. T 1
62. T 1
63. T 3
64. T 2
65. F 2
66. F 2
67. (b) 1 (c) 2
68. (a) 1
69. (c) 4
70. (a) 2

71.	(b)(c) 1; (d) 2		88.	(c)(d) 1
72.	(a) 2		89.	F 1
73.	F 1		90.	F 1
74.	F 1		91.	F 1
75.	F 1		92.	F 2
76.	F 2		93.	F 2
77.	T 2		94.	T 5
78.	F 6		95.	(b) 1 (a) 2
79.	F 1		96.	F 2
80.	F 1		97.	F 2
81.	F 1		98.	T 1
82.	F 1		99.	T 2
83.	F 1		100.	F 1
84.	Unscored		101.	F 1
85.	Unscored		102.	T 2
86.	F 3		103.	T 2
87.	T 1		104.	F 1

Highest score possible this section ___230___

My score _____

Analyzing Your Score: Identifying Strengths and Weaknesses

A theoretically perfect score on this 462-item questionnaire would be 928, with section totals as follows:

Section 1	Resources	109 points
Section 2	Interests	135 points
Section 3	Motives	211 points
Section 4	Expectations	100 points
Section 5	Skills	143 points
Section 6	Traits	230 points

Based on our sample populations, the scores fall into five general categories following a normal bell-curve distribution. The scoring ranges indicate the probability of an individual being a successful parent. And remember, there is little if any significant difference between a score of 818 and 825; or between 778 and 790, and so on.

PROBABILITY OF BEING A SUCCESSFUL PARENT

a score above 775 indicates a *very high* probability
a score between 774 and 704 indicates a *high* probability

a score between 703 and 425 indicates an *average* probability
a score between 424 and 355 indicates a *low-average* probability
a score below 355 indicates a *low* probability

Excellence on particular questionnaires should be considered carefully, and we will pay close attention to section totals in order to analyze your score meaningfully. (Perhaps your overall score is in the average range but you are close to a perfect 120 in the resources section). But even the breakdown by sections will not give us information as precise as we should have: If you are close to perfect in resources, are you close to perfect in all resources or just some? Or perhaps in all resources except energy?

No matter what range your score falls within, we'll also want to ascertain whether there may be one specific subsection (or even just a single questionnaire item) that may be pulling your section totals or your overall score down from its otherwise possible total.

Keep your pencil handy, and let's break down each section of the questionnaire into the specific variables or qualities it's been intended to measure.

Questionnaire 1 attempted to find out whether you have a good degree of the four basic resources that can get you off to a good start if you become a parent: Maturity, Health, Home, Money.

Maturity items are worth more points than any other resource category. Add your score for maturity items 2, 6, 11 through 14, 27, 44 and 45.

> Total possible maturity points _56_
> My total points on these items ____

Financial items are the second most heavily weighted because these indicate not just your level of affluence but your attitude about money, your priorities for spending it, and possibly present self-indulgent habits. Add your score for money items 1, 18 through 26, 28 and 29, 32, 33, and 43

> Total possible money points _27_
> My total points on these items ____

Health items are 3, 4, and 5; 7 through 10; 15, 16 and 17

> Total possible health points _14_
> My total points on these items ____

Items relating to *home environment* are 30, 31, 34 through 42

> Total possible home points _12_
> My total points on these items ____

Now, please fill in where indicated below:

The resource I have that seems closest to the possible ideal score is _____ ; the resource it seems I most need to develop is _____ .

Questionnaire 2 measures your interest in children and liking for children. Your *overall* liking for children is indicated by Items 1–15.

Total possible liking-for-children points<u> 60 </u>
My total points on these items____

Your positive response to and interest in infants and young children is focused on by Items 16–34.

Total possible infants and young children points <u> 26 </u>
My total points on these items____

The degree to which you seem drawn to school-age children is measured by Items 35-59.

Total possible school-age child interest points <u> 24 </u>
My total points on these items____

Your feelings about teenagers is the concern of Items 60–75.

Total possible teenage-interest points <u> 25 </u>
My total points on these items____

Now, please fill in where indicated below:
The age group of children I seem most interested in is _____ and least interested in is _____
and my overall "liking for children" score is: (check one)

good: 50-60 ____
moderate: 30-50 ____
low: 0-30 _._

Questionnaire 3 assesses motivations for parenthood that have some risk attached. The presence of a high score within each category given below will indicate the *absence* of the mentioned high-risk motive; and an overall high score will imply that any desire for a child that you have is likely to be affectionate or altruistic.

    Egoistic motives are measured by Items 1 through 18.

Highest score possible Items 1–18 23
My score Items 1–18 ____

    Whether you might want to compensate for an *unpleasant job* by having a child is the concern of Items 19–34.

Highest score possible Items 19–34 21
My score Items 19–34 ____

    An *unhappy marriage* as a possible motivator is focused on by Items 35–57.

Highest score possible Items 37–57 85
My score Items 35–57 ____

    An *unhappy family background* is investigated by Items 59–67.

Highest possible score Items 58–67 11
My score Items 58–67 ____

    Sex-role insecurity is measured by Items 68–84.

Highest possible score Items 68–84 35
My score Items 68–84 ____

    Social isolation is determined by Items 85–94.

Highest score possible 85–94 18
My score total Items 85–94 ____

Motives of *conformity* might be indicated by a low score on Items 95–105.

Highest score possible 95–105 <u>18</u>
My score on Items 95–105 ____

Please fill in where indicated below:

My score is highest in motivation areas_____ and _____ ; therefore, I am least likely to have these two risky ("wrong") motives as part of my thinking. My score is lowest in motive areas_____ and _____; therefore I am more likely to have these two risky or "wrong" motives.

Questionnaire 4 investigates your expectations about parenthood and children.

How realistic are my expectations regarding:
nature of children (Items 1–11)

Total points possible 1–11 <u>24</u>
My total points on these items ____

effect of children on individuals and their marital relationship (Items 12–20; 30–32; 35–37)

Total points possible these items <u>53</u>
My total points on these items ____

what parenthood is really like (items 28, 29, 33, 34)

Total points possible these items <u>20</u>
My total points on these items ____

Please fill in where indicated below:
"A set of expectations I need to change in the direction of realism is_____."

Questionnaire 5 measures skills.

Nurturing skills are measured by Items 1–20 in this section.
> Total possible points   1–20 _31_
> My total points Items   1–20 ____

Ability to discipline children is measured by Items 21–44.
> Total possible points 21–44 _27_
> My total points Items 21–44 ____

Teaching skills are measured by Items 45–64.
> Total possible points 45–64 _28_
> My total points Items 45–64 ____

Ability to mediate is demonstrated by Items 65–82.
> Total possible points 65–82 _41_
> My total points Items 65–82 ____

Organizing ability can be seen in Items 83–96.
> Total possible points 83–96 _16_
> My total points Items 83–96 ____

Please fill in where indicated below:
My best parenting skill(s) seem to be_____ and the skills I would most need to develop are_____.

Questionnaire 6 examines traits helpful to parenthood.

Patience is assessed by Items 1–12 in this section.

> Total possible points 1–12 _18_
> My total points Items 1–12 ____

Flexibility is measured by Items 13–27.

> Total possible points 13–27 _20_
> My total points 13–27 ____

Independence is assessed by Items 28–38.

> Total possible points 28–38 _73_
> My total points 28–38 ____

Practicality and *realism* are measured by Items 39–55.

> Total possible points 39–55 _36_
> My total points 39–55 ____

Selflessness is examined by Items 56–72.

> Total possible points 56–72 _32_
> My total points 56–72 ____

Stability is judged by Items 73–95.

> Total possible points 73–95 _37_
> My total points 73–95 ____

Humor and *optimism* are estimated by Items 96–104.

> Total possible points 96–104 _14_
> My total points 96–104 ____

Please fill in where indicated below:

My most promising trait(s) that are compatible with parenthood seem to be _____ and my trait(s) most in need of development seem to be _____.

We are now ready to consider how to improve your score, section by section.

Chapter 8

How Can I Improve
My Score?

If your high-range score hints that you may be cut out to be a mother or father, you may feel pleased—or you may feel rather like you've been handed free blueprints for a new house, but you like your present one just fine, thanks. If this questionnaire suggests that you could probably be a good parent, it is certainly not telling you that you should or must be one.

The aptitude may be yours—but so is the choice.

If, on the other hand, your score was lower than you'd like, let's respond to one final question:

Either my numerical score or my personal reaction to this questionnaire suggests I'm not really parent material. My feeling about this is:
a) I'm just as glad because I don't want kids anyway. My interests lie elsewhere.
b) I'm disappointed. I'd like to be a parent, but now I wonder if I should wait or skip it.
c) I distrust the test. I want to be a parent and I think I know myself better than any questionnaire does.
d) I'm curious. I feel I'd be a successful parent, but I'm going to have another look at my score card to see where my problem areas might be.
e) I feel worthless.

Give yourself a lot of credit for *any* of the above responses except the last!

Parenthood aptitude has about as much to do with overall personal worth as does the ability to write poetry or mix a perfect martini. Seeming to have good parenting potential does not guarantee that one has other desirable traits or human vir-

285

tues—leadership, for example, or cultural vision or a host of personal talents.

And, regardless of your score, whatever you choose to do about having children is totally up to you—with the strong possibility that, indeed, no matter how carefully this questionnaire was designed, your chances for success will rest more on your own decisions and actions than on any numbers on an answer sheet.

The numbers can play a useful role, however, by indicating areas of real challenge or potential problems. You can prepare for these challenges and problem areas, and, in a sense, raise your score.

While it's true that theories of aptitude imply that a person's potential abilities are fairly stable, that isn't totally true. If somebody gave clear evidence today of skill at math but lack of vocal talent due to tone deafness, we would, of course, be surprised if these aptitudes had reversed themselves by next week. But over longer periods of time, people do and have changed to that extent. Circumstances have a way of bringing out capabilities that may have been lying dormant and unnoticed, while formerly visible talents can shrink through simple lack of exercise or interest.

There are several specific ways to bring about score improvement on this questionnaire of parenthood aptitude. Four major ones are:

elapsed time
experience
effort
evasion (there's sometimes a way around a weak skill area)

We might begin with the simplest of these, elapsed time. One easy way to improve your score is simply to wait a while—perhaps a year or so—and take the test again. Skills and aptitudes can emerge given more maturity and readiness for a task. Perhaps in a few years your financial situation will be more stable, your relationship with your mate more established, your career and personal ambitions more realized.

Your score can also be improved in some areas, such as resources, by an effort to consciously reorder your priorities or change your standards. Could you substitute sensible spending habits for impulsive ones? Do you really need the book club and the country club when there are libraries and rural areas nearby?

Experience can raise your score dramatically—and in at least one case, quickly. Having just been through the experience of pondering realistic *vs.* unrealistic childbearing *expectations*, for example, it's possible that your score in this area could have risen in the last two hours or so!

Evasion? Well, if neither you nor your spouse has any interest in the at-home care of very young children, as you investigate day-care possibilities, you could be said to be delegating one of your parental responsibilities—or *evading* it—by calling in a support system in your stead. In practice, this last technique works just fine; it won't raise your score, however.

Let's consider the various questionnaire sections specifically.

Conservation of Resources

Only a few financial resource points (7 of 27, to be exact) can be won by present level of affluence, savings in hand, or even future income prospects. That's not to say it wouldn't be an excellent idea to try to earn those seven points if you don't presently have them—by saving $2000, finding a job that offers a comfortable income in a secure field, and so on. But far more important are your ways of using the resources you presently have. Altered habits and attitudes can effectively add to your spending income, even if your earned income doesn't increase by a penny.

This is where effort is required to change those habits and attitudes.

If any of us lost points because of certain spending habits, we can try to reform those habits. If we are known for a stylish way of dressing, we can start being known for something else. If we do not presently comparison shop, we can learn to. Though we love our front-row seats, we could investigate the balcony.

Even the attitudes which underlie these spending practices can prove malleable. If we presently hold live-for-today or quest-for-experience attitudes, there are at least two ways in which we can significantly change these operating outlooks: We can consciously decide that we want to change our attitudes to ones more compatible with parental caretaking. Or we can simply wait a while.

If we find it enjoyable right now to let whatever money we get in hand slip pleasurably through our fingers, it's not absolutely necessary to clench our fists and try to rush headlong toward fiscal restraint. Elapsed time can work for us, can often bring a gradual shift toward more conservative spending habits. Often, living for today has an appeal whose days are numbered, and, often, experiences quested for are found and we spend less time in costly pursuit of them. Accumulated experiences that discretionary income can buy may change your personal resource picture, making it likely that priorities indicated by Item 43 in Questionnaire 1 will shift. Having satisfied many other life-style ambitions that depend on unstructured spending, one can feel that a budget *now* would not be a frustrating restraint. One can feel *ready* for the kinds of financial choices that childbearing will require.

All twenty-three points relating to home environment can be picked up with effort and planning, too. If your home is not presently one you feel happy to be in (at home in), pay a little attention to your personal surroundings. If necessary to avoid a stifled or cramped feeling (now or later), you might want to change your address as well as your wall hangings and those fragile figurines that would otherwise have to be off limits. You should, if your plan for a child is serious, even look at new neighborhoods from a child's viewpoint if you possibly can.

You don't have to move from the city to the suburbs or from a high-rise to a rural area—but you should be aware of how close playgrounds are; whether there are any play-group notices posted at the nearest shopping areas; how close the schools are; how convenient transportation seems; whether you see any children in the neighborhood and, if so, how old they are.

Even health attributes and resources can respond to improvement efforts.

If you presently have your own personal energy crisis—can't get out of bed in the morning, feel high-strung—it's worth asking whether your diet is a high-starch mess, what your daily exercise typically consists of, and how long it's been since you saw a vitamin at close range.

A pregnant woman is urged by her physician to exercise, quit smoking, drink moderately, and take nutritional supplements. Is there any reason not to get the body into good shape well before a pregnancy?

After the birth the mother is not the only parent who will need energy, stamina, resistance to childhood diseases, and the ability to keep going in spite of a cold or other mild illness.

And by the way, if you did indicate you sometimes have low energy or feel high-strung, it might be worth while to look into whether one or both might be metabolic or psychological.

Before having a child or even considering it, you really should feel in good enough shape to cope with the normal requirements of a childless day.

Maturity is considered the most important area within the resources section, comprising fifty-six total points as opposed to an average of twenty-one points for the other resource areas. Elapsed time will certainly tend to add many of these points to your score. This won't necessarily happen automatically, for maturity as we have discussed it involves such factors as feelings of self-worth and a sense of personal direction in life, and there are people who drift through life with neither. Perhaps the very fact that you are reading this book indicates that you are not one of those drifters, however: You are taking important bearings before possibly changing your course in life by becoming a parent. You are seeking self-knowledge, and that in itself is important.

Sustaining present relationships will add several points in this area over time. Absorbing experiences and reflecting on them and observing year-by-year social changes will gradually allow for a meaningful future perspective, gradually making it possible for you to decide just where you fit into the general scheme of things, what your important personal goals are. With your goals established, you are more likely to feel in the future—if you do not now—that your day-to-day activities matter, are important, since they will relate to some objective you have thought about and established for yourself.

And of course some of these points in the maturity area will come effortlessly, since, with time, one does predictably get older.

Can You Learn to Like Kids?

Overall liking for children is considered the most important area within the interests section of the questionnaire, comprising a total of sixty points, as opposed to about twenty-five each for positive interested response to a specific age or developmental period of childhood. And it is certainly possible for *liking* to be learned—to be enhanced if not created by exposure and experience. Just as there are some who never liked football until they went to a game and others who thought opera silly until they attended a performance, it is similarly possible to learn to like children by getting to know them! In fact, the points attached to all fifteen questionnaire items dealing with liking for children could possibly be gained if you gave attention to just the two or three crucial items which specifically reflect your experience with children. You can easily find ways to build experience points; you could extend the following list of general suggestions almost endlessly over a period of time until you might almost be said to have given yourself a period of trial parenthood.

1) First, for a period of at least a month, get accustomed to taking care of something that is less demanding than a child but that is totally dependent upon you (and/or your spouse) and, ideally, that has a schedule. Have you or could you be responsible for the care and nurture of a plant? a pet?

2) Offer to baby-sit for friends—one child, for one evening, to start with.

3) Move on to a weekend experience with that same child, then repeat (2) and (3) with several children of different ages, sexes, temperaments.

4) Offer to give friends, relatives, or co-workers a chance for a brief vacation by keeping their child in your home for a week or more.

5) Get to know a variety of children by volunteering for an in-city tutorial or recreational project.

6) Join Big Brothers, Big Sisters (and by the way, both partners should have this experience).

7) Consider taking a foster child into your home for a period of time.

In sum, as Questionnaire Items 2–2, 2–3, and 2–8 almost specifically direct, work with children in some way if you have not. Find a child whom you can befriend . . . invite children to share your home for a period of time. Subsequently, you may find that you have gained more than just the experience points attached to the mentioned items. You may, from your experience, find that certain of your attitudes toward children are changing as well. You may find yourself thinking that kids don't necessarily get away with murder, that they sometimes deserve to be heard as well as seen, and the like.

What's happening? You're just gaining some general sympathy and liking for children, that's all.

Internalizing the experience principle and actually reflecting on child behavior and child development—gaining an appreciation for *the way kids see things*—can also help make children more genuinely appealing to you. At the very least, it should provide a novel detour from your own adult perspective. If there is one generalization that can be made about children with total accuracy, it is that children are nonadult. To the adult view, a child's attention span is short, his behavior baffling, his sense of propriety unstably developed and any concept of manners totally dormant, his grasp of cause and effect shaky—but his interpretation of ordinary statements frustratingly literal. A child, for instance, thinks, "wait a minute" means "wait one minute." This all takes some getting used to.

By adult standards, children can seem impractical, selfish, thoughtless. This also takes some getting used to! For an adult to behave the way the child Johnny does, for instance, in the following scene from *My Heart's in the Highlands* would be intolerably rude. For Johnny, it's just natural.

MAC GREGOR: Young man, could you get a glass of water for an old man whose heart is not here, but in the highlands?
JOHNNY: What highlands?
MAC GREGOR: The Scotch Highlands. Could you?

JOHNNY: What's your heart doing in the Scotch Highlands?

MAC GREGOR: My heart's grieving there. Could you get me a glass of cool water?

JOHNNY: Where's your *mother*?

MAC GREGOR (*Inventing for the boy*): My mother's in Tulsa, Oklahoma, but her heart isn't.

JOHNNY: Where *is* her heart?

MAC GREGOR (*Loud*): In the Scotch Highlands. (*Soft*) I'm very thirsty, young man.

JOHNNY: How come the members of your family are always leaving their hearts in the highlands?

MAC GREGOR (*In the Shakespearean manner*): That's the way we are. Here today and gone tomorrow.

JOHNNY (*Aside*): Here today and gone tomorrow? (*To MacGregor*) How do you figure?

MAC GREGOR (*The philosopher*): Alive one minute and dead the next.

JOHNNY: Where's your *mother's mother*?

MAC GREGOR (*Inventing, but angry*): *She's* up in Vermont, in a little town called White River, but her heart isn't.

JOHNNY: Is her poor old withered heart in the highlands, too?

MAC GREGOR: Right smack in the highlands. Son, I'm dying of thirst.

(JOHNNY'S FATHER *comes out of the house in a fury, as if he has just broken out of a cage, and roars at the boy like a tiger that has just awakened from evil dreams*)

JOHNNY'S FATHER: Johnny, get the hell away from that poor old man. Get him a pitcher of water before he falls down and dies. Where the hell are your manners?

Now, there are two distinct possibilities.

You will either find these things charming or you will not. The latter possibility does have to be considered. It simply may be that this entire set of get-to-know-kids suggestions just won't work for you. After all, exposure nurtures affection only sometimes; hence the continuing currency of an old saying about absences and fonder hearts. But if your experiences with children are not causing any flow of warm feelings, don't try to railroad your emotional responses in what you think would be the right direction—not if some inner stop signals are flashing.

You are not a terrible person if you have incompatibilities with nonadults; the only mistake would be in failing to acknowledge those incompatibilities and their implications, at least for now.

Motivation Modification

Existing motivations within an individual can be changed by:

1) psychoanalysis
2) psychological self-help
3) group therapy
4) positive thinking
5) consciousness raising
6) all of these
7) some of these
8) none of these

Depending on what you read, all human motivations result from fear of death or the search for the mother; fear of failure or the search for honor and power; or perhaps fear of castration and the search for the penis.

Whatever their source, motives are indisputably powerful personality forces. Psychologist Gordon Allport was among the first to point out that motives can even achieve "functional autonomy," surviving independent of their original animating principle. Thus a businessman may continue packaging mergers as though pursued by demons long after he has accumulated the fortune that was his original goal; an entertainer may mercilessly drive himself through nightclub and TV circuits long after he has won the fame he originally sought.

There is no easy way to remove from the personality any deeply rooted motives of ego, compensation, conformity. However, *we can at least partially control the ways in which we allow such motives to express themselves.* We may be deeply motivated by a desire for wealth, but we need not rob. We may have profound and unmet ego needs, but chances are we can keep them away from the sphere of childbearing. And it would be well worth the effort to do so, since ego needs focused on a child are easily as destructive to the child as they are unsatisfying to the parent. The ego need shown in a belief that you always love your own child just because it's yours will easily be frustrated, because no child can be "yours" in the sense that ego wants. Our children can make us no promises to grow tall, become doctors, or think that we are "the greatest."

By acknowledging in advance the likely limits of ego satisfaction that a child of ours could give us, we may see that our ego needs can be more reliably served in almost any other way than by having a child.

Even though we may then still have high, unmet ego needs, we can then get a perfect score on Questionnaire Items 3-1 through 3-18 if we simply determine that we will send our desires for recognition in other directions. Want recognition, do we? Of course; who doesn't? But if we can learn to earn it from other sources, find it in existing roles, we won't have to look to a future child for it. We can then let Jody choose not to seek recognition if that's her preference (or his).

Conforming motives are really not separate from egotistic ones. In fact, conformity is often the refuge of an ego inadequately housed, one seeking public shelter or group identification.

But of course this safe housing can gradually become so comfortable that impulses of individuality are lost. The literal meaning of *conform* alludes to loss of one's own form, shape, and contour as one nestles snugly within group norms. And it is not as large a step as one might think from resigning individual choice of the shape of one's clothing to the shape of one's opinions or feelings or actions.

Conscious efforts to avoid conformity, even if only in small ways, in effect take a weak ego for short walks, then gradually longer ones as the ego strengthens and eventually becomes autonomous.

The opposite of conformity is autonomy, not nonconformity. If everyone you know reads the New York *Times* and you suddenly refuse to, you are not necessarily being autonomous: both those who embrace a norm and those who spurn it are still taking their cues from it and are still dependent on it. True autonomy begins with awareness of a wide range of choices and options, whether regarding life-style or morals, or clothing, or newspapers. Wearing unconventional clothing does not prove autonomy; being able to be comfortable in whatever you are wearing does, for faith in the self is thereby declared; as it is, similarly, in being unafraid to acknowledge being in therapy regardless of anticipated reactions. The excessively conforming personality will see leadership and individuality as synonymous, for those who conform too much tend to see any individual as a leader. It is a little surprising how clear our tendencies to conform can seem to us, given even slightly sterner habits of thinking. And it is particularly important for prospective parents to think sternly about their levels of conformity in areas other than the reproductive—if only to be in practice for an honest answer to the question of whether they are about to make a childbearing decision autonomously or under the influence of group norms. "Having children is an obligation I must fulfill" is a good indicator: do you believe that, autonomously? And if you do not, who influenced you to believe that? Asking yourself such questions will bring advantages to your prospects for parenthood far beyond eighteen added points in Questionnaire 3.

Ego manifestations can be diffuse, and even differences between autonomous and nonconforming behaviors a little hard to figure out, at least until we get the hang of it. But most of us can know—quite clearly and quickly—if we are unhappy with our work, disappointed with our social life, feel our marriage is on the rocks, or have some other major discontent. If we just sit still for a few minutes, the truth about these matters tends to surface.

If there are areas of dissatisfaction, then we can go on to ask, Are they serious enough for me to want a baby to make up for them?

We'll hope for a "no" response to the above question, since compensatory motives are considered the most potentially dangerous of any within the motives section of the questionnaire: in fact, 170 of a possible 211 points within this section are devoted to ascertaining compensatory motives for parenthood.

In this area, however, accurate diagnosis of what is troubling us can lead to real cure, not compensation—and more easily and directly, at that.

If we have an unhappy job situation, we do not have to have a child to compensate: We can change jobs.

If we feel socially isolated we do not have to have a child to compensate: We can cultivate companionship and friendship.

If our marriage feels tense and loveless, we don't have to have a child in what we inwardly know would be a foolish attempt at compensation: We can work to improve the marriage (or end it).

If we are worried about our masculinity or femininity, the adequacy of our bustline or paycheck, the correctness of our dominance or delicacy: we can try consciousness raising, not child rearing!

If we take the latter course or courses of action, our point totals for each group of questionnaire items alluded to should rise fairly close to the possible maximum. And if a desire to be a parent remains with us, then at least we have improved the chances that we are drawn to parenthood because we find it an intrinsically attractive prospect—not merely an attempt to escape from trouble in another quarter of life.

Expect No Miracles

Like the predictions on paper slips in fortune cookies, expectations about parenthood sometimes come true. Of course, the more modest they are, they more likely they are to materialize; and the loftier they are, the less probable they become. And "Parenthood is largely fun," "My child will be like me," and the like are lofty expectations indeed.

A child of yours might be like you.

But that likelihood will not be aided by your counting on it or employing it as an unconscious incentive. Parenthood is more aptly compared to standing before an emerging canvas than peering into a mirror for our own reflection. Gregory Zilboorg has said,

> A man cannot be a true father without being a creator of something, something that he wants to flourish before him rather than have molded in his image. A true father must be an artist, otherwise he becomes a violator of the creative spirit of man, by trying to mold a child to be exactly the way he the man is. . . .

And more and more, social forces other than the family will frustrate any such attempts to mold a child, in any case.

But you know such things by now. In fact, you probably know enough about the thwarted expectations that typify parenthood to not only earn a perfect score on Questionnaire 4 but to deliver your own lecture on almost every questionnaire item. The next stage is to bring this general questionnaire procedure closer to your own situation.

Do you know some parents whose expectations are being met and some whose are not? If they are being met, what predisposing conditions of marriage, personal satisfaction, maturity, and other factors can you identify? Can you define your own expectations and speculate on their chances of being met? To a large extent, you should be able to do so. It is not at all futile to try to predict life-style changes that will follow childbirth and determine how these changes relate to what you expect or hope for. Accurate observation of others' experiences and careful thinking about your own hopes can tie your expectations to real possibilities and tangibly increase the chances of your expectations in fact becoming real.

Building Skills and Taming Traits

Some skills have a simple physiological base. Fine embroidery requires good eyesight; virtuosity on a musical instrument calls for manual dexterity; instantaneous logarithmic calculations are aided by fortuitous connections in the brain.

It would be convenient if skills involved in parenting could be so easily traced to sources of muscle and tissue. Then skill improvement might be a simple matter of mechanical or instrumental correction like eyeglasses, practice of piano scales, or memorization of logarithmic tables.

But parenting skills have a more complicated structure. Teaching skills, for example, have many bases, including:

1) sensitivity to student as well as knowledge of subject
2) sense of priorities
3) knowledge of teaching techniques
4) willingness to teach
5) philosophical perspective on teaching tasks

Each of those five factors can be acquired, though some will come more easily than others. In some cases the questionnaire itself may serve not only as a measurement of your present skills, but potentially it may serve as a vehicle for improvement of your ability to teach as well.

Before you read the questionnaire, for instance, you may not have considered that knowing who you are teaching can be as important as knowing what you want to teach. Previously, you may never have given a thought to what priorities you would set for teaching preschoolers (courtesy or the alphabet). You probably had not pondered questions of teaching techniques, either (what techniques teach values, and what ones teach shoe-tying). By this time you have also come face to face with your own degree of willingness to teach (do you generally give directions when asked), and just by coming to grips with statements like "Praise success, ignore failure" and responding to them, you have begun to develop a philosophy of teaching.

But there is a sixth factor vital to good teaching, and it is revealed by the questionnaire item "Stupidity irks me." If your response to that statement was true, then all the other factors more or less go out the window because your potential teaching skill ultimately grows from an underlying trait: patience.

The other parenting skills, too, grow from traits of character that lie deep enough in the personality to be untouched by simple efforts at improvement. Traits are considered the focal points of the personality, formed in childhood and continued throughout life. Habits can be altered by will power, attitudes respond to new facts and information; but traits, while they are not immutable, can be strongly resistant to change.

Further, the links between parenting skills and traits are often very close ones. To be able to nurture and teach, you need selflessness and patience; discipline requires independence, flexibility—and patience; mediating skills grow from practicality, flexibility—and patience. Therefore, to talk about building our parenting skills inevitably draws us to discuss traits and trait theory as well.

Trait theory has received some challenge from psychologists, to be sure, and, not incidentally, from the feminist movement. As an example, feminists would argue that although women have typically had the trait of *dependency*, women can become more independent if they are given responsible roles which require independent action; they can become more independent after consciousness raising, and so on.

Case by case, the feminist contention could be challenged: a woman executive who has recently become more forceful in her business life might be seen to have simply shifted her dependency traits to domestic or social settings; a woman who, after consciousness raising, no longer seems dependent on her spouse may have simply transferred her dependency to her c-r sisters, needing their approval for her actions as she once needed her husband's.

Nonetheless, if we look keenly around us, we know that some people do manage to control traits they find counterproductive to their well-being.

There are dependent people who never cling; there are impatient people who seldom burst out in anger. There are people who, lacking flexibility themselves, will nonetheless allow you to be late. There are selfish men and women who somehow manage to give. And whether such individuals are managing to conquer their basic tendencies or have effected only a temporary truce perhaps matters less than the fact that *they are managing that truce*! And the importance of the truce with rebellious traits can easily (only too easily!) be imagined in parenting situations. To lose patience with a child can damage that child; to fail to give nurturance freely to a child can cause serious deprivation; to be dependent upon a child for one's own emotional satisfaction can distort the child's emotional development.

Since the trait of patience seems to underlie so many parenting activities, let's consider how that trait can be encouraged or its opposite controlled. A suggestion we think of some value comes from Myrtle McGraw, one of the most prominent figures in the child-development movement. McGraw believes that *attentiveness to and involvement with a child's phases of development can in great part create or reinforce patience.* Clearly communicating her own fascination with the developmental processes of young children, she writes,

> There's nothing more exciting than the unfolding of behavior during the first three years. When you think of this little bit of protoplasm, right out of the uterus, and in three years he has to become human. He has to get on his two feet; he has to learn to talk, and in your language; and he can give you a damn good argument by three years. That's a fantastic development! *Now if you see something significant in what's going on, nobody would ever have to tell you, "Be patient." Just stop to watch what the child is doing and patience is there—because you're interested.* (emphasis ours)

That advice might sound good enough to wrap up and take home immediately; or it might seem more to you like spurious, inspirational, or magical wishful thinking. But attentiveness to a situation at hand, if it can be managed, should at least help control impatience.

For example, let's suppose that you are waiting with your child in a pediatrician's office, it is one hour past appointment time, and you are getting very impatient and angry. If (following McGraw's advice) you had watched your child's play activities intently, watched his efforts to talk to other children, paid attention to books and magazines he picked up, it is just possible that you'd have been sufficiently absorbed that the hour would have seemed to pass quickly.

Another practical way to deflect impatience away from a child is suggested by Judge Gertrude Bacon of Parents Anonymous: "Just take your anger *out* on somebody *other* than your child!" Choose your target carefully if you can; if you can, identify who or what is really to blame for a situation that is causing your loss of patience. In that same pediatrician's waiting room, rather than lash out at a child because you're frustrated by the wait, Bacon's advice would be to make trouble for the pediatrician or possibly for an appointments secretary who scheduled children's visits too closely.

There is also a theory of behavior modification which holds that "acting out" an emotion, far from dispelling the emotion, rather sustains and reinforces it. For example, you are nervous; you smoke a cigarette, and instead of becoming calmer you become more nervous.

Whether or not this applies to the trait of patience (you are impatient; you express anger; by expressing anger you define and exacerbate your impatience) may vary from individual to individual. Still it did seem fairer on questionnaire items 6-1, 6-2 and others dealing with patience to ask whether you could "respond in a controlled manner" rather than feel no impatience at all.

Patience is a central virtue according to this questionnaire design. If you acquire most or all of the points related directly to it (18 points in Questionnaire 6), you should also raise your point totals within skill areas of nurturance, teaching, and mediation by about 25 points (Questionnaire 5). Patience also plays a role in certain interest questionnaire items; for example, it may well help determine how you felt about the mother waiting silently for her two-year-old to climb a flight of stairs on his own.

But possibly something quite different should be said about patience at this point. If, to us, patience seems like a central virtue, there's no denying it could seem to others like a rather dull trait or personal attribute. While, based on our successful-parent sample, patience does seem to go hand-in-glove with good parenting, let's say right now that even the best parents take their gloves off sometimes! Then, too, we suspect there exist somewhere impatient parents who also manage in their own way to be successful parents; who manage to lose their tempers without terrorizing their children; and whose kids may even say to their peers such things as, "Doesn't your mom ever do anything interesting, like yell?"

There is no one rigid, predictive, apple-pie profile for good parenting. While the chances are very good that your score on this questionnaire carries much predictive meaning, this might be as good a time as any to mention that, whether or not exceptions can be counted on to prove rules, exceptions, as well as rules, most certainly exist.

There are no recipes for revising other traits measured by the questionnaire—selflessness and flexibility *vs.* their opposites of self-centeredness and rigidity—but in all cases principles similar to those just discussed could be employed. It is possible, we imagine, to become more selfless through encouraging your own interest in others; by deflecting expressions of any self-centeredness you have away from your child; or by trying not to let self-centeredness find expression very often at all. These are not impossible tasks. For example:

If you are virtually required to selflessly abandon something you'd like to do today to take care of your child, then be "selfish" about garnering the time you want by pulling back from others rather than your child.

If child-caused chaos frustrates your deep desire for order in your home, you can exercise your more characteristic precision and meticulousness at the office (but meanwhile leave your five-year-old's half-built castle where it is so that he can finish it tomorrow).

It is perhaps worth suggesting that while the traits we've so far talked about improving (patience, selflessness, flexibility) are important in raising children, their opposites—that we're trying so hard to suppress—can have their own utility in other situations.

Maybe there's nothing intrinsically wrong with impatience,

or even with rigidity or selfishness. Impatient people often have high standards; inflexible people organize well and produce results; selfish people tend to be characterized by high creativity and personal growth. If *you* seem to yourself to lack one or more traits central to good parenting, weigh the utility of that present trait against your desire to reform or change it to facilitate parenthood. It could be that more than a few of us who are impatient, lack selflessness, and so on would be just as well off to say to ourselves, "Well, that's the way I am," accept the possibility that parenthood could make nervous wrecks of us, accept ourselves as we are nonetheless—and remain childfree.

There is one trait, however, that is not only inimical to good parenting but inimical to most everything else we might approach in life as well: dependency. This has been heavily weighted in the scoring because of its potential dangers to both parent and child (comprising a total of 73 points in the Traits section and affecting all Skill areas as well).

Dependency is the exclusive trait of the infant, the overriding trait in the young child, still a predominant trait in school-age youngsters, and a significant part of even the adolescent personality. But it has less and less a legitimate place in our emotional pattern as we grow older. Certainly all humans have needs that can be met only by others. But in healthy relationships dependencies are interchanged—need and support flow two ways. One-sided dependency blocks the dependent person from autonomous actions, development of standards, and sometimes even realistic perceptions. (The difference between reciprocal and unilateral dependency is the difference between symbiosis and parasitism.) Traditional sex-role concepts tried for a long time to insist that even extreme dependency was natural for women (who were to act only according to their partners' wishes, see only through their eyes, etc.), but the truth is that even strong men find a helpless woman frightening; and not many were ever charmed by this trait for very long, unless it was thought to be an act.

The trait of dependency cannot be conquered by cleverly

gathering sufficient support; extra emotional crutches don't do much to help anybody walk. A man who sees seven women a week avoids seeming dependent on any one of them, as do dependent parents of large numbers of children. But such people aren't conquering their dependency; they're just redistributing it.

A consensus among psychologists suggests that dependency can be challenged in two ways: by establishing a balance among several life roles, and by personal achievement. Both can build autonomy. Both should be goals consciously worked toward by men or women with excessive dependency needs, and those who are already parents have a particular responsibility to do so. Consciousness raising or professional therapy have certainly been known to aid both processes.

The matter of excessive emotional dependency, or neurotic need, seems worth some emphasis since it is a trait that can underlie other variables in parental aptitude. It can not only sabotage efforts to develop skills such as discipline, its preoccupying nature can prevent the emergence of any genuine interest in children or liking for them. If you need something, can you judge at all whether you like it? Do addicts "like" opium? Do alcoholics "like" gin? Dependency can sternly police inner thinking about parenthood to keep expectations rosy so that the needed child will be produced. Dependency can even get mixed in with all the wrong motives. Egotistic, compensatory, and conforming motives can result from a need to feel important, a need to make up for lack of autonomy in other roles, and a need to find comfort in conformity.

It therefore seems likely that the worst reason of all to have a child is because you need one. Need destroys objectivity, sinks judgment, prevents the dignity of decision making. You can't well ask yourself whether or not you *should* have a child if you are gripped by the panicky feeling that you *must*!

In a slightly different context, Jo Coudert wrote in *Advice From a Failure* as a final word of guidance to those contemplating marriage:

Ask yourself a last, odd question: what would the other's life be like without me? If you have a sneaking suspicion that it would be a perfectly good life, go ahead and marry. If you have an equal suspicion that you, too, would manage reasonably well, you can marry with double assurance, for you can then assume that you want each other more than you need each other, and wanting is a much better long-range basis for marriage than needing. . . .

That is not a bad final advisory guideline for those contemplating parenthood, either. Could you get along all right if you never had a child? Then you will probably manage well enough if you do have one, for choice is a better dynamic for parenthood than need.

Chapter 9

What Are My Alternatives to Parenthood?

Why Even Ask?

She almost didn't make it to the television station by noon.

Rushing in just in time to have her microphone attached so that she could answer five minutes of questions on this Saturday's local public-affairs program, her interviewer opened with an unexpected question: "Why were you late?" Laughing a little, Pam explained that her morning had been an active one; she'd just come from an origami class, and before that a Sierra Club meeting, and before that breakfast at the marina with her husband and some friends, and before that a trip to get supplies for a late afternoon sailing party . . .

Since the purpose of the interview was to ask Pam her reasons for choosing to be a nonparent, the interviewer understandably remarked, "Well, I see why you don't have children—you're too busy."

"Oh, but I *do* have children," Pam protested. "Let's see . . . I'm almost forty now . . . so I've had . . . why, thousands and thousands of children." She was, of course, a teacher.

It seems to us that Pam might have made a marvelous mother. But she found an alternative to parenthood that she preferred—in a ninth-grade classroom.

Have you thought about what your own alternatives to parenthood might be?

If parenthood were really a profession like any other, we wouldn't even raise the question (any more than we would ask, "What are my alternatives to banking?").

But parenthood can be seen, not just in its occupational

311

outlines, but as a central life role involving our best human, caring impulses. And this role holds both appeal and potential rewards for many men and women who would not be happy parents—at least, not in the traditional sense.

Peter Stein, author of *Single in America*, has remarked, "We cannot all be married. And those who can be, cannot all be married in the same way." Stein is among those who believe that marriage will be jeopardized as an institution if we continue to see it as the inflexible, legally binding, one-size-fits-all contract it has been in the past. Fortunately, where marriage is concerned, the trend toward adapting traditional concept to individual needs is already well established.

Perhaps parenthood, too, needs a more flexible definition. Perhaps it's been too closely tied to biology. Perhaps it needn't always involve twenty years of adult life. Perhaps if it were less obligatory it could be more authentic. To adapt Stein's statement, we cannot all be parents. And those who can be, cannot all be parents in the same way. Fortunately, ways are being found to allow men and women with nurturing potential to fill a parenting role without attempting to fit within parenthood's traditional, procrustean framework.

In the Israeli kibbutz a highly respected parental career open to both men and women is that of the *metapelet* (the Hebrew word *metapel* means "to take care," hence a *metapelet* is one who cares, in this case, for children).

Sociologist Jessie Bernard has reported,

> The term *mother* is used to refer to anyone, regardless of sex, who is nurturant. There is a strawberry mother, a cow mother, a chicken mother, an orchard mother. These are people who love and cherish strawberries, cows, chickens, orchards. There are even mothers who are cherishers and protectors of machinery and tools. . . .

It is the function, not the fecundity, of the caretaker that constitutes such "motherhood."

There is as much wisdom as whimsy in this outlook; for many of us do have the capability and the desire to care for something; but for only some of us will a suitable "something" be our own progeny. Therefore, if we can view parenthood from a more flexible and varied perspective, we can find alternatives—not all of which will be restricted to experimental communities, many of which can be integrated easily with an existing life-style, and some of which may have more value to us than traditional, biological parenthood.

Parenthood Without Pregnancy: The Close-to-Parenthood Alternatives

Adoption and foster care provide one such set of alternatives; teaching and counseling provide another.

To be an adoptive parent is of course to be a parent, period. It can be considered an alternative only because our traditional norm closely links parenthood to the biological processes of pregnancy and childbirth. However, the very nonbiological nature of adoptive parenthood seems to give adopting parents a few advantages that are far from insignificant.

The fact that adoption never happens by accident is a decided advantage. There is no chance at all for hand wringing or for self-accusing "how did this happen?" questions. Nor, within a marriage, can adoption result from a decision made by only one of the partners: the requisite thought and planning must occur over a period of time between husband and wife.

The nature of that planning is more multidimensional than is the matter of planning to biologically conceive a child. The adopting couple can choose the sex of their child as well as the nationality and age preferred. Recent trends such as liberalized abortion laws and attempts by young mothers to keep their babies at least initially have meant that more and more adopting couples are welcoming older children into their homes, and this fact brings yet another advantage to the adopting couple. Since, typically, it is infancy from which fathers tend to retreat, the arrival of a posttoddler can mean close husband-wife cooperation in child raising from the very first.

Adopting couples are also given professional guidance at each stage of the adoption procedure (and even in some cases a trial period after the adopted child enters the couple's home). Family specialists have long noted the relatively greater family happiness and the relative freedom from parenting problems that adopting couples have. Perhaps a significant reason for the greater success of such couples is that they must, as part of their adoption screening, confront many questions raised in this book, questions seldom suggested for natural, biological parents to consider. There is, for example, no rushing into the experience of parenthood without adequate resources: Agencies require evidence of sufficient resources before adoption is approved. Thus chances for financial problems are less. And, among other factors, agencies are also alert to the quality of the marriage and personal maturity of each of the partners.

Because adoption is not biological, parents who adopt need not view age thirty-five or forty as a now-or-never deadline for decision.

Automatically, they are also freed from certain of the egotistic motives. The adopting mother is in no danger of responding narcissistically to the attentions the pregnant woman receives—neither she nor her partner can very well be impelled to adopt in order to see their exact features reproduced.

Therefore, there is typically a different balance of ego and altruism for adopting parents than for biological ones. The taking over of a responsibility someone else created but could not fulfill has a different dynamic than does assuming responsibility for a child whom you brought into existence—a dynamic that has much selflessness inherent in it.

An illustration of this selflessness is found in Bertolt Brecht's *The Caucasian Chalk Circle*. In an early scene of the play, an upper-class woman escaping a local revolution is more concerned with saving material possessions than with saving her child. To a servant she calls "Quick! Bring the child to the carriage! No! First bring my dresses to the carriage . . ." with the result that the child is left behind. Oblivious to her fellow servants' warnings that rescuing the child will court danger since the child's high birth is hated by the revolutionaries, the servant woman Grushka can say only, "But he's looking at me . . ." to explain why she feels she must carry the child away with her. While it would have been both moral and responsible for the child's natural mother to rescue the child, it would have been merely a typical *expected* responsibility. But Grushka's act represents an extraordinary responsibility. To Brecht, Grushka's rescue of the child represents a very high moral principle, involving a risk that she need not have taken.

Adoptive parenthood combines motherhood or fatherhood with a concept at once more profound and simpler: brotherhood.

The same could be said of temporary adoption, or foster care. Foster parenthood is usually temporary, though there are rare exceptions when a child or sibling group remains with foster parents until maturity. The short-term nature of this particular alternative to parenthood will seem an advantage only to some (and, at that, some who initially see it as an advantage may change their minds when it is time for their foster children to leave).

At any given time, particularly in urban areas, there are more children needing foster placement than needing adoption. Some parents simply become unable to care for their children for reasons such as illness, loss of home, marital breakup, general family instability, abuse of children, or inability to control children. Typically, the child from such a home needs an interim family setting between the immediate institutional placement he is normally given and eventual adoption. Such children are often of at least school age and not infrequently are in their teens.

In addition, however, more and more children born to adolescent mothers are given up ("relinquished") sometime between their first and third birthdays as the responsibilities of child care become too great for the natural mother to meet.

Obviously, due to the typically stressful family life they have just come from, foster children may have physical or emotional problems requiring the utmost patience and sensitivity.

That is why many couples frankly feel that foster parenthood is the most difficult kind of parenthood alternative there is. "Of course the foster-parent role is the toughest one to do well," said one woman in a group we interviewed; "that's why you're paid to do it." (Foster parents are generally paid for board while children are in their homes; in addition, money for clothing and medical and dental expenses is provided.)

Like adoption, foster care offers a couple their choice as to the sex and age of the child they feel they can care for temporarily. This can be a decided advantage.

One couple who has had almost continuous foster experiences over the past twelve years explained that, to them,

> This kind of parenthood feels like being a specialist instead of a general practitioner . . . you don't get total experiences of what parenthood is like. We've never had infants or very young children, for example. But we seem to be real good with six-year-olds on up to preteenage children. That is the age

range we've always asked for and gotten. You develop a lot of insight into what the problems of that age group are. You do all you can for the children while you have them, then hope that somebody takes over and does just as well. Even so, you have the satisfaction of knowing you've done what you could, given these kids things they might not otherwise have had.

For those truly drawn to children, this category of parenting offers the advantage of knowing and working with more children than the average parent possibly could, no matter how many Scout troops she or he might sponsor over the years.

Tess and Henry Cohen of upstate New York are one couple who, while not biological parents, have almost totally immersed themselves in guiding children for half a century. For forty years, "Henny" Cohen was a popular and successful teacher, guidance counselor, and coach of baseball, soccer and basketball in New York public schools. In addition, the Cohens founded a summer camp for underprivileged children which they maintained personally until their recent retirement.

Asked to estimate the number of youngsters he has worked with, Henny replied that the task was impossible.

Teaching aside, for thirty summers we directed a camp which one thousand underprivileged kids attended: and beyond thirty thousand I'm just not going to count. . . . Let's just say that for forty-two of our fifty years of work we've been involved with children, and helped them in ways that many still remember. Just this week, a fifty-year-old man stopped me on the street and thanked me for advising him through some problems he had in high school. Now, that's my kind of parenthood. . . .

Part-Time Parenthood: Big Brothers, Big Sisters, Just Friends

"On Wednesday afternoons and Friday nights, I am a father," explained Tom, a bachelor who owns his own plastics fabrication operation. "Sometimes on weekends, too," he adds.

Tom, now twenty-eight, has been a Big Brother since his senior year in college, and now has his fourth Little Brother, Larry, who visits Tom's home or office to talk about schoolwork on Wednesday afternoons, goes to a movie or a ball game with Tom on Friday nights, and sometimes gets together with Tom on weekends to "just mess around."

Larry was eleven years old when he was drawn into a crowd of boys who lied habitually, shoplifted, and took drugs. Larry's father had left home for good when Larry was three. His mother, who felt she had done a "good enough" job raising her boy in spite of having to work long hours, became alarmed at Larry's new associates and called Big Brothers.

"There's no guarantee that I'm going to work any magic," Tom admitted, "but there's a built-in success factor in the Big Brothers program. Because kids like Larry know that those of us who are their Big Brothers don't have to be with them—we spend time with them because we *choose* to—they're a little careful to live up to what we expect. In the program, you may not do a lot of good. You may do only a little bit of good. But it's a little bit of good that wouldn't have gotten done otherwise."

The same thought was echoed by Gail, who has been a Big Sister for about a year and a half. "My cousin has a child who's nine, the age of my Little Sister. She's always worried about 'giving her child enough,' whatever 'enough' means. I don't have that worry. If I buy Sarah a little plastic bracelet, bring her a book or a souvenir from a trip, or tell her a funny story, it seems like the greatest thing in the world to her—because it's something she wouldn't have otherwise."

What Big Brothers and Big Sisters mainly give to their children, though, is experience: one Saint Louis Big Sister said, "When I realized there were kids living in this city who'd never seen the city arch; who had no idea what the Kentucky bluegrass was—something only a state away that *I* loved to drive to with my family when I was a child—it took me about one millisecond to decide to join . . ."

Teaching and counseling occupations have several elements in common with adoption and foster care, for these roles, too, are volitional, nonbiological, and, essentially, charitable. They are also extremely flexible.

One can choose to teach or counsel at any level from prekindergarten to postcollege and choose subject areas of greatest personal interest. There is also choice as to whether a teacher wants to train for and work with slow-learning, "normal," or gifted students. In a few school systems and private schools, it is still possible to choose to teach only boys, or only girls.

After-school clubs and extracurricular activities give teachers a chance to establish extremely close friendships with students and countless informal opportunities to give help and guidance. One teacher remarked, "I think I've got the best parts of parenthood . . . I don't have the overall hassle, the arguments about what time Jimmy got home last night. But I'm the one every kid seems to come to when there's something important going on in his life; I'm the one to share a problem, a victory, a decision about college—or for that matter the latest John Denver album. I know that I'm closer to a lot of these kids right now than their own parents are; and in some cases I'm even giving them more 'parenting' than their own parents are. It's very satisfying—very. I love it. I wouldn't trade my job for anything.''

Within schools there is also an increasing need for special security officers, particularly in urban areas. School security work might seem to have more in common with police work than with parenthood, given the problems of arson, assault, extortion, vandalism, illegal drinking, and pot smoking and the like with which security personnel have to deal. Yet the essence of this job is more psychological finesse than physical force. It seems to lie in establishing oneself as comrade and friend to troublemakers; as someone that students will both look up to and want to behave for. ''The only method of maintaining order is to become a liked and respected authority figure,'' said one officer who has his own fan club within a very rough Detroit school. ''In some cases, you're the first authority figure these kids have ever had. It's a big responsibility; it has its dangers; there are a lot of kids you lose as well as a lot you help; and the pay is lousy. But I'd rather be slugging it out here than in some safe desk job. Not many of the kids are basically bad. And once in a while something really good happens. After half a year of hassling with two of the school's toughest pushers, they came to me and asked if they could be my deputies. I felt like some goddamn real-life TV hero. . . .''

Taking part in such a guidance program might be seen as an easy way to assume some parental responsibility. You do not have to cope with all the ages, developmental stages, and typical problems of childhood. You can request the kind of child you feel best suited to help, relate to, and give to. You have the additional advantage of looking at the program either as an alternative to parenthood or as a preparation for it. Finally, if your hopes for the child are not realized, it is not ultimately your fault or responsibility.

Naturally, you don't have to look for a structured, part-time parenthood program. It is often easy enough to find and create your own. There may be a child you know, or know of, who needs a friend, who has never seen a museum, or who does not have the money to join a Brownie troop or go to summer camp.

You may enjoy being "aunt" or "uncle" to children, as the couple who wrote, "We try to be happy, useful influences in the lives of our relatives' children. We also have a god-daughter with whom we have a delightfully warm relationship, and we know many younger people who look to us for friendship and even counsel. As we look ahead to old age, we don't feel we will be deserted. We intend to be continuously interested in the current world, and to have continued strong relationships with the boys and girls our siblings and cousins had."

It is also possible, from time to time, to respond to youth groups needing sponsorship within your community or through a local Y or church group.

And there is such a thing as being just friends.

Katharine Hepburn, who by choice has no children of her own, is said to strike up friendships with children very easily whenever she encounters them.

The two boys who recently appeared with her in *Olly Olly Oxen Free* were initially awed by her, but she instinctively put them at ease. "On the third day of production," a friend reported, "one of the boys blew his lines and Hepburn said, 'My fault. My fault.' The boy asked, 'How could it be your fault? I forgot the line.' And she replied, 'Because I delivered *my* line too fast, making you forget.' " It seemed to be just a ploy to put the young actor at ease, but it is just this ability, her friends say, that greatly endears Katharine Hepburn to young people she meets and works with.

Any friendship between an adult and a child (even if it's only a fifteen-minute conversation) almost inevitably takes on some characteristics of a parent-child relationship.

Doris Lessing tells of one such friendship in her novel, *Memoirs of a Survivor*. Against the background of a collapsing city and civilization, a child is brought to the apartment of the woman narrator of the novel by a stranger who says simply, "This is Emily. Look after her." The older woman cares for Emily, sees her through preadolescence to young womanhood. Their relationship becomes one of deep mutual loyalty—a loyalty that stands out in ever-greater relief as the society around them becomes increasingly barbaric.

Sometimes friendships seem to spring up just as suddenly in real life.

A retired teacher who now lives in Cold Spring, New York, has had a close friendship with a little boy named Jay Jay for about five years now—a friendship that began when Jay Jay wandered by the teacher's house one day and said, "Hi. D'you want to be my friend?"

And that, explains Mr. Nathan Drut, was that.

Jay Jay stops by every day after school now to have tea and orange juice; fix a snack; go for a walk; watch the birds at the feeder; listen to music; watch TV; or just talk. Sometimes the two just sit and enjoy being with each other.

Mr. Drut emphasizes that he does not think of Jay Jay as a son: "No, no, of course not. Jay Jay has a father. He doesn't need another one. He needs an adult friend, which believe me I take pleasure in being to him. Being a father involves much more responsibility, though. I feel that I have, now, the best part of a fatherly relationship without any of the awesome worries, fears, and concerns which would be a part of fatherhood. I don't feel that I need a son, either. To some people, that is very important. But to me, I cherish my relationship with Jay Jay for just what it is—the kind of friendship you don't find too often, no matter how long you live; and no matter how many acquaintances or relatives—or children—you have."

Just *Friends?*

Although Mr. Drut and others in his situation sometimes speak of their relationships with children as "just friendships," it would be a mistake to think that such friendships exist without real love on both sides.

Sometimes the love even seems to have a romantic quality. Mr. Drut, in fact, articulated this thought by explaining, "Let's compare not having your 'own' children to not having your 'own' husband or wife. By not marrying, you want to remain free to fall in love with others over a period of time, rather than commit your love to one man or woman exclusively. By not having your 'own' children, you're free to 'fall in love' with other children you meet—like Jay Jay."

Mr. Drut's niece, Marcia Rothstein, during the years when she was a schoolteacher, had a number of such close experiences. One began, simply enough, with a hand-delivered letter from a second grader. The letter read simply,

Dear Mrs. Rothstein,
Do you have kids? And do you like kids? Are you nice to them?

Susan

to which Marcia replied in her own letter,

Dear Susan,
I do not have any children. I want to keep on teaching. I like

children very much. I hope you think that I am nice to you.

Sincerely,
Marcia Rothstein

That exchange began a correspondence that has lasted seven years now. Susan and her family moved away the summer after second grade, but as her former teacher explains, "Her letters have never stopped. I've watched her style and way of expressing herself change—from childlike exuberance that was close to the conversational, and minimal punctuation, to more thoughtfully crafted communications. I've been 'with' her as she's grown from a little girl into a young woman almost fifteen years old now. I've been her confidante in many ways, even at great distance. I know being this sort of 'pen pal' is a long way from being a parent. It's not real parenthood—any more than it would be a real marriage if my husband and I lived seven states apart. But I feel a little like a mother. And that 'little,' while it wouldn't be nearly enough for some people, happens to suit me just fine."

Global Parenthood

While on a research trip to New Guinea in the 1950s, Dr. Carleton Gajdusek decided to remain there a while and live among the Fore tribes with the intention of trying to find a cure for a fatal nerve disease that had run rampant through these tribes for generations. He did in fact discover both etiology and effective treatment for the dreaded *kuru,* and was awarded the 1976 Nobel Prize in Physiology and Medicine for this investigative work. Since the Nobel Prize confers more than just honor and glory, Dr. Gajdusek found himself with

$160,000 in prize money. How did he decide to use it? For the education of "his children": this bachelor scientist has adopted—so far—sixteen youngsters of the South Pacific! This might make him eligible for another, unofficial honor; he might well be called a leading citizen of our small world or "global village."

Gajdusek's example of global parenthood is not unique. There was an American millionaire who carried on a one-man, one-airplane crusade to airlift orphans from Vietnam; a Chilean poet who personally saved one thousand exiles from French camps during the Spanish Civil War and found them homes in South America; and Joan Ganz Cooney, who sought to enrich the lives of all American children by improving the quality of television fare offered them.

And if efforts to better life for an entire community or nation of children may be considered parenthood, might not those such as Ralph Nader or Stewart Mott be considered symbolic "fathers" of a million children? Surely Nader's vigilant attention to auto and air safety, food additives, and the quality of public services have touched the life of virtually every American child, as have Mott's tireless efforts to achieve political reforms, more honest and responsive government, an end to the complacent national psychology which could threaten the lives of today's children, here and elsewhere, by creating tomorrow's Vietnams.

Arthur Mitchell, whose passionately pursued goal has been to introduce black children to the world of dance (and who left a leading professional ballet company at the height of his career to do so), describes himself as a "father" to the children he teaches.

And what of Anna Freud, who patiently studied children, then described how their perceptions of self developed as well as how normality and pathology in childhood might be determined?

What of Italian educator Maria Montessori, who provided

the first *casa dei bambini* in the slum tenements of Rome and whose theories of learning (the Montessori method) revolutionized the education of children around the world?

And what of Maurice Sendak, who has been called the Picasso of children's books, whose children's literature is perhaps loved by more children than that created by any other author; and whose *Where the Wild Things Are* inspired one emotionally damaged little girl who had never spoken before to say her first words: "Can I have that book?"

Nonparents all, such men and women have yet enriched the lives of countless children.

A concept of morality developed by Bertolt Brecht in several of his works is quite synonymous with nurturing and motherliness. It defines itself by asking: "Do you work to fulfill other humans' needs, wherever met?" The childless men and women just described could answer yes to Brecht's question.

Actually, their kind of parenthood has been the role of many nonparents throughout history. During the many centuries when children in Europe were not treated tenderly but instead seen as "little adults" with the right to hire themselves out for twelve hours of labor a day, whatever benefits poor youngsters received were often got from childless religious people—priests and nuns—who not only maintained the orphanages and institutions of the day but whose role it was to try to meet physical and spiritual needs of all children. (It is likely no accident that the word for "priest" is, in French, *père*; in Spanish, *padre*; in Russian, *batiushka*—in all languages, *father*.)

But the same spirit of wishing to reach out to children in other human communities can be, and frequently is, expressed in less cosmic ways. We are probably all familiar with the foster-parent plans through which sponsors pay a small amount of money per month to help support a poor child somewhere in the world. A New Jersey woman who sponsored a child in Ecuador told us, "If Patricia's letters to me telling me how her life has changed since I adopted her were not enough to fill my heart, her recent photographs would be. My first view of her was of a wasted little girl in rags, staring blankly at the camera. Though her later pictures are still in black and white, they almost seem to me to be in color: Patricia is decently clothed—*and smiling* . . ."

In fact, one need not even be an adult to be a foster parent through such a program. William Lederer tells the following story in *A Nation of Sheep:*

> One mother I know suggested to her twelve-year-old daughter that she adopt a Korean orphan as a 'brother.' The adoption cost fifteen dollars a month. Naturally this was too expensive an undertaking for the twelve-year-old to do alone. The mother asked if perhaps her classmates at school wouldn't like to join in the project. The classmates were delighted; and each contributed fifty cents a month to the orphan's upkeep. But, of course, the thirty girls didn't want to adopt a child from a land about which they knew nothing. Because their new 'brother' lived in Korea, they had to find out something about its history and customs. They began studying what people in Korea eat, what kind of clothes they wear, what the major occupations are, the customs and traditions. What are the summers like? The winters? What about the songs and the dances?
>
> In this manner, thirty American children learned in a personal way about a foreign land. . . .

Such kinds of parenthood may seem as far removed from traditional procreative hallmarks as cigars and bassinets, baby showers, and bronzed shoes. But they are not far at all from the kind of affectionate nurturing that is the basis of all good parenthood; in fact, they well exemplify that nurturing principle.

Children of the Mind

The child as we know her or him today is a relatively modern being, having existed, in fact, for not much more than a hundred years. Solicitude for children, we learn from landmark works such as Lloyd de Mause's *The History of Childhood*, is not an age-old phenomenon.

In primitive times parents at their best provided only the bare means of survival; their very struggle to attain that survival prevented the kind of nurturing interaction we value so much today.

Later, in feudal and agrarian eras, the grueling labor of peasant mothers and fathers was not conducive to parent-child interaction, and even among the educated, parental involvement with children was minimal. Upper-class families sent their children away to be raised by others or employed servants within the home to do the job.

It was not until the late eighteenth century that children began to be seen as worthy of the interest of intelligent adults. Exulting in this new idea, Victor Hugo wrote, "Christopher Columbus only discovered America: I have discovered the Child." Rousseau could make a similar claim. He publicly deplored regular beatings and other endemic antichild practices, insisting that children were basically good. Far from needing harsh treatment to subdue their innate evil impulses, they needed their good qualities brought out by patient nurturing, within their own homes, by their own parents, he said.

It is only the century of Hugo and Rousseau that gave birth

to the Child, that devised the nursery and developed the idea of home as nest wherein one generation kindly devoted itself to nurturing the next. "Mothers were summoned from social pleasures to seek the joys of running a nursery, while fathers were encouraged to feel it not beneath their dignity to romp with infants, and to keep a close eye on their development," de Mause's collected essays tell us. Rousseau typically has the heroine of his novel *La Nouvelle Heloise* declare her life's goal to be ". . . to make my children happy. This was my first prayer when I became a mother, and my efforts are perpetually directed to its fulfillment."

It seems that children had been severely neglected for so long that the force of the new, enlightened ideas caused an overreaction. The time was ripe for the beginning of an idealization of the home and nurturance, the glories of which were wondrously described by a hundred lesser Rousseaus in a trend that would not end before many homey nests came to be perceived by their occupants as cages. The century of the child would become oppressive to the private lives of many adults.

The fact that public responsibility for children not one's own awakened simultaneously, however, gave a richer dimension to the century of the child, making the time also ripe for the emergence of the strikingly humane philosophy of *generativity*. Generativity is defined by Erik Erikson as the concern of one generation for establishing and guiding the next. However, within this philosophy, Erikson seemed to recognize that such a task was not for everyone, or at least not in the same way.

In his works on generativity, Erikson carefully explained,

Although generativity is primarily the concern for the next generation, there are individuals who, through misfortune or because of special and genuine gifts in other directions, do not apply this drive to their own offspring. [Therefore] I have always called the dominant task of adulthood *generativity* rather than *procreativity* because I want to allow for a variety of activities other than parenthood: generativity can mean man's love for his ideas and his works as well as his children. . . .

That ideas could be viewed as children has a history of interesting poetic and philosophical expression.

Legend has it that Socrates was instructed in this view by a learned woman of Mantinea called Diotima; supposedly Diotima told him,

> Animals as well as men seek to perpetuate themselves and thereby become immortal. But for man there are various stages in the hierarchy of this desire. The lowest is that of the animal inspired by the desire for children of the body, but as one ascends there is realization of the possibility of producing *children of the mind:* who would not prefer the poetic offspring of a Homer or a Hesiod . . . ?

During all the centuries since, it has not been unusual for artists to further that analogy. Just as the creativity involved in raising a child aims for the moment when the child can take on a life of her or his own, painters and writers have often declared that at a certain point in their artistic creativity, a work of art or literature takes on a life of its own.

Ben Shahn has been quoted as saying, "There arrives a period during the painting when the painting itself makes certain demands. . . . It definitely becomes a living thing."

Bruno Walter has written, "The *thematic idea,* this child of truly creative musicianship, is a live birth and has individual qualities; and in treatment, shaping, and development of it, its progenitor should have regard for the 'child's' nature, and not proceed in an arbitrary fashion. The true composer does not behave like a tyrant toward his thematic substance; but he watches like a provident father for signs suggestive of individual development, and lets his creative phantasy be directed by these. . . ."

Norman Mailer is among novelists who have stated repeatedly, "A book takes on its own life in the writing," and musician Liz Swados, explaining to a reporter why she had no interest in acquiring a husband or family, said, "When I say I'm married to music I'm not using a corny metaphor: these works are my children."

Even those of us not endowed with the talents of a Homer or a Hesiod (or a Ben Shahn or Bruno Walter) would do well to ponder the idea of children of the mind. We too can give as much care to developing our own accomplishments as we would to developing physical progeny.

A modest example is provided by a personal essay which appeared in the *Village Voice* around Mother's Day, 1974. A young woman wrote that, as she approached age thirty, her work as a free-lance writer and editor suffered because of increasingly frequent "writer's block." Taking this problem to her therapist, she wondered if these blocks might be due to a nagging guilt that she had not become a mother (and in fact felt little or no inclination to do so). After the therapist's simple suggestion to "Make your writing your baby," her writer's blocks disappeared. She has since gone on to write a well-received psychological self-help book, a biography of a famous film star, and a promising first novel. She believes she could not have conceived of or brought any of these projects to fruition had she had a child three years ago, at the time of her conflict on the matter.

But a child of the mind need not be thought of as something so imposing as the published word.

An Indiana woman's chosen alternative to childbearing was the creation and development of her own small business, initially a shopping service for business executives which has now branched out to include two of her own specialty and gift shops. "My business is like a child to me," she consciously admits, "and why not? Men have always nurtured their careers, not children. I think that women should start to have that option, too."

Many—indeed, perhaps *most*—family-science professionals would agree. Dr. Teresa Marciano of Fairleigh Dickinson University comments, "An unwise pregnancy can cause a kind of 'psychological abortion' for today's woman, shutting off from possible life any incipient talents or ambitions which might otherwise be explored—not necessarily with the goal of fame in mind, but for the *self-satisfaction* that personal achievement can bring. The self-esteem that results from achievement of any sort is both valuable in itself; and it can only make a person a better parent if, eventually, he or she does have a child." Personal achievements, she insists, should not be viewed as "substitute children." "They're 'substitutes' only if you insist on children as a near-universal norm; more properly, they are *alternatives.*"

The range of such alternatives is too wide for a brief overview. It would include not only the creation of a book or a small business, but successful progress in an established job; the exploration of new interests; the development of untried skills; the enhancement of appreciations; the sharpening of citizen awareness; a devotion to worthy causes; ongoing exposure to new experiences; the pursuit of cultural or recreational experiences; the growth of self-knowledge.

Singly or in some combination, such alternatives provide nurturance of the adult self, which, from psychological perspectives, can be seen as a worthy alternative to parenthood. The man or woman who cultivates these elements of the self is involved in a creative process not likely to lead to a frenzied, mid-life search for identity. His or her identity will have been soundly built.

For some, this creative task of self-development will prove incompatible with parenthood; for those the choice to develop the self should be respected just as much as the choice to be a parent.

For others personal growth will only result from giving the self to others—intimately, unreservedly, continuously—through having a child or children of their own. For these men and women, a Big Brother program holds no more appeal than being a Sunday painter would to Leonardo da Vinci; children of the mind appears a meaningless abstraction, and nurturance of the self an irrelevant exercise. For such men and women, even lofty sounding pursuits like the enhancement of appreciations will have an arid sound unless applied to children (but will come to life if viewed as the enhancement of appreciations, of a child's development). The rewards such gifted individuals will find in parenthood will not be known to many of their childless peers.

"Birth allows us all to be little gods," wrote Joseph B. Tamney in *Family and Fertility*—and so indeed does the painting of a masterpiece, the reformation of a nation, or the structuring of a well-lived life; but never in a way involving such intense commitment as reproduction. Those who have children and raise them successfully deserve perhaps the statues typically raised only to artists and statesmen, for such parents make possible the continuance of a civilization within which art and social law have meaning.

Yet nowhere is it written in stone that each of us should have 2.1 children, or in fact any children at all. Whether or not we do so is now our own choice and no one else's. The only catch is that, when we were all merely following a near-universal norm in having children, at least we personally did not have to hold ourselves responsible if things went wrong. We could just blame bad luck (or those near-universal norms). But knowing we have choices imposes a responsibility to try to make the wisest ones we can, for ourselves and others—for the community around us and for the children we may have.

This book, perhaps, has been a guide. But it is only that. The choice to follow, or reflect on, or reject its suggestions is also yours alone.

Can each of us make our own choice wisely, based on qualities we feel we have within us?

It is admirable to have selflessness, patience, compassion, concern for others, and other virtues characteristic of good parents. But as much as such traits and qualities are to be admired, not all of us are wisely destined to work to fulfill other humans' needs, wherever met. Some of us will be better suited to nurturing our own potentialities. Erich Fromm has remarked in *The Art of Loving*, "Eventually the mature person has to come to the point where he is his own mother and his own father." That is a central task for all adults, a task of encouraging full growth of whatever qualities lie within us, so that we may move beyond the points at which we might have stopped developing and move instead toward the point that measures all we may become.

Bibliography

Ames, Louise Bates, and Ilg, F. *Between Parent and Child.* New York: Avon Books, 1965.

Aries, Philippe. *Centuries of Childhood.* New York: Vintage Books, 1962

Bernard, Jessie. *The Future of Motherhood.* New York: Dial Press, 1974.

Bettelheim, Bruno. *The Children of the Dream.* New York: Avon Books, 1969.

Brim, Orville. *Education for Child Rearing.* New York: The Free Press, 1975.

Carmichael, Leonard. *Introduction to Psychology.* New York: Houghton Mifflin and Company, 1972.

Chess, Stella. *How to Help Your Child Get the Most Out of School.* New York: Dell Books, 1974.

Comer, James, and Poussaint, Alvin. *Black Child Care.* New York: Pocket Books, 1975.

deBeauvoir, Simone. *The Second Sex.* New York: Bantam Books, 1952.

deMause, Lloyd. *The History of Childhood.* New York: Psychohistory Press, 1974.

Dobson, James. *Dare to Discipline.* New York: Bantam Books, 1970.

Dodson, Fitzhugh. *How to Parent.* New York: Signet Books, 1970.

Dyer, Everett. "Parenthood as Crisis: A Re-Study." *Marriage and Family Living* 25 (1968): 198.

Erikson, Erik. *Childhood and Society.* New York: W.W. Norton, 1963.

_____. *Insight and Responsibility.* New York: W.W. Norton, 1964.

_____. *Life History and the Historical Movement.* New York: W. W. Norton, 1975.

_____. *Youth: Change and Challenge.* New York: Basic Books, 1963.

Figley, Charles. *Readings in Intimate Human Relationships.* Lafayette, Ind.: Purdue University Press, 1974.

Fromme, Allan. *The ABC of Child Care.* New York: Pocket Books, 1965.

Gilbert, Sara. *What's a Father For?* New York: Warner Books, 1975.

Ginott, Haim. *Between Parent and Child.* New York: Avon Books, 1975.

_____. *Between Parent and Teenager.* New York: Macmillan, 1969.

Goodman, David. *A Parent's Guide to the Emotional Needs of Children.* New York: Hawthorn Books, 1959.

Gordon, I. *Baby Learning Through Baby Play.* New York: St. Martin's Press, 1970.

Hamachek, Don. *Encounters with the Self.* New York: Holt, Rinehart and Winston, 1971.

Hobbs, Daniel. "Parenthood as Crisis: A Third Study." *Journal of Marriage and the Family* 27 (1965): 367–72.

Holland, J. L. *Making Vocational Choices: A Theory of Careers.* Englewood Cliffs, N.J.: Prentice-Hall, 1973.

Jacoby, Arthur. "Transition to Parenthood." *Journal of Marriage and Family* 31 (Nov. 1969): 720–7.

Kieren, Dianne, Henton, June, and Marotz, Ramona. *Hers & His.* Hinsdale, Ill.: the Dryden Press.

Lazarus, Richard. *Psychological Stress and the Coping Process.* New York: McGraw Hill, 1966.

LeMasters. "Parenthood as Crisis." *Marriage and Family Living* 19 (1957): 353.

LeShan, Eda. *How to Survive Parenthood.* New York: Warner Books, 1965.

Lynn, David. *The Father: His Role in Child Development.* Monterey, Calif.: Brooks/Cole, 1974.

Myers, Walter. *The World of Work.* New York: Bobbs-Merrill, 1975.

Myrdal, Alva, and Klein, Viola. *Women's Two Roles.* London: Routledge and Kegan Paul, 1968.

Peck, Ellen, and Sanderowitz, Judith. *Pronatalism—The Myth of Mom and Apple Pie.* New York: T. Y. Crowell, 1974.
Pugh, Thomas, et al. "Rates of Mental Disease Related to Childbearing." *New England Journal of Medicine* 268:1224–8.

Radl, Shirley. *Mother's Day is Over.* New York: Charterhouse, 1973.

Renee, Karen. "Correlates of Dissatisfaction in Marriage." *Journal of Marriage and the Family* 32 : 54–66.

Rogers, Carl, and Stevens, Barry. *Person to Person.* New York: Pocket Books, 1967.

Rosenblatt, Paul. "Behavior in Public Places: Comparison of Couples Accompanied and Unaccompanied by Children." *Journal of Marriage and the Family* (Nov. 1974, Vol. 36, No. 4).

Schell, Robert, ed. *Developmental Psychology Today.* New York: Random House, 1975.

Senn, Milton. *Speaking Out for America's Children.* New Haven, Conn.: Yale University Press, 1977.

Shaw, Charles. *When Your Child Needs Help.* New York: Barnes and Noble, 1972.

Super, Donald, and Crites, John. *Appraising Vocational Fitness by Means of Psychological Tests.* New York: Harper & Row, 1962.

Sweet, James. *Women in the Labor Force.* New York: Seminar Press, 1973.

Wells, J. Gibson. *Current Issues in Marriage and the Family.* New York: Macmillan, 1975.

Wrightsman, Lawrence, and Sanford, Fillmore. *Psychology: A Scientific Study of Human Behavior.* Monterey Calif.: Brooks/Cole, 1975.

Woolfolk, William, and Woolfolk, Joanna. *The Great American Birth Rite.* New York: The Dial Press, 1975.

Answer Sheet

This form is your personal record of responses to all question-naire items. Simply circle T or F to indicate whether you agree or disagree with the items. In the case of multiple-choice items, circle the letter indicating the response that comes closest to what you believe your own response would be. Two answer sheets are provided, so that each partner will have one.

Questionnaire 1

1.	T	F			16.	T	F
2.	T	F			17.	T	F
3.	T	F			18.	T	F
4.	T	F			19.	T	F
5.	T	F			20.	T	F
6.	T	F			21.	T	F
7.	T	F			22.	T	F
8.	T	F			23.	T	F
9.	T	F			24.	T	F
10.	a	b	c	d	25.	T	F
11.	a	b	c	d	26.	T	F
12.	a	b	c		27.	T	F
13.	T	F			28.	T	F
14.	T	F			29.	T	F
15.	T	F			30.	T	F

31. T F
32. T F
33. T F
34. T F
35. T F
36. T F
37. T F
38. T F

39. a b c
40. T F
41. T F
42. T F
43. a b c d e f g
    n i
44. T F
45. T F

Questionnaire 2

1. T F
2. T F
3. T F
4. a b c d
5. T F
6. T F
7. T F
8. T F
9. T F
10. T F
11. a b c d
12. T F
13. T F
14. T F
15. T F
16. T F
17. T F
18. T F
19. T F
20. a b c d

21. a b c d e
22. a b c d e f
23. T F
24. T F
25. T F
26. a b c d e f g
27. T F
28. a b c d
29. T F
30. a b c d e f g
31. a b c d e f
32. T F
33. T F
34. a b c d e
35. T F
36. T F
37. T F
38. T F
39. a b c d e f g
    h i j k l m n

40.	T	F
41.	T	F
42.	a	b	c	d	e	f	g
43.	a	b	c	d
44.	T	F
45.	a	b	c	d	e	f
46.	a	b	c	d	e	f
47.	a	b	c	d	e	f
48.	a	b	c
49.	a	b	c	d
50.	a	b	c	d
51.	T	F
52.	T	F
53.	a	b	c	d	e
54.	T	F
55.	T	F
56.	T	F
57.	T	F
58.	T	F

59.	a	b	c
60.	T	F
61.	T	F
62.	T	F
63.	T	F
64.	T	F
65.	T	F
66.	a	b	c	d	e
67.	a	b	c	d	e	f	g
68.	a	b	c
69a.	a	b	c	d	e	f
69b	a	b	c	d	e	f
70.	a	b	c	d	e	f
71.	a	b	c	d	e	f	g
72.	a	b	c	d	e	f	g
73.	T	F
74.	a	b	c	d
75.	a	b	c	d	e

Questionnaire 3

1.	T	F
2.	T	F
3.	T	F
4.	T	F
5.	T	F
6.	a	b	c	d	e	f
	g	h	i	j	k
7.	T	F
8.	T	F

9.	T	F
10.	T	F
11.	T	F
12.	a	b	c	d
13.	T	F
14.	T	F
15.	T	F
16.	T	F
17.	T	F
18.	T	F

19. T   F   39. T   F
20. T   F   40. T   F
21. T   F   41. T   F
22. T   F   42. T   F
23. T   F   43. T   F
24. T   F   44. a   b   c   d   e
25. T   F   45. T   F
26. T   F   46. T   F
27. T   F   47. T   F
28. T   F   48. T   F
29. T   F   49. a   b   c   d
30. T   F   50. T   F
31. T   F   51. a   b
32. a   b   c   d 52. T   F
33. T   F   53. T   F
34. T   F   54. a   b   c   d   e
35. a   b   c   d   e   55. T   F
36. T   F   56. T   F
37. T   F   57. T   F
38. T   F

(Responses to Items 35–57 are to be written by you according to how you believe your spouse responded.)

(35.) a   b   c   d   e   (45.) T   F
(36.) T   F   (46.) T   F
(37.) T   F   (47.) T   F
(38.) T   F   (48.) T   F
(39.) T   F   (49.) a   b   c   d
(40.) T   F   (50.) T   F
(41.) T   F   (51.) a   b
(42.) T   F   (52.) T   F
(43.) T   F   (53.) T   F
(44.) a   b   c   d   e   (54.) a   b   c   d   e

(55.)   T   F   84.   T   F
(56.)   T   F
(57.)   T   F   *68–84 for men*

58.   T   F   68.   T   F
59.   T   F   69.   T   F
60.   T   F   70.   T   F
61.   T   F   71.   T   F
62.   T   F   72.   T   F
63.   T   F   73.   T   F
64.   T   F   74.   T   F
65.   T   F   75.   T   F
66.   T   F   76.   T   F
67.   T   F   77.   T   F
                                 78.   T   F
68–84 for women   79.   T   F
                                 80.   T   F
68.   T   F   81.   T   F
69.   T   F   82.   a   b   c   d   e   f   g
70.   T   F   83.   a   b   c   d
71.   T   F   84.   T   F
72.   T   F
73.   T   F   85.   T   F
74.   T   F   86.   T   F
75.   T   F   87.   T   F
76.   T   F   88.   T   F
77.   T   F   89.   T   F
78.   T   F   90.   T   F
79.   T   F   91.   T   F
80.   T   F   92.   T   F
81.   T   F   93.   T   F
82.   T   F   94.   T   F
83.   a   b   c   d   e   f   g   95.   T   F

96.	T	F
97.	T	F
98.	T	F
99.	T	F
100.	T	F

101.	T	F	
102.	a	b	c
103.	T	F	
104.	T	F	
105.	T	F	

Questionnaire 4

1.	T	F
2.	T	F
3.	T	F
4.	T	F
5.	T	F
6.	T	F
7.	T	F
8.	T	F
9.	T	F
10.	T	F
11.	T	F
12.	T	F
13.	T	F
14.	T	F
15.	T	F
16.	T	F
17.	T	F
18.	T	F
19.	T	F

20.	T	F
21.	T	F
22.	T	F
23.	T	F
24.	T	F
25.	T	F
26.	T	F
27.	T	F
28.	T	F
29.	T	F
30.	T	F
31.	T	F
32.	T	F
33.	T	F
34.	T	F
35.	T	F
36.	T	F
37.	T	F

Questionnaire 5

1.	T	F
2.	T	F

3.	T	F
4.	T	F

5.	T	F				38.	a	b	c	d
6.	T	F				39.	T	F		
7.	T	F				40.	T	F		
8.	a	b	c	d	e	41.	T	F		
9.	T	F				42.	a	b	c	
10.	T	F				43.	a	b	c	d
11.	T	F				44.	a	b	c	
12.	a	b	c	d		45.	T	F		
13.	T	F				46.	T	F		
14.	T	F				47.	T	F		
15.	a	b	c	d		48.	T	F		
16.	a	b	c			49.	T	F		
17.	T	F				50.	T	F		
18.	a	b	c			51.	T	F		
19.	T	F				52.	a	b	c	d
20.	T	F				53.	a	b	c	
21.	T	F				54.	a	b	c	d	e
22.	T	F				55.	T	F		
23.	T	F				56.	T	F		
24.	T	F				57.	T	F		
25.	T	F				58.	T	F		
26.	T	F				59.	a	b		
27.	T	F				60.	a	b	c	d
28.	T	F				61.	T	F		
29.	T	F				62.	a	b	c	d
30.	T	F				63.	T	F		
31.	a	b	c	d		64.	T	F		
32.	T	F				65.	T	F		
33.	T	F				66.	T	F		
34.	T	F				67.	T	F		
35.	a	b	c			68.	a	b	c	d
36.	T	F				69.	a	b	c	d	e
37.	T	F				70.	T	F		

71. T F
72. T F
73. T F
74. T F
75. T F
76. a b c d
77. T F
78. a b c d e f
79. a b c d e
80. a b c d e
81. T F
82. T F
83. T F

84. T F
85. T F
86. T F
87. T F
88. T F
89. T F
90. T F
91. T F
92. T F
93. T F
94. T F
95. T F
96. T F

Questionnaire 6

1. a b c d e
2. a b c d e f
3. T F
4. T F
5. T F
6. T F
7. T F
8. a b c d e
9. T F
10. T F
11. T F
12. T F
13. T F
14. T F

15. T F
16. T F
17. a b c d
18. T F
19. T F
20. T F
21. T F
22. T F
23. T F
24. T F
25. T F
26. T F
27. T F
28. T F

29.	T	F				
30.	T	F				
31.	T	F				
32.	a	b	c			
33.	T	F				
34.	T	F				
35.	T	F				
36.	T	F				
37.	a	b	c	d		
38.	a	b				
39.	T	F				
40.	T	F				
41.	T	F				
42.	T	F				
43.	T	F				
44.	T	F				
45.	T	F				
46.	T	F				
47.	T	F				
48.	T	F				
49.	T	F				
50.	T	F				
51.	T	F				
52.	T	F				
53.	a	b	c	d		
54.	T	F				
55.	T	F				
56.	T	F				
57.	a	b	c			
58.	T	F				
59.	T	F				
60.	a	b	c	d		
61.	T	F				
62.	T	F				
63.	T	F				
64.	T	F				
65.	T	F				
66.	T	F				
67.	a	b	c			
68.	a	b	c	d		
69.	a	b	c	d		
70.	a	b	c			
71.	a	b	c	d	e f g
72.	a	b				
73.	T	F				
74.	T	F				
75.	T	F				
76.	T	F				
77.	T	F				
78.	T	F				
79.	T	F				
80.	T	F				
81.	T	F				
82.	T	F				
83.	T	F				
84.	T	F				
85.	T	F				
86.	T	F				
87.	T	F				
88.	a	b	c	d		
89.	T	F				
90.	T	F				
91.	T	F				
92.	T	F				
93.	T	F				
94.	T	F				

95. a b c d e	100. T F
96. T F	101. T F
97. T F	102. T F
98. T F	103. T F
99. T F	104. T F

Answer Sheet

This form is your personal record of responses to all questionnaire items. Simply circle T or F to indicate whether you agree or disagree with the items. In the case of multiple-choice items, circle the letter indicating the response that comes closest to what you believe your own response would be. Two answer sheets are provided, so that each partner will have one.

Questionnaire 1

1.	T	F		16.	T	F
2.	T	F		17.	T	F
3.	T	F		18.	T	F
4.	T	F		19.	T	F
5.	T	F		20.	T	F
6.	T	F		21.	T	F
7.	T	F		22.	T	F
8.	T	F		23.	T	F
9.	T	F		24.	T	F
10.	a	b	c d	25.	T	F
11.	a	b	c d	26.	T	F
12.	a	b	c	27.	T	F
13.	T	F		28.	T	F
14.	T	F		29.	T	F
15.	T	F		30.	T	F

THE PARENT TEST

31. T F
32. T F
33. T F
34. T F
35. T F
36. T F
37. T F
38. T F

39. a b c
40. T F
41. T F
42. T F
43. a b c d e f g
    h i
44. T F
45. T F

Questionnaire 2

1. T F
2. T F
3. T F
4. a b c d
5. T F
6. T F
7. T F
8. T F
9. T F
10. T F
11. a b c d
12. T F
13. T F
14. T F
15. T F
16. T F
17. T F
18. T F
19. T F
20. a b c d

21. a b c d e
22. a b c d e f
23. T F
24. T F
25. T F
26. a b c d e f g
27. T F
28. a b c d
29. T F
30. a b c d e f g
31. a b c d e f
32. T F
33. T F
34. a b c d e
35. T F
36. T F
37. T F
38. T F
39. a b c d e f g
    h i j k l m n

ANSWER SHEET

40. T F	59. a b c	
41. T F	60. T F	
42. a b c d e f g	61. T F	
43. a b c d	62. T F	
44. T F	63. T F	
45. a b c d e f	64. T F	
46. a b c d e f	65. T F	
47. a b c d e f	66. a b c d e	
48. a b c	67. a b c d e f g	
49. a b c d	68. a b c	
50. a b c d	69a. a b c d e f	
51. T F	69b. a b c d e f	
52. T F	70. a b c d e f	
53. a b c d e	71. a b c d e f g	
54. T F	72. a b c d e f g	
55. T F	73. T F	
56. T F	74. a b c d	
57. T F	75. a b c d e	
58. T F		

Questionnaire 3

	9. T F
1. T F	10. T F
2. T F	11. T F
3. T F	12. a b c d
4. T F	13. T F
5. T F	14. T F
6. a b c d e f	15. T F
g h i j k	16. T F
7. T F	17. T F
8. T F	18. T F

96. T F
97. T F
98. T F
99. T F
100. T F

101. T F
102. a b c
103. T F
104. T F
105. T F

Questionnaire 4

1. T F
2. T F
3. T F
4. T F
5. T F
6. T F
7. T F
8. T F
9. T F
10. T F
11. T F
12. T F
13. T F
14. T F
15. T F
16. T F
17. T F
18. T F
19. T F

20. T F
21. T F
22. T F
23. T F
24. T F
25. T F
26. T F
27. T F
28. T F
29. T F
30. T F
31. T F
32. T F
33. T F
34. T F
35. T F
36. T F
37. T F

Questionnaire 5

1. T F
2. T F

3. T F
4. T F

ANSWER SHEET

5. T F	38. a b c d
6. T F	39. T F
7. T F	40. T F
8. a b c d e	41. T F
9. T F	42. a b c
10. T F	43. a b c d
11. T F	44. a b c
12. a b c d	45. T F
13. T F	46. T F
14. T F	47. T F
15. a b c d	48. T F
16. a b c	49. T F
17. T F	50. T F
18. a b c	51. T F
19. T F	52. a b c d
20. T F	53. a b c
21. T F	54. a b c d e
22. T F	55. T F
23. T F	56. T F
24. T F	57. T F
25. T F	58. T F
26. T F	59. a b
27. T F	60. a b c d
28. T F	61. T F
29. T F	62. a b c d
30. T F	63. T F
31. a b c d	64. T F
32. T F	65. T F
33. T F	66. T F
34. T F	67. T F
35. a b c	68. a b c d
36. T F	69. a b c d e
37. T F	70. T F

THE PARENT TEST

19. T F	39. T F
20. T F	40. T F
21. T F	41. T F
22. T F	42. T F
23. T F	43. T F
24. T F	44. a b c d e
25. T F	45. T F
26. T F	46. T F
27. T F	47. T F
28. T F	48. T F
29. T F	49. a b c d
30. T F	50. T F
31. T F	51. a b
32. a b c d	52. T F
33. T F	53. T F
34. T F	54. a b c d e
35. a b c d e	55. T F
36. T F	56. T F
37. T F	57. T F
38. T F	

(Responses to Items 35–57 are to be written by you according to how you believe your spouse responded.)

(35.) a b c d e	(45.) T F
(36.) T F	(46.) T F
(37.) T F	(47.) T F
(38.) T F	(48.) T F
(39.) T F	(49.) a b c d
(40.) T F	(50.) T F
(41.) T F	(51.) a b
(42.) T F	(52.)· T F
(43.) T F	(53.) T F
(44.) a b c d e	(54.) a b c d e

ANSWER SHEET

(55.) T F   84. T F

(56.) T F

(57.) T F   *68–84 for men*

58. T F   68. T F

59. T F   69. T F

60. T F   70. T F

61. T F   71. T F

62. T F   72. T F

63. T F   73. T F

64. T F   74. T F

65. T F   75. T F

66. T F   76. T F

67. T F   77. T F

                    78. T F

68–84 for women   79. T F

                    80. T F

68. T F   81. T F

69. T F   82. a b c d e f g

70. T F   83. a b c d

71. T F   84. T F

72. T F

73. T F   85. T F

74. T F   86. T F

75. T F   87. T F

76. T F   88. T F

77. T F   89. T F

78. T F   90. T F

79. T F   91. T F

80. T F   92. T F

81. T F   93. T F

82. T F   94. T F

83. a b c d e f g   95. T F

71. T F   84. T F
72. T F   85. T F
73. T F   86. T F
74. T F   87. T F
75. T F   88. T F
76. a b c d   89. T F
77. T F   90. T F
78. a b c d e f   91. T F
79. a b c d e   92. T F
80. a b c d e   93. T F
81. T F   94. T F
82. T F   95. T F
83. T F   96. T F

Questionnaire 6

1. a b c d e   15. T F
2. a b c d e f   16. T F
3. T F   17. a b c d
4. T F   18. T F
5. T F   19. T F
6. T F   20. T F
7. T F   21. T F
8. a b c d e   22. T F
9. T F   23. T F
10. T F   24. T F
11. T F   25. T F
12. T F   26. T F
13. T F   27. T F
14. T F   28. T F

ANSWER SHEET

29. T F		62. T F	
30. T F		63. T F	
31. T F		64. T F	
32. a b c		65. T F	
33. T F		66. T F	
34. T F		67. a b c	
35. T F		68. a b c d	
36. T F		69. a b c d	
37. a b c d		70. a b c	
38. a b		71. a b c d e f g	
39. T F		72. a b	
40. T F		73. T F	
41. T F		74. T F	
42. T F		75. T F	
43. T F		76. T F	
44. T F		77. T F	
45. T F		78. T F	
46. T F		79. T F	
47. T F		80. T F	
48. T F		81. T F	
49. T F		82. T F	
50. T F		83. T F	
51. T F		84. T F	
52. T F		85. T F	
53. a b c d		86. T F	
54. T F		87. T F	
55. T F		88. a b c d	
56. T F		89. T F	
57. a b c		90. T F	
58. T F		91. T F	
59. T F		92. T F	
60. a b c d		93. T F	
61. T F		94. T F	

THE PARENT TEST

95. a b c d e   100. T F
96. T F   101. T F
97. T F   102. T F
98. T F   103. T F
99. T F   104. T F